Archives
OF
Memory

love
Howie

Archives
OF
Memory

A SOLDIER RECALLS
WORLD WAR II

Alice M. & Howard S. Hoffman

THE UNIVERSITY PRESS OF KENTUCKY

Frontispiece: Howard Hoffman at Longwy, France, January 1945

Copyright © 1990 by The University Press of Kentucky
Scholarly publisher for the Commonwealth,
serving Bellarmine College, Berea College, Centre
College of Kentucky, Eastern Kentucky University,
The Filson Club, Georgetown College, Kentucky
Historical Society, Kentucky State University,
Morehead State University, Murray State University,
Northern Kentucky University, Transylvania University,
University of Kentucky, University of Louisville,
and Western Kentucky University.

Editorial and Sales Offices: Lexington, Kentucky 40506-0336

Library of Congress Cataloging-in-Publication Data

Hoffman, Alice M., 1929-
   Archives of memory : a soldier recalls World War II / Alice M. &
Howard S. Hoffman.
      p.   cm.
   Includes bibliographical references (p.) and index.
   ISBN 0-8131-1718-6
   1. Hoffman, Howard S., 1925-   . 2. World War, 1939-1945-
-Personal narratives, American.   3. World War, 1939-1945—Campaigns-
-Western.   4. Soldiers—United States—Biography.   5. United States.
Army—Biography.   6. Oral history.   I. Hoffman, Howard S., 1925-
. II. Title.
D811.H648   1990
940.54'21'092—dc20   90-12759
[B]   CIP

The stream of thought flows on; but most of its segments fall into the bottomless abyss of oblivion. Of some no memory survives the instant of their passage. Of others, it is confined to a few moments, hours or days. Others again, leave vestiges which are indestructible, and by means of which they may be recalled as long as life endures. Can we explain these differences?

—*William James*

Contents

Maps

Foreword

Forrest C. Pogue

It is a pleasure to contribute this foreword to Alice and Howard Hoffman's study of his memory of experiences as a young soldier in World War II. Going beyond transcription of taped interviews, the authors have analyzed the reliability and stability of long-term memory and have checked Howard's recollections against accounts of the same incidents recorded shortly after they occurred. In the process the Hoffmans have talked with Howard's fellow soldiers and have examined unit histories, personal documents, after-action reports, official journals, and other written accounts. They have also endeavored to check their conclusions about memory against the writings of psychologists. The result is a striking contribution to oral history.

My own interest and experience in what is now called oral history brought me into contact with Alice Hoffman at the second National Colloquium on Oral History at Arden House, New York, in November 1967. At this meeting the new Oral History Association adopted a constitution and elected officers. I was asked to be a speaker. Alice Hoffman recalls that during the meeting Cornelius Ryan and I made contradictory statements about the value of interviews for the historian; she says that these statements gave her the idea for the experiment she and her husband have since conducted, on which the present book reports.

Cornelius Ryan, whose *The Longest Day* (1959) was an extremely popular book on the Normandy invasion, questioned the value of the interviews conducted by the army's combat historians, adding that he had interrogated 6,000 men for his book and had failed to find one who could tell him whether the water in the Channel had been hot or cold or at what time the troops had attacked a particular objective. I spoke later at the meeting to explain the army's purpose and methods in the World War II interview program, in which I had been involved. I did not remember ever asking anyone about the relative coolness of the water on D-Day. I had been on the water that day, but its temperature was officially recorded by weather experts. As for time of attacks, we had soon learned that most soldiers claimed to have been too busy staying alive to check their watches. Some veterans, alternatively, asked us at what time they were supposed to attack and then said that this was the time at which they *had* attacked. We found it more realistic to ask the veterans to estimate how much time had elapsed after the main artillery preparation before they attacked, for we knew that coordination of infantry movement with artillery fire had to be precise and that the time was carefully recorded in artillery records.

Combat historians, knowing that they would have journals, after-action reports, and daily summaries supplemented by combat photographs and official art, were trying to fill in the part of the story that official records did not always provide. And we tried to get this information as soon as possible after the action so that we could actually inspect some of the area of combat or elicit from fighting men their immediate impressions of what had happened in their own small areas.

Valuable as the combat history program proved to be for the writing of official history, it still did not give historians the complete coverage they wanted, and it sometimes neglected important phases of the war. Even now efforts are still being made to interview surviving veterans of World War II. Writers on military history and students of other historical developments can feel encouraged by the study the Hoffmans have provided. Howard Hoffman's account, drawn from his memory by the expert questioning of his wife, a long-time oral history professional, expresses the anxieties of the uninitiated soldier about the perils of service in the war zone and realistically conveys the bewilderment, weariness, and fear during moments now more than forty years past.

The authors are fervent believers in the value of oral history. But they are equally convinced that the transcript of an oral interview must pass the same tests required of any written memoir. It is necessary, in other words, to ask: (1) is the writer speaking from personal knowledge; (2) is there any basis for doubting the validity of the testimony because the witness had a faulty memory, wanted to enhance his own role, wanted to cover up his shortcomings, or omitted salient factors; and (3) does the witness follow a pattern of truth—does he hate to let facts ruin a good story, does he avoid unpleasant facts because they might damage a friend, or does he tell slightly different versions of his story to different people? Historians must approach oral statements with the same skepticism that they bring to written memoirs.

Reminiscences are nonetheless important, however, and history that rules out the personal memoir, written or oral, risks loss of color and personality, which are as vital as "facts." As a historian and biographer trying to pin down details of combat, a political controversy, or a critical decision in war or peace, I still look to participants when I want to feel the hot breath of history. Their testimony can give life to dry journals and meaning to the most admirably constructed after-action report. In this connection it is of more than passing interest to as what people remember for the rest of their lives and how they remember it. The Hoffmans' book shows that the interview occupies an essential place in history as it increases our appreciation not only of past events but also of the significance of memory.

Foreword

Charles T. Morrissey

In this landmark book Alice Hoffman applies oral history as a technique of inquiry to Howard Hoffman's spoken recollections in order to assess their reliability, their validity, and related aspects of long-term memory. That oral history here serves as both method and matter highlights the pluralism of the term; as a field of study it relies upon anthropology, folklore, sociolinguistics, and other academic specialties for research skills and draws upon such disciplines as literary analysis, gerontology, and especially psychology to ascertain its evidential character. All oral history interviewers deal inevitably with the psychological dimensions of oral recollections, but they usually do so only superficially. After twenty-seven years of conducting tape-recorded interviews, I find that I have been fumbling and amateurish in the way I have confronted the psychological factors involved when I ask informants to speak their memories. Michael Frisch has aptly labeled memory "the elusive core of oral history."[1] To appreciate the Hoffmans' achievement, an observer of the oral history movement may note that Trevor Lummis remarked as recently as 1987, "To establish the way in which memories are shaped, forgotten and interpreted is an essential task which, as yet, oral historians have not seriously tackled."[2] But oral historians are not alone in being to blame for this lack of attention; as David Lowenthal has noted, the absence of large-scale inquiries into how people see, value, or understand the past is astounding.[3] Michael S. Gazzaniga laments the same dearth of inquiry by memory researchers: "If I had to assign the blame for the present state of affairs, I would trace it to the limited resources assigned to the study of memory. Only a relatively few scientists are working on the problem."[4]

Now we can thank the Hoffmans for tackling what Lummis calls "the essential task." Their collaboration is also welcomed because it invites an agenda enlarging upon their recommendations for pursuing the interconnectedness between oral history (both as a technique and as spoken recollections) and the psychological study of autobiographical memory. If other oral history interviewers could secure the cooperation that Alice got from Howard, in our various endeavors to build rapport with oral respondents, we might not continue to stumble awkwardly in the darkness which obscures our efforts, feeling perplexed by the absence of dependable findings about the ways memories work in oral history exchanges. The half dozen questions discussed below have beguiled me during several years of interviewing.

Vividness. Among oral historians generally, I sense a tendency to accept vivid memories as likely to be authentic where accuracy and impact are concerned. Because they persist graphically in reminiscences and are recalled explicitly, their credibility seems indisputable. But in terms of historical causation I encounter instances when vivid memories are overstated as explanations of significant changes. For example, one source recalls that a community devastated by a major catastrophe, such as fire, flood, or a divisive labor-management confrontation, never fully recovered from the setback, whereas other sources describe economic decline as having preceded and accompanied the disaster. Do vivid memories project greater decisiveness as turning points than warranted by dispassionate historical analysis of the contexts in which they occur?

Exactitude. Historians who interview can mislead themselves if they conclude that a respondent's memory for accurate detail signifies as well an understanding of the overarching meaning of past events. When Arthur Mann was preparing his biography of Fiorello LaGuardia, the feisty mayor of New York City, he began his interviews by informally testing the memories of informants by asking for dates, addresses, the names of associates, how names were spelled, and so forth. "Thus, in the case of LaGuardia's World War I orderly and Greenwich Village barber, I accepted his credibility as a witness when he remembered the exact day that the Germans broke through at Caporetto, the middle names of his commanding officers, and the day and the time of day that LaGuardia's first wife was buried in 1921 as well as the street address and the name of her undertaker."[5] I would argue that some detail-minded interviewers are not talented at evoking the scenes they can reconstruct with factual accuracy and also that the converse applies: memoirists with poor retention of detailed information can be very adept at describing the dynamics of past events even if they can't date them or name all the participants. What explains these differences?

Autobiographical Voices. When interviewees describe themselves in the third-person singular, instead of the first-person "I," they depict themselves quite differently from the ego-centered narrator who speaks as a main character on the historical stage and embraces a remembered past. Paul Knaplund deliberately chose to narrate his memoirs in the third-person singular because "the 'I' of today is not the 'I' of yesterday. The old 'I' has vanished like a winter's snow."[6] Some admirers of *The Education of Henry Adams*—a memoir that all oral historians should read—contend that the Adams memoir is a classic because the narrator's use of a third-person-singular viewpoint strengthens the authorial viewpoint. But others fault Adams for hiding behind the third-person perspective. John W. Blassingame has noted that Jeremiah W. Loguen, a Tennessee slave who became a minister and an agent for the Underground Railroad when he achieved freedom shortly before the Civil War, has caused a few scholars to doubt that the slave narrative he published in 1859 was genuine because Loguen chose to present his account in the third-person singular.[7] Question: what happens to memory when a memorist shifts from the first-person singular to the third-person singular?

Layering. I've been tempted to ask interviewees who have recounted social interactions from many years earlier in their lives whether I could borrow their lists of people with whom they annually exchange Christmas cards. Would a correlation emerge? Would figures who loom significantly in reminiscences tend to be those with whom the respondent has kept in touch through the intervening years? Contrariwise, do those who fall out of historical narratives tend to be those who do not maintain connections with the original group? Analyses of scrapbooks and photo albums might reveal similar correlations—or, interestingly, the absence of them. Such studies could pursue the research by Bahrick, Bahrick, and Wittlinger which Alice cites in chapter 1 of this book. We need to know whether remembered historical significance is a consequence of latter-day layering of relationships.

Transformations. It is my hunch that individuals who have made dramatic changes in their life courses have more perceptive memories of the persons they once were but abandoned for self-chosen lifestyles or career trajectories. Likewise, people who voluntarily migrate from their native haunts or childhood scenes often have sharp pictures of the communities they left behind. The best local history often involves oral history interviews of former residents now living outside the community whose history is the focus of research. But local historians often assume, mistakenly, that the best sources are the long-timers who have remained in the community. Is it generally true that continuity dulls recollection, and change enhances it?

Historical Consciousness. For more than a decade I have asked adults in oral history courses, at workshops, and in the audience when I speak about oral history skills and applications whether they are keeping diaries of some sort on a regular basis. From the number of raised hands I surmise that the portion hovers around 6 percent. But because these respondents tend to be well educated and have already gathered to observe history-centered occasions, the percentage of diarists among them may exceed that for the American population as a whole. We need to know more about diary keeping—the extent to which it occurs, who the diarists are, what they write and omit, what they preserve or discard, and (most important for the impetus that the Hoffmans give us) how the act of writing affirms the memory being described. Put another way, do the memories of nondiarists differ from those of diarists?

Howard Hoffman was not a diary keeper in World War II. Military strictures prohibit foot soldiers from recording diary entries which would disclose troop movements and other such information to enemies if these soldiers were captured or if their diaries were removed from their pockets while they lay wounded or dead. The experiences that Howard endured during World War II conditioned the manner in which he summoned his memories. With "makers and shakers" in America's power elite, I find it important to ascertain how much personal and professional loyalty they retained toward institutions which nurtured their success because intense loyalty often inhibits frank revelations. Howard believed that loyalty to the U.S. Army was part of his duty as a soldier temporarily enlisted in his nation's service at a time of crucial need; he did not feel a lifetime conviction toward defending his government which other oral history respondents might feel if they were interviewed about their experiences. Likewise, Howard's memory consists of visual images. To extend the study Alice has initiated, we need to know how other interviewees, especially those who remember verbally, not visually, articulate their memories.

Neuroscientists are hailing the 1990s as "the decade of the brain" because many functions of cognitive systems, which have long defied efforts to explain their operation, are within the reach of understanding as research solves persistent mysteries. The 1990s could similarly be a decade of advances toward unraveling some of the perplexing aspects of oral history as it relates to the psychology of memory. The Hoffmans demonstrate how collaboration can be rewarding. They helpfully point the way.

Introduction

History is not a recreation of the past but a story about the past created from extant artifacts and documents. To tell this story, the historian gathers memory claims from a variety of sources and selects those which seem significant, interesting, and perhaps explanatory of the contemporary situation. In so doing, historians have long been suspicious of their sources and careful to subject them to rigorous analysis. Thucydides stated in his introduction to *The History of the Peloponnesian War*, "My conclusions have cost me some labour from the want of coincidence between accounts of the same occurrences by different eyewitnesses, arising sometimes from imperfect memory, sometimes from undue partiality for one side or the other."[1]

Thucydides' successors have often recognized that their informants were likely to be biased, able to give only a small part of the picture, sometimes romantic, and sometimes self-serving lying rascals. Throughout the nineteenth and twentieth centuries, chroniclers came to rely more and more upon written documents. In the twentieth century, however, historians found that, while their documents became ever more voluminous, they were no longer likely to contain thoughtful discussion of events, notes on alternative courses of action, or analysis by one actor of the other participants in the drama. Such information is now more typically shared and conveyed in person or by telephone.

The revolution in transportation and communication has not only created the global village but has paradoxically made it increasingly difficult to know what really informs the decisionmakers in that village. We are drowning in documents created expressly for the media and designed deliberately to mislead and obfuscate or at the least to put the best face on any given situation. Thus it was virtually inevitable that historians, lamenting the quality of the available sources, would hit upon the notion of questioning informants, tape-recording their responses to ensure their accuracy, and promising them that the information would be preserved for the future but would not be available to embarrass them in the present.

The historian who is usually credited with having institutionalized this method is Allan Nevins, who set up at Columbia University the first organized oral history program. By 1966, practitioners of the art of preserving oral records archivally were numerous enough to warrant defining the technique and creating the Oral History Association. Oral history, it was agreed, consisted of "recorded interviews which preserve historically significant memories for future use."[2]

At the time that this "new" technique was gaining momentum, I was hired by the Department of Labor Studies at Pennsylvania State University to retrieve the archival records of Pennsylvania labor organizations. The department was aware that the dearth of scholarship with respect to Pennsylvania labor history was due in large measure to the lack of accessible sources on the labor movement, particularly those dealing with the history of the rise of the great industrial unions in a drama where much of the action took place in the steel towns of Pennsylvania. As I began to gather the records from various union halls, I found myself disappointed. The documents were studded with notes and memos reading approximately as follows: "Dear Sir [or Dear Brother]: Proceed as we discussed on the phone." The papers before me held no trace of the strategy and the rationale for it. In sum, the records contained little, if any, information about process but reflected, and only rather dimly at that, the end product of the historical development.

I identified other problems in the attempt to document labor organizations. Their history has been controversial. Much of primary—that is, contemporary—written source material is biased in viewpoint, either positively or negatively where the organization is concerned. In addition, individuals who have been important in the development of the organization have typically not kept diaries or recorded the specific details of the organization's growth. I decided that perhaps the only solution to these problems was to find the people who had been present at the organization's founding as observers or as policymakers, to interview them, and to tape-record their answers to such questions as "What was it like?" "How, where, and when did it happen?" and "Who was responsible?" I had thus formulated the standard rationalization for an oral history project, and I became an oral historian. I spent the next nineteen years seeking informants who could describe for me their memories of significant events in labor history, transcribing the interviews, and placing them in the Labor Archives of the Pennsylvania State University.

At the second national colloquium on oral history, where the Oral History Association was founded, Forrest Pogue, the biographer of General George C. Marshall, was a principal speaker. He described the combat interview program that was started by the army's historical project in 1943. This project assembled a team of army historians to interview soldiers just coming off the line.

The interesting part about this type of interviewing is, they liked the idea that you were also experiencing what you were asking about. This is really history while it's hot, because you have to stay alive to ask questions about their being shot at. And we were always running into people with a pixyish sense of humor. You'd go up to a Command post and you'd say, "I'd like to talk to Sergeant so and so who we understood took the hill yesterday" or "the man who wiped out four Germans in the pillbox" or something of that sort.

Well, you know, [they'd say,] he's out there—firing, about 200 yards, he's with a machine gun out there, and it's not quite safe for you to go out there just now unless you'd like—[us to] put up some smoke and send you out.

Well, we always said that our colonel, when he sent us out, had said that he wanted living history, but also living historians. And we cooperated with him fully in this regard.

Seriously speaking, three of [these army historians] were killed, and I think at least four badly maimed.[3]

This talk profoundly affected my own thinking. I saw that because of the work of this army team of interviewers, the history of World War II could differ from previous histories of war. It could include the perceptions of the foot soldiers, so that it would be possible to assess the meaning of the experience in a new way. The idea also had implications for my own work: labor history could employ this technique to preserve the actions and attitudes not just of labor leadership but of the rank and file as well.

At this same colloquium Cornelius Ryan, author of *The Longest Day*, the story of the D-Day invasion, criticized the interview process. He had read through the army combat interviews produced by Forrest Pogue and others and also claimed to have conducted some 6,000 interviews of his own. He described his conclusions:

I discovered that interviewing is not reliable. I never found one man who landed on Omaha Beach who could tell me whether the water was hot or cold. I never found one man who landed on Omaha Beach who could tell me the exact time when some incident occurred. . . . Gathering the material after was very, very difficult indeed, and it did not lend itself to total accuracy. . . .

It has been said before that anyone who dares write history, when faced with a statement of fact, must ask himself first the question: "Who said so, and what opportunities had he of knowing it?"

Now, the historian, when he subjects his materials to this test, discovers very quickly that much that is considered evidence tends to dissolve. And indeed, in my kind of writing, one fact stands out more than any of the others—the very worthlessness of human testimony. Unless—and I underline the word "unless"—unless it can be substantiated by documents supporting the testimony.

In writing *The Longest Day,* I rejected at least ninety percent of the testimony I received in interviews. I did this simply because I was unable to substantiate or confirm what the person said. I do not say that their testimony was wrong, but there was no way to prove it.[4]

The questions that Ryan raised have preoccupied oral historians and their critics ever since.

I discussed the problem of verifying recorded testimony with my psychologist husband, who was well schooled in the scientific study of learning and memory. Our conversations led me to break the question into two parts: how reliable is human memory, and how valid is it? In this connection reliability can be defined as the consistency with which an individual will tell the same story about the same event on a number of different occasions. "Validity" denotes the degree of conformity between the reports of the event and the event itself as recorded by other primary source materials, such as documents, diaries, letters, or other oral reports.[5]

My experience in conducting oral interviews had led me to the hypothesis that the memories being tapped might be special in character. I had had one particularly compelling experience. In an interview, John Mullen, who had been an employee of the Carnegie-Illinois Steel Company in Clairton, Pennsylvania, had described the means by which the company had attempted to force him to provide information on the union activities of his fellow employees. Some months later I found an anonymous interview which also described the attempts to recruit industrial spies. It appeared in a book by Robert R. Brooks published in 1940, which was based on his research on the earliest attempts of steelworkers to organize.[6] The interview quoted by Brooks and mine, conducted thirty years later, read almost word for word the same![7] How could the remarkable similarity be explained? I imagined that the story had been told and retold over the years until it had become well rehearsed, but when I questioned Mr. Mullen, he answered that while he had had occasion to tell the story at various times, at the time I interviewed him he had given that particular incident little thought for many years. I concluded that this particular memory had remained remarkably stable and reliable from youth to old age.

I was also aware, however, that when the story was compared with other testimony and documents on industrial espionage such as that uncovered by the LaFollette Senate committee to investigate the violation of civil liberties,[8] Mullen's testimony showed discrepancies with the preponderance of other available sources. Thus while the information was reliable to a remarkable degree, various aspects of its validity were in question.

At length Howard and I devised a plan to examine the reliability and validity of memory utilizing the combined analytical methodologies of psychology and history. Experimental psychology has discovered a great deal about the basic processes of memory which could prove useful for historical analysis. In view of the obvious connections between the two disciplines, historians and psychologists have had surprisingly little interaction.[9] In designing our study we were influenced by Forrest Pogue's description of the army combat interviews. We were preparing to examine the long-term autobiographical memory that typically comes into play in an oral history interview, however, and not the short-term episodic memories of Pogue's after-action interviews.

We decided that Howard would serve as an oral history interviewee, and I would ask him about his experiences forty years earlier as a combat solider in World War II. I would conduct the interviews and attempt to locate whatever official records might be available to corroborate or disprove the stories that Howard told. The plan was to conduct the interviews in three phases.

First, in order to assess the reliability or stability of the memory, we would conduct two sets of interviews based on free recall and separated from one another by several years. In these interviews we would tape-record and transcribe the memories elicited by the request "Tell me about the war." Questions would be asked merely to clarify or expand upon the information provided. This method represented a departure from the standard interviewing practice of oral history. Ordinarily, an interviewer would familiarize herself with the available documentation and engage the interviewee in a rigorous dialogue based upon that research. For the purposes of this project, however, we wished to develop two interview documents that could be compared with one another to assess reliability and could subsequently be compared with a document produced by the standard oral history methodology.

In the years separating these two interviews, Howard would try to avoid situations that might stimulate him to rehearse or further explore his memories of World War II. He would avoid war films and books and would go about his business of teaching and research, activities which offered little occasion for him to think about, let alone discuss, his term as a soldier. Once the two reliability interviews were completed, a third set of interviews would be conducted on the basis of any documentary evidence that could be located. This group of interviews would more nearly constitute the typical oral history interview and would enable us to assess the validity of the memory store.

The first set of interviews was begun in late 1978. In that year John Neuenschwander published an article in the *Oral History Review* entitled "Remembrance of Things Past: Oral Historians and Long-Term Memory," in which he focused on studies made by experimental psychologists. He concluded with the following plea: "Oral historians can and must begin to seriously study long-term memory. What is needed are studies of how interviewee memory claims differ over time. Re-interviewing narrators after five, ten, and fifteen year intervals may provide helpful insights on long-term memory. Oral historians should also build into their interview format questions about memory. Explanations of how interviewees think their memories work could prove helpful."[10] We were intrigued by Neuenschwander's article because it suggested that our approach would meet a need.

The second set of interviews was conducted in 1982. Meanwhile, I was fortunate to find that a careful and detailed record existed of the daily activities of Howard's company (Company C, Third Chemical Mortar Battalion) at the army archives in Suitland, Maryland. In addition to an account of the daily battle statistics for Company C, this record contained a detailed daily log of the activities in which Howard had been engaged for the entire time that he was overseas. Thus it became possible to compare the free recall interviews with this log and to conduct the third set of interviews.

In the third set of interviews we used photographs taken by the U.S. Army Signal Corps as well as secondary sources, cartoons, and photographs taken by the subject himself with a "liberated" German camera. In addition, we made a trip to Edgewood Arsenal, Maryland, where Howard had served in 1943 as a subject in some poison gas experiments. The trip made it possible to test Howard's memory claim about his participation in these experiments and to identify some ways in which Howard's memories might be affected by a return to the scene where some events had taken place. I was careful not to expose Howard indiscriminately to these sources. I showed them to him systematically and interviewed him after each exposure. By proceeding in this way, we hoped to be able to assess the affect upon the memory store of various classes of recognition items.

At the end of the project Howard assembled a set of maps which appear in this volume. In order to make these maps, he painstakingly compared the records in the daybook with detailed maps and examined each and every description of the routes taken and the towns near which the company had bivouacked. In this process he was necessarily subjected to considerable documentation against which we could further check his memories for events and places.

In the course of this research, we discovered that the Third Chemical Battalion had been holding periodic reunions. We had not previously known of these meetings, but after the second interview we contacted the group and met with a few of the veterans near York, Pennsylvania. We later met with the entire reunion group at its biannual convention in Baltimore in July 1986. We recorded several interviews at these meetings and then recorded Howard's reactions to the meetings. We used all of these documents to examine our questions about the memory process.

In the following pages we share with the reader what we learned. The first chapter contains a brief history of the field of memory research and sets out some of the issues that have been central in the debate on the nature of long-term memory. The ensuing chapters are divided into four parts. Each part includes a section of the first recall document followed by an analysis based upon a comparison of the first recall document with both the second interview and the validity interviews and documents. Portions of both the company log and the second recall document are included in appendixes. We did not include the entire second recall document because it was nearly identical to the first recall document even though it was conducted four years later. The final chapter offers some conclusions and suggestions for further research. While the present book takes as its subject the memory of one individual, Howard and I hope, like other memory researchers before us who have focused on one subject, that it will provide information of general utility.[11] The project was initially my idea and was jointly planned and executed. Howard not only served as the subject of the study but also contributed his considerable talents as a psychology professor who had devoted a lifetime to scientific research on behavior. The research and commentary are principally my own work, however, and the first-person pronoun, in the analytical sections below, as in this introduction, refers to me.

Alice M. Hoffman

Biographical Note
on Howard S. Hoffman

Howard's parents met and married in New York City. Neither of them attended college. Since they were both grand master bridge players, they would probably have been able to earn college degrees if they had had the opportunity. His mother was born in Canada and immigrated to this country as a young adult. Howard's father spent most of his life working as a salesman. Although he had yearnings to climb the ladder of success, things just never seemed to work out for him. He tried a variety of schemes, including a luncheonette on the boardwalk at Long Beach, Long Island, and a ladies' handbag store in a hotel in Miami Beach. None of these efforts produced enough surplus income for the family to buy a car, let alone contemplate a college education for the three sons. In 1936, Howard's father moved the family to Harrisburg, Pennsylvania, where he worked as the assistant manager of Bond's Men's Store.

Howard did not spend the entire period of the war in the army. He enlisted in May 1943 just before turning eighteen. He went overseas in March 1944, fought in the battle for Cassino, and participated in the capture of Rome. In August 1944, Howard was a part of the invasion of southern France and fought with troops making their way north to link up with the Allied troops that had invaded Normandy. He was rushed to the defense of Bastogne and fought at the Bulge. His outfit continued in support of infantry troops until it met the Russians at the Elbe River in May 1945.

Shortly after Howard's discharge from the army, he used the GI Bill to enter the University of Chicago, where he began to major in physics. While he was waiting for a new semester to begin, however, he received a gift of oil paints and discovered that he had some natural talent as an artist. In an effort to decide upon a career, he sought help from the Veterans Administration, which administered a battery of tests designed to assess his interests and abilities. To his chagrin the psychologist who interpreted the tests informed Howard that according to the results he should be either an artist or a physicist and that the government would support his education in either field. Armed with this set of "clear" directions, he decided to go to New York and try to be an artist. He attended the School for Art Studies and studied under Moses Soyer.

At length Howard's funds from the GI Bill ran out. But he continued to paint and shared his flat with the now celebrated author William Styron. The two men lived an impoverished bohemian life and attended several of the rather strange parties described in Styron's first novel, *Lie Down in Darkness*.[1] During this period Howard obtained a position as a teacher's assistant in one of the New York day care centers, where he became intrigued by children of nursery school age. In particular he began to wonder what made them behave as they did. This curiosity prompted him to take courses in psychology at the New School for Social Research, and in 1952 he graduated with a B.A. By this time he had become caught up in the effort to study behavior systematically and was convinced that his career should center on this interest. He went on to take a master's degree in psychology at Brooklyn College, and afterward he attended the University of Connecticut, where he received his Ph.D. His doctoral research employed synthetic (machine-made) speech and focused on the rather specialized question of how a listener is able to discriminate between the voiced stop consonants *b*, *d*, and *g*.

Howard joined the faculty of the Pennsylvania State University in 1957, where he stayed until 1970, when he was invited to join the faculty of Bryn Mawr College. Throughout his career his research has focused on the scientific analysis of behavior and in particular on the mechanisms of learning and retention. In an early article he sought to discover how long a pigeon would retain learned material. He was unable to find any evidence that the pigeon forgot as a function of elapsed time.[2] Recognizing that learning was affected by emotional state, he began to study the startle mechanism as an indication of emotionality. Soon he was interested in the startle phenomenon itself. He also published studies on imprinting. After teaching courses on sensation and perception, he developed techniques for teaching the art of drawing that tapped existing knowledge of how the eye and the brain work together to see. He began to teach a course called "The Psychology of Visual Art." The results were dramatic. Students who had previously been unable to draw were now able to do so sensitively and accurately. These efforts led him to write a book entitled *Vision and the Art of Drawing*, published in 1989 by Prentice-Hall. The book gave Howard considerable satisfaction because it united the dominant interests in his life at last. The tests at Chicago were almost right; instead of indicating that he should either be a scientist or an artist, they should perhaps have suggested that he could be both. Howard has in fact never ceased to draw and paint and respond to the world as both an artist and a scientist.

1 A Psychological Overview of Memory

Psychologists have been investigating memory for at least 100 years. It has usually been defined as the capacity or faculty of retaining and retrieving impressions from the past by means of recalling them or by recognizing them when some aspect of the impression is presented. This definition is generally accepted. A debate arises when we ask how the process works. Where and how are the impressions stored? Which impressions are stored—all of them or just some, and if just some, how are they selected for storage? What strategies are used for retrieval from memory, and what factors may impinge upon retrieval? Are these impressions susceptible to change and/or decay over time? The investigation of such issues has resulted in debate and the creation of opposing camps of theorists.

In fact, two of the earliest pioneers in the study of memory, Hermann Ebbinghaus (1885) and F.C. Bartlett (1932), took different approaches to the task of attempting to understand memory processes which have not as yet been brought into one organic conception. It is possible when studying most of the contemporary scientific literature on memory to assign a study either to the Ebbinghaus or to the Bartlett tradition.[1]

It was primarily German professors who began to study the processes of the mind experimentally. Their own training was in areas where the laboratory method was well established, such as physics or physiology. Hermann Ebbinghaus, who had been so trained, observed that the experiments being conducted by most of his colleagues were restricted to the analysis of sense perception. He wanted to go a step further and use laboratory methods to look at "the workings of the mind and to submit to an experimental and quantifiable treatment the manifestation of memory."[2]

He recognized the inherent difficulties in the task he had set himself. "How," he asked, "can we keep constant the bewildering mass of causal conditions which, insofar as they are of mental nature, almost completely elude our control, and which, moreover, are subject to endless and incessant change?"[3]

Ebbinghaus attempted to provide appropriately controlled conditions by inventing the nonsense syllable, which consisted of a vowel surrounded by two consonants that did not form a three-letter word. He made up 2,300 such syllables and then proceeded to make lists of varying lengths and measure the amount of time and the number of trials which he needed before he could recite the list without error. He also attempted to determine the number of trials required to relearn a list after the passage of time had caused him to forget it. He was the principal subject of his own experiments, and while he realized that his tests would be primarily of individual significance, he hoped nevertheless that his experiments would provide a generally valid set of relationships. In conception and aim, then, our own study belongs to the Ebbinghaus tradition.

It must be observed that Ebbinghaus did exceedingly well—so much so that at a centennial symposium held at the twenty-sixth annual meeting of the Psychonomic Society in Boston in 1985 a group of memory theorists honored his contribution and agreed that his empirical techniques and conceptual framework are still a useful guide for research in the field. In the 100 years since Ebbinghaus made his studies, psychologists have been preoccupied with testing his propositions and with analyzing and extending their applicability to a wide variety of learning tasks. Ebbinghaus found, for instance, that attributed meanings cause the syllables to be learned more quickly. He discovered a savings effect, namely, that when material must be relearned, it can be mastered more quickly than when the first attempt to learn it was made. The implication is that, while the material is not available for recall, some memory trace must facilitate relearning the material.

Ebbinghaus found that learning is more efficient when sessions are distributed than when the same amount of time is spent in one session. And he plotted a forgetting curve which demonstrated that information is lost from memory rapidly at first but that the rate of loss levels out over time. This curve has proven valid for many types of learned material over a wide range of circumstances.

In 1932, Frederick C. Bartlett, professor of psychology at Cambridge University, published a book entitled *Remembering*. He was critical of the use of nonsense syllables and unrelated word lists to study memory. Bartlett believed that it is impossible to ensure that all experimental subjects begin the effort to learn and recall material unaffected by previous experience with the material to be remembered. He observed, as had Ebbinghaus, that the human subject makes innumerable associations in the effort to remember even nonsense syllables. But he carried his observation to the conclusion that the memory process is in and of itself inextricably bound up with the development of structural organization, or what he termed "schemata," and he suggested that a study divorced from the history of the subject and from the natural tendency to seek meaning and association has a doubtful claim to be focusing upon memory at all.

He asked his subjects to remember pictures and stories. In one study he presented subjects with a series of five postcards, each with a picture of a man in one branch or another of the British armed forces. Since the study was being made during World War I, his subjects were quite familiar with the fighting services and were generally interested in them. Each of his twenty subjects was given ten seconds to examine each card and was then asked to describe the cards and to answer a series of questions about them, for example, "Which man has a mustache?" or "Which man is smoking a pipe?" After a period of two weeks or so, each subject was again asked to describe the cards and to answer questions about them. Bartlett tested for accuracy in the sequence in which the cards had been presented. He found that his subjects made frequent errors in this regard, although none was wrong as to which card had been presented first. This finding is of particular interest, for as will be seen there is a considerable primacy effect in Howard's recollection of his World War II experience. That is, he recalled the first time he did or experienced something more vividly and more accurately than he recalled similar subsequent events.

Bartlett also found that his subjects could be divided into two groups: those who relied primarily on visual images and those who relied upon language cues in attempting to recall the cards. Those who relied upon the image were more sure of the correctness of their response, but in fact there was no difference in the number of errors made by the two groups. Bartlett remarked that, in strategies for recall, "seeing is believing."[4]

Elizabeth Loftus in her work on memory reports the same phenomenon with respect to the confidence of visual imagers in their memories. Like Bartlett, however, she found that they were not more accurate in their ability to recall than those who processed their experiences verbally.[5]

In another set of experiments, Bartlett presented a story to his subjects that was derived from an Eskimo folktale. It concerned two young men who went to hunt seals. When his subjects repeated the story, Bartlett found that they showed a clear tendency to shorten it, to reduce it to its gist, and to reproduce that essence. He also found that subjects tried to make the story accommodate their own viewpoint and experience. Thus "something black came out of his mouth" became "foamed at the mouth" in many of the reproductions. And canoes frequently became boats. He further found that, once the story had been rationalized to fit constructions satisfying or understandable to the subject, subsequent reproductions remained stable and were subject to very little, if any, change.[6]

Since Bartlett's publication of his findings, there have been relatively few studies of the accuracy of report over time. His contribution did not receive the attention that it deserved until quite recently. Most studies of memory have been concerned with very short retention periods. In many cases, in fact, they have involved retention periods of less than a minute.

There are a number of reasons for this emphasis. First, psychologists have suggested that there are two stages of memory, short-term memory and long-term memory.[7] Short-term memory is information stored for only a few seconds, for example, a telephone number, which may be stored for no more than the time required to dial it.

Material retained for any appreciable amount of time beyond a minute belongs to the latter classification, and the basic processes involved are perhaps not effectively different whether one is examining retention for a day or a week or years. Therefore, the experimental analysis of the basic process involved is facilitated if shorter time intervals are used. Second, individual differences are smaller in memory over short periods. Information retained over long periods of time is affected by a host of potentially confounding variables, such as perceived importance, interest, comprehensibility, knowledge, personality, attitudes, temperament, prejudices, and so forth. Obviously at some point all these individual factors will have to be taken into account and controlled for, but experimental psychologists have deemed it wise to attempt to understand the underlying mechanisms first and to look at ways in which people or animals perform similarly with the expectation that such a strategy is more likely to uncover these basic mechanisms. Third, longitudinal studies are inherently difficult because over time the original group of subjects may die, become ill, or otherwise be unavailable to the researcher. Fourth, it is unfortunately true that longitudinal studies require a great deal of time between their conception and their completion, and in the academic environment of publish or perish few psychologists can afford a lengthy delay.

While studies on memory over long periods of time are relatively rare, some do exist. In the early twentieth century, there were a number of studies on the accuracy of report over time. These studies corroborate Bartlett's observation that the reports show considerable inaccuracy and that the inaccuracies tend to be in the direction of bringing the report of the event into congruence with expectation or with accepted norms and standards. Moreover, a more recent study by H. Kay suggests that memory is very much influenced by its original encoding process or by the storage process itself. In other words, the assimilation of the material greatly affects its retrieval. Kay asked sub-

jects to listen while he read two short passages. They were then asked
to write a verbatim account of these passages. When they had done so
he read a correct version to the subjects. A week later they were asked
to reproduce the passages. This process was continued for seven
weeks. In each case, subjects remembered their own reproductions far
more accurately than the correct version even though at each session
they were presented with the correct version.[8]

Obviously the fact that they had to write out their own version may
have produced more powerful and persistent learning of their own
version. It would be interesting to replicate the study with tape-
recorded responses from the subjects rather than written responses to
see what effect the change might have on the results. It is perhaps
noteworthy, however, that, when Michael Howe replicated the study
and obtained substantially the same results, he found that, according
to subjects' reports of their subjective experience, they knew they were
reproducing their own version and not the correct version but that they
were able to recall only their own version. It might also be interesting to
see whether subjects could correctly identify their own version and the
correct version when both were presented. In this way their recognition could be tested as well as their ability to recall the material.

Howe concluded that "when we speak of distortions in memory it
would often be more accurate to speak of distortions in the material as it
enters the retention system; once the material is stored, it is unlikely
that much further distortion occurs."[9]

Such findings have led many psychologists to conclude with D.B.
Bromley that "short-term memory declines with age, whereas long-
term memory is relatively unaffected except by disuse."[10] There is
ample evidence that short-term memory declines with age; the ability
to retain a telephone number long enough to dial the number correctly,
for example, is a skill which deteriorates considerably with increasing
years. The evidence that long-term memories are affected, however, is
less clear-cut. It is, in fact, unclear whether memory is, or is not, a
unitary process. There may or may not be a variety of kinds of memory.
Furthermore, it is not clear exactly what memory is. Is it a chemical
change in the brain? Is it the result of changes in neuronal pathways?
Are memories laid down in a specific geographical location, or are they
diffused in some way throughout the brain? These questions are cur-
rently under intense investigation. While some progress has been
made, psychologists seem to agree that it is not yet possible to say with
certainty where or how memories are stored in the brain.

Karl Lashley spent a lifetime looking for the specific location of
memories. He systematically removed parts of the brain of rats that had
learned a maze. No matter where he cut, however, memory survived,
and finally, he gave up the search.

In 1951 Wilder Penfield, a Canadian brain surgeon, reported a study which generated considerable interest both in the scientific community and in the popular press. Brain surgery is usually performed under local anesthesia because the brain itself is not susceptible to pain. As a result the patient is conscious throughout the operation. Penfield reported that he could elicit specific memories in human patients who were undergoing brain surgery. If he touched a particular spot in the temporal lobes of the brain, patients would report a particular recollection. Moreover, it seemed to run off in time rather like a tape recording would.

Penfield's work gave credence to the notion that the brain functions rather like a tape recorder and that not only specific memories can be evoked but also the associated perceptions, which have also been recorded. Moreover, Penfield believed that all experience is preserved and that any experience is available for replay if it can be appropriately evoked or retrieved.[11] There are however a number of difficulties with Penfield's results. The most basic problem involves the difficulty of knowing whether the responses being evoked by the surgeon's probe are in fact actual memories of real events or rather some kind of hallucination. Furthermore, no other neurosurgeon has reported similar findings.[12]

The suggestion that the memory is rather like a storehouse of audio and video tapes available for replay, however, has been an attractive one. It fits in with studies showing that memories can more easily be retrieved if some part of the experience can be brought to consciousness. For example, some studies show that, if a student can arrange to take a test in the same room in which he or she studied, the amount of material available for recall will increase substantially. In other words, the environment itself serves to cue or set in motion the retrieval process.[13]

In 1980 Duncan Godden and Alan Baddeley suggested that this environmental effect would serve to enhance recall but not recognition.[14] They distinguished between intrinsic context and extrinsic context. They defined intrinsic context as those aspects of a stimulus which are inevitably processed when the stimulus is perceived, such as the voice in which an item is spoken or the typeface of a word on the page. Extrinsic contexts are irrelevant to the perceived item, such as the color of the walls in the room. They found that recall is enhanced by both intrinsic and extrinsic contexts but that recognition is enhanced only by intrinsic contexts. In other words, if you know that you will be given a multiple choice or true/false test, it would not enhance your performance to study in the room where you will take the test, but if you are to take an essay-type exam, then studying in the room where you will take the test may be advantageous.

Much of psychoanalysis is based on the assumption that all memory is retained somewhere in the recesses of the mind and that by application of categorical or contextual cues (that is, pieces of information or word associations), the patient can be led to retrieve memory that has been suppressed and has hence been unavailable for recall.

Sigmund Freud suggested that forgetting is due, in large part, to the repression of events which, if brought to the conscious mind, would cause anxiety or fear. Efforts to find evidence of repression in laboratory experiments on memory processes have, on the whole, not been successful. One study that seems to provide evidence for repression was cited by I.M.L. Hunter. In the study, subjects were asked to produce all the memories which they could recall of their first eight years of life, and then to rate them as unpleasant, pleasant, or neutral. On the average they reported about 50 percent pleasant, about 30 percent unpleasant, and 20 percent neutral.[15] The preponderance of pleasant memories over unpleasant could be attributed to repression, but the more optimistic view might be that most people simply have more pleasant experiences than unpleasant ones.

In any case, if one hypothesizes that all experience leaves a memory trace in the brain (which has been a matter of considerable dispute among memory researchers), one might expect to be able to enhance the reproduction of long-term memory through the use of diaries, scrapbooks, photo albums, and a return to the scene. Bahrick, Bahrick, and Wittlinger provide some data regarding this possibility.[16] In their experiment, 392 high school graduates were tested for their memory of names and faces selected from their high school yearbook. The retention interval ranged from two weeks to fifty-seven years. In other words, these investigators took a cross-sectional approach to the study of long-term memory. This strategy had an advantage over typical laboratory studies in that it more nearly resembled real-life learning situations. In real-life situations there is prolonged acquisition of information and the information is preserved for a much longer period than is evident from typical laboratory experiments. Moreover, laboratory experiments typically impose a much greater interdependence upon free recall and recognition than is in reality inherent in the functioning of the memory system. This study permitted the use of a more naturalistic method to study memory. It shows that the number of items retrieved through free recall correlates neither with class size nor with recognition performance. Recognition was greater than recall. "Apparently the context serves as a mediator for retrieval of information; once the association of mediator and target item is lost, the item can no longer be retrieved for recall but can still be identified on recognition tasks."[17]

The results of this study indicate that recognition remains approximately 90 percent correct for fifteen years independent of class size and that it declines with negative acceleration to 60 percent, even up to the forty-eighth year. Moreover, social context is shown to be a powerful determinant of recall performance and less important in recognition. This study made no distinction, however, between extrinsic and intrinsic context, although social context could be assumed to be both intrinsic and extrinsic in nature.

One can deduce from this study that information which is important for the subject has a high degree of validity in recall performance and that an even greater amount of material is reliably available for recognition if a context can be provided which will mediate in the retrieval process.

A large proportion of the studies of memory have presented the material to be remembered to their subjects. More recently, however, psychologists have reexamined the work of F.C. Bartlett and found much to be commended in his insistence on meaningfulness as an essential concept in the study of memory. Moreover, the findings of both ecology and cognitive psychology have led researchers to attempt to study memory in its more "naturalistic" manifestations.

In 1972, Endel Tulving, a Canadian psychologist, published a book entitled *Organization of Memory.* In this work, he suggested that it would be analytically useful to consider two types of memory, episodic and semantic. Episodic memory consists of specific experiences from an individual's past, such as what one ate for breakfast or an event which occurred during your first year of school. This class of memories is often called autobiographical memory. Semantic memory refers to the general knowledge and abstract principles that have been derived from past experience. Examples include the knowledge that cars have four wheels; that three plus four equals seven; that George Washington was the first president of the United States, and so on. Each of us has derived a storehouse or library of such information which we call upon in our daily lives.

That such a dichotomy exists is perhaps underlined by my own recent experience in trying to understand unfamiliar psychological terms. I was able to remember very clearly having looked up a particular word. I remembered where I was when I looked it up, the time of day, and so forth. But I was unable to recall the meaning of the word. Thus my episodic memory was functioning, but semantic memory had failed.

Episodic memory has not until very recently been studied by psychologists, but it has preoccupied philosophers.[18] One explanation for this fact is that the means to validate reports of autobiographical memory have not been readily available to psychologists conducting studies. Whitten and Leonard, for example, asked college freshmen to recall one teacher from each grade from one to twelve under three conditions. In condition 1 the subjects were asked to provide the names of teachers from grades 1 to 12; in condition 2 they were to list them from grades 12 to 1; and under condition 3 they could list the teachers in any order. Those students who were asked to make the list from grades 12 to 1 were able to complete the task much more effectively than students from conditions 1 or 3. These results led the researchers to conclude that "the probability of recalling an item from autobiographical memory is primarily a function of recency."[19] This study, however, provides no means of ascertaining whether the names recorded are in fact the names of the teachers that the students had in any particular grade. Moreover, the study does not recognize that in grades 1-6 there typically are many fewer target names than in grades 7-12.

In a more recent book entitled *Elements of Episodic Memory,* Tulving discusses additional types of memory, namely procedural memory and declarative memory. The latter is conceived as encompassing his original two systems of episodic and semantic memory. Procedural memory is the knowledge of how to go about doing something, and it may include the process by which one engages in a memory search. Individuals may use a variety of memory procedures, processes, or skills in an attempt to retrieve items from memory, and these processes can in themselves be acquired, learned, and stored. Tulving himself recognizes that the experimental evidence for his system of classification has barely begun to be accumulated. Clearly his postulation of a variety of kinds of memory has stimulated a whole new area for experimental investigation.[20]

Ulric Neisser, a psychologist from Cornell University, has echoed the argument that memory should be studied in as naturalistic (and hence as meaningful) a manner as possible. He assembled a series of studies of memory which he felt met the criterion of naturalism in a book entitled *Memory Observed.* Neisser ridiculed the work of the memory theorists in the Ebbinghaus tradition. He stated that, in a study done by Kreutzer, Leonard, and Flavell in 1975, it was shown that the generalizations derived from laboratory studies of memory are already familiar to the average third grader.[21] This accusation has of course been frequently made in connection with experimentally derived information. Some individuals knew all along that the world was round, but the point was not conclusively shown until someone had circumnavigated the globe by sailing in one direction.

The fact that we know a great deal about processes of the mind which can subsequently be experimentally demonstrated is reassuring, for it demonstrates that we do in fact live in a world governed by cause and effect and not by random meaningless inconsequential events. Therefore, our behavior has been reinforced when in attempting to learn and remember we have used such processes as attributing meaning to the material to be remembered or by understanding that material once learned can be relearned in less time than we needed for the first attempt. We feel that we know this information intuitively. What we feel we know intuitively is not always accurate, however. We often assign causality to events that are simply related in time (post hoc ergo propter hoc). It is important to validate experimentally what we think we already know.

In his introduction to *Memory Observed,* Neisser admits that, while we do indeed know more about memory than third graders do, psychologists have nevertheless been asking fundamentally wrong questions. He suggests that studies which focus on the functions of memory are likely to yield more useful information. He says that memory is used to provide self-definition; to confirm our impressions of what happened; to plan future activity; to enable us to preserve language, poetry, theater, and music exactly as written; and to preserve information. Because it is used for all these essential tasks, naturalistic memory as it is used in real-life situations is worthy of study.

Neisser's collection of naturalistic studies emphasized an important new focus for the study of memory, and several of the studies in the book were of direct relevance and application to the present work and to our developing hypothesis. For instance, Roger Brown and James Kulik report a study in Neisser's volume on what they call "flashbulb" memories. In these memories, they contend, you recall a powerful event with great significance and important consequences in terms of your precise location at the time you experienced or learned of the event, and you remember your surroundings in considerable visual detail. Forty white and forty black Americans were asked to respond to a questionnaire regarding the circumstances under which they heard the news about the assassinations of Medgar Evers, John F. Kennedy, Malcolm X, Martin Luther King, and Robert Kennedy and about attempts to assassinate some other public figures.

The results enabled the authors to demonstrate that the personal consequentiality of the news is an important determinant in flashbulb memories: there was a very large difference between blacks' and whites' experience. Many more blacks than whites had such flashbulb memories of the assassination of Martin Luther King. Conversely, more whites reported such memories of Robert Kennedy's assassination, and all subjects in both groups reported detailed memories of the moment when they learned of the assassination of John F. Kennedy. Thus significance to the individual is an important determining factor in creating flashbulb memories. Rehearsal also appears to be important. Seventy-three percent of the white subjects and 90 percent of the black subjects reported overt rehearsal with friends and family of where they were when they heard the news. Most subjects reported that such rehearsals had occurred between one and ten times.[22]

Brown and Kulik suggest that the hypothesis of a physiological psychologist named Robert B. Livingston may aid in the interpretation of flashbulb memories. Livingston postulated what he called a "Now Print" mechanism for memory. This mechanism, a deliberate mental process, enables a person to save a particular bit of experience from the oblivion of the stream of all conscious experience and to do so through the mechanism of either overt verbal rehearsal or covert interior rehearsal. This idea finds further elucidation, if not corroboration, in the work of neurophysiologists, who report that "memories . . . appear to be stored in a distributed and redundant way in the cortex."[23] This observation may illuminate Lashley's inability to remove a memory surgically from the rat's brain. Recent studies of so-called flashbulb memories have yielded data which cast doubt on the existence of a special class of memory that creates a vivid, detailed, veridical, and permanent memory store. Memories of highly consequential events, such as the explosion of the space shuttle *Challenger*, are apparently as subject to distortion, reconstruction, and error as any other long-term memories.[24]

Marigold Linton contributed to Neisser's collection a study recalling the work of Ebbinghaus in that she herself was the subject, but in this case real world events were involved. Each day Linton selected two or three unique events and made notes about each one on a card with the date. Once a month she picked seventy-five pairs of cards at random and tried to state which of the two events in the pair had occurred first. When she was unable to recognize an event, the card was discarded. At the end of the first year, 1 percent of the cards had been discarded, and in each of the next two years about 6 percent more of the cards were discarded. On the basis of this longitudinal study, Linton drew several conclusions. An event is likely to endure in memory if (1) it is perceived as highly emotional at the time it occurs; (2) if the subsequent course of events makes the event appear to be instrumental or causes it to be perceived as a turning point; and (3) if it remains relatively unique (and is not made less distinct by repetition).[25]

Neisser's collection also includes a chapter by Elizabeth Loftus, who has done seminal work in uncovering the sources of error in eyewitness accounts of events.[26] She shows that it is relatively easy to interfere with memory by supplying subsequent information; the implication is that memory is a reconstructive and active process. According to this view, the mind is constantly endeavoring to combine information from a variety of sources in reconstructing memory and to bring it into congruence with "what must have been."

Neisser's collection includes work by Ulric Neisser himself. His chapter compares the transcription of the tapes recorded in the Oval Office to John Dean's recollections of these conversations in his testimony before the Senate committee that investigated the Watergate crisis. Neisser's careful and systematic analysis of the two transcripts leads him to conclude that, while John Dean believed his account of the conversation to be accurate, he was in fact, like Bartlett's subjects, reporting only the gist. Moreover, he showed some tendency to exaggerate his own role and to report things he had said when in fact they were more likely to be things which on reflection he wished he had said. Nevertheless, the comparison of the documents reveals that, while his memory was influenced by these mental scripts, or "schemata," he was "essentially giving a true account of the facts."[27]

The cognitive psychologists, by emphasizing the more naturalistic manifestations of memory, have made important contributions to our understanding, although the conclusions from the neuroscientists and physiological psychologists may prove in the long run to be the most explanatory. Many of the cognitive psychologists, however, have exhibited a distressing tendency to attack their more behaviorally inclined colleagues without finding it necessary to support their arguments with data. Endel Tulving, for instance, has asserted that man is the only animal capable of traveling back into the past in his own mind.[28] It is not clear to me how Tulving can possibly substantiate such a statement, but he apparently does not consider it necessary to try. Moreover, many of the cognitive psychologists have been much influenced by ecology and the need to study a phenomenon in its naturalistic setting. Thus to perceive man as unique rather than as a part of a continuum in nature is a strange departure from the perspective of biologists, who ordinarily emphasize the importance of ecological considerations.

The emphasis on episodic or autobiographical memory in the more recent literature undoubtedly made the present study of autobiographical memory feasible by creating a climate of inquiry that would permit it to be considered within the scope of reasonable discourse.[29] I must admit that I felt uneasy, however, when I read the following statement and others like it in the more recent literature: "Ebbinghaus explicitly rejected the study of personal memory on the grounds that the study of consciousness was bad methodology. . . . Experimental psychologists overwhelmingly chose the Ebbinghaus route. It is only recently, with the reduction in the methodological constraints of behaviorism . . . , that the study of autobiographical memory has been able to make a comeback."[30]

I was disquieted because the subject of this study has been a hard-nosed rat runner—the very object of the cognitive psychologists' scorn.

What primrose path was my Skinnerean behaviorist about to set his feet upon? And all because of an unfortunate alliance with an oral historian, that most nonempirical of souls? Despite misgivings, however, we persevered where more sensible precautionary types might have demurred. We felt that it was not only unnecessary but counter-productive to discard the work of laboratory scientists following the Ebbinghaus tradition. It was Tulving himself who distributed the survey that he had done on the accomplishments of 100 years of memory research at the Psychonomic Society meetings in 1985. He asked seventy-five memory researchers to vote on empirical findings, theoretical ideas, and methods which in their judgments had stood the test of time.[31] The list was impressive and included contributions from a wide range of theoretical camps including behaviorists.

In summary, an analysis of the history of memory research reveals that, while much has been accomplished, many questions remain unanswered. In fact, Marigold Linton is correct when she asserts that at the present stage of memory studies taxonomy and description may still usefully be pursued. Like the ethnologist or the population biologist, according to Linton, one may yet ask the question: "What is there?" Linton has attempted to chart what exists in her own memory. In her contribution to Rubin's *Autobiographical Memory,* she reports remarkable stability of memory over time, and she has described her search strategies and reflected on how their efficacy has changed as a function of time. She reports a tendency to retain positively toned events better than negatively toned events.[32] Her leads merit further investigation by future researchers.

Other memory questions which may still usefully be addressed in a descriptive fashion include the following:

1. Is memory reliable over time? That is, could one expect to elicit substantially the same account each time if that account were repeatedly called for over a period of years? Alternatively, would an analysis of a particular memory store reveal considerable reconstruction and elaboration from one recall session to another?

2. Would subjecting an informant's memories to comparison with other historical documents serve to corroborate them or not? Certainly memory studies with the capacity to compare various descriptions of the same events have been rare indeed. The methodologies most frequently used in even the most recent studies of autobiographical memory have not allowed for an assessment of the validity of the memories studied.

3. What kind of lapses or gaps occur in the memory? Do forgotten events show any pattern or consistency that might provide information with regard to how the memories were encoded, stored, and retrieved?

4. Are all memories retained, even those which are not ordinarily accessible for recall? Are some memories available only for recognition? Once a memory has been recognized, does the recognition process stimulate further recall? Or have some experiences from the past been absolutely forgotten, leaving no discernible trace in the mind?

5. What function does context serve as a cue for recall or recognition? Does a return to the scene stimulate further recall? Does interaction with others who shared the same or similar experiences stimulate recall of previously inaccessible memories?

These questions continued to intrigue us after we had completed our study of the memory literature. Our study of Howard's memories of World War II, we think, provides information that bears on these questions and suggests avenues for further collaborative investigation by psychologists and historians.

2 Stateside Experiences
First Recall Document

AH: This is an interview with Howard S. Hoffman on his World War II experiences. The interview is being conducted by his wife, Alice M. Hoffman, in their kitchen on the first of March 1978.

Howard, I think we'll just begin, since we're going to focus exclusively on your memories of World War II, with the circumstances of your enlistment. You enlisted in the army, is that correct?

HH: Yes, that's right. Initially I was hoping to enlist in the navy. This was not strictly a patriotic effort. I knew that I was going to be drafted at one point or another. I was hoping to exercise some options by enlisting.

AH: Was it patriotic in some sense, though? What were your feelings about the United States and this war that it was about to enter into?

HH: I felt that it was appropriate for us to be in the war. I was surprised that it had taken us so long to get into it. Pearl Harbor had occurred, of course.

AH: How old were you when Pearl Harbor occurred?

HH: Well, I was in high school; I was probably sixteen or seventeen, I would imagine. The reason I'm saying that is because I'm using as a reference point the fact that I went into the army within a week or so of my birthday, which was May 23—my eighteenth birthday.

AH: So in December 1941 you were sixteen years old.

HH: Yes. December 7. And I do remember the news that Pearl Harbor had been bombed.

AH: How did that affect you?

HH: Well, it meant that we were definitely going to go into the war.

AH: Did you think about that in terms of its effect on you personally?

HH: Well, I was still sixteen; I wasn't yet old enough to be drafted or to even suspect that I was going to go into the war. I didn't know whether the war would be over by the time I would be old enough to fight. However, within a year or so of that, it became clear that I was very likely to be drafted, and most likely that I would be in some kind of combat. That's what I envisioned.

AH: You did envision being in combat?

HH: Oh, yes, sure. I figured if I was going to be drafted, they'd do whatever they wanted with me. They'd put me in the navy or the infantry. They could put me in tanks, anything. I wanted to go to college. I envisioned myself as having the potential for doing some kind of work as a scientist, hopefully as a physicist. First thing that I thought about was maybe I could go into some area that was related to physics, but not necessarily physics, that would have useful potential for the war effort. I remember I applied to Kenyon in Gambier, Ohio, and in fact I got accepted there, at Kenyon College, as I recall, but then discovered that the tuition there was absolutely prohibitive. The reason I had applied to Kenyon was because they had a meteorological program and I had taken some special examinations that got me into that program, but then it turned out that I had to pay a very great amount of tuition and we simply didn't have the money and I couldn't go. I decided to enlist in the navy because they had an Officers Training Program where they would again send you to college and teach you to fly, and you would be in the Naval Air Corps. That was of interest to me. I thought that maybe I could do that. I remember going up to somewhere like Lancaster or Middletown to take the special physicals they had for that program. But I failed the physical on the basis of color vision. It turned out that I have some color weakness. I have a red/green weakness; I am an anomalous dichromat. [Laughter]

AH: What was your parents' attitude toward your impending military service?

HH: Well, I think they were supportive; they didn't argue with what I did and what I hoped to do. The other thing that I did was that I took a series of tests for ASTP—Army Specialized Training Program—and in that program the army sends you to college. I remember taking the test; the way the test operated was that, if you took the test and you got a high grade on the test, you could then enlist, and after you completed basic training they would send you to, or the chances were good that they would send you to college. I took the test, and I don't remember whether I learned what my grades were or whatever, but I remember feeling that I had done pretty well on them and that it was possible that if I enlisted I would very likely be sent to college after I completed basic training.

AH: What were your parents' feelings about the war?

HH: Well, we all deplored the war. I can't imagine their feelings were any different from your parents' feelings. I mean, Germany was an enemy and Japan was an enemy and they were destroying the world and they had to be stopped. It wasn't the way people felt about Vietnam.

AH: Did your mother express any of her fears to you, or did she keep those to herself?

HH: No. She expressed her fears. I had the same fears. I was very frightened of what might happen, what would happen to me. I wasn't sure I would be able to take it, whether I would be able to be a man. I was seventeen at this time and I didn't know what my capacities were, what my potentials were for this. I certainly didn't want to die. I was very frightened; I was frightened as to how would I tolerate simply being away from home at that age. I'd never been away from home before.

AH: You enlisted in May of 1943?

HH: No, no. I enlisted a month or two before that, maybe a couple of months before that. But I knew they wouldn't draft me; I couldn't be called until I turned eighteen. But as it turned out I was called within a week of turning eighteen.

AH: So you went down to an army recruitment center in Harrisburg?

HH: Yes, to enlist, right.

AH: How was that enlistment handled?

HH: As I recall, they had a physical. I don't remember whether the physical was at the time of the enlistment. I think it was. It may have been the induction. I just don't remember when the physical came, but I remember. . . . You see, you had many physicals in the army. And I almost failed the physical—I think it was the enlistment physical, and I almost failed it because they detected something in my urine. It may have been sugar or something like that in my urine, and they had me provide another sample. They pulled me aside because of that, but that was the only thing that was holding me back there. And then they said "Go ahead."

AH: You went back home after the physical?

HH: Yes, after the physical I went home.

AH: And they said that you would hear from them by mail?

HH: Yes, that's right.

AH: Okay. So, when you got the letter what did the letter say?

HH: "Greetings." Then it told me to appear, I think it was Indiantown Gap or downtown at the induction center in Harrisburg to be transported to Indiantown Gap. I think that's what it said. I had a few days, maybe a week. I don't remember how much time there was in the letter; it wasn't very much. I think I got the letter a day or so after my eighteenth birthday. I didn't feel good about it. I was very frightened, in the sense of not knowing whether I would be able to hold up under being away from home. Would I be homesick? How would I do without people that I knew? Would I be in with a lot of older men who were much more mature than I was and more able? I remember getting on the bus, and there were all kinds of people on the bus, all ages. Very few of the people were volunteers. If you were a volunteer, you had a one in front of your number. My number was 13158418, my serial number. So that indicated somebody who had enlisted as opposed to someone who was drafted. They had a three or four or some other number.

AH: Was there any special kind of privilege for people who enlisted?

HH: No. You quickly lost your identity in the sense that you became a number very quickly or an item. I was very depressed by the whole situation. Because, for example, in the induction center you take these tests, but the conditions under which you take them are often very, very bad. They rush you into here and they rush you into there, and they'll take you to physicals, or take you here, between your physical and your lunch, you rush in and suddenly you're sitting down and you're taking an IQ test or a test of your ability at code or a test of your ability at mathematics or in visualizing matrices and squares and things like this. Of course, you know, you might take the test late afternoon or early morning or even in the evening. You could be very tired. And you knew that what you did on the test was going to determine, in part, what was going to happen to you. Maybe whether you'd live or die, because it would determine what kind of a situation you might be in. You might be lucky and get to be a company clerk or something in the rear, you know, in supply, or never leave the States. You know, for every combat man there were twenty support people who never saw combat.

AH: You knew that, then?

HH: I was pretty well aware that most people didn't go into combat, but I just felt very unlucky. I was depressed by the anonymity; I was especially depressed by the thought that what happened to my life was going to be determined by maybe what some pusillanimous clerk had for lunch. Because he would be faced with thousands, or hundreds of sheafs of paper, and he would pick up one and he would take this one and put it in this basket, pick up that one and put it in that basket. And whichever basket he happened to put it in, that determined where you, as a living, breathing individual, was going to go. And if I got assigned to this or assigned to that was a matter of chance and the whim of whoever was handling these things. You felt very much at the mercy of circumstances and not your own person.

AH: So the lost control was very threatening to you?

HH: Very, very threatening, very threatening.

AH: And moreover, what I hear you saying is that you were banking very heavily on these tests as a means of avoiding the potential terrible consequences of the war and as a possible way of realizing your own goals.

HH: Which I couldn't realize because we didn't have the funds to do it otherwise.

AH: So that the fact that the tests were given to you under adverse circumstances heightened your anxiety about how you might do on them.

HH: Tremendously. Tremendously.

AH: How long were you at Indiantown Gap?

HH: Maybe a week.

AH: What was your day like there? Can you reconstruct it?

HH: I can reconstruct a little bit of it. I remember being in the lines and going through the buildings where they handed out clothes. You go to one thing and some guy would measure you real quickly and throw you a shirt. Somebody would measure your waist, measure your seam, and throw you a pair of pants. Then you'd get a pair of boots, you know, you'd stand on a thing and [they would] look at the size of your foot and they would throw you a pair of boots. Zip, zing, zing, in fifteen minutes you had an overcoat, you had more than you could carry, a duffle bag. All of a sudden, there you were, no more civilian clothes. You packed your civilian stuff up, and I don't remember whether I sent it home or what I did with it, but within the first twenty-four hours, I was in uniform, there to remain for the next several years.

AH: Did you make any relationship with any of the other people that were going through these lines with you, or was it really pretty anonymous?

HH: It was pretty anonymous. I mean, you know, I talked to people, but I don't remember having any friends, making any close friendship with anybody in that period. People would talk to each other; I don't remember anybody I was particularly close to or that I could do anything with. Maybe I went to a PX with somebody, but I don't even remember doing that. We were really sort of stripped of everything.

I do remember lying in bed, you know, the first night and thinking to myself, "I've got no control." I didn't cry or break into tears or anything, but I felt very, very much threatened; I felt that I was now in the grip of forces that I couldn't do anything about; that what was happening to me was largely a matter of chance; that I was at the very bottom of the totem pole. There were officers, and there were sergeants and there were corporals, and everybody else was up above me and I was at the bottom, the very bottom of the barrel, and I had to do whatever anybody told me to do. We were taught how to salute and how to address an officer and how to stand at attention, how to clean the latrines, things like that. The meals were . . . there was enough to eat, but it simply wasn't very good.

AH: How did you feel on that day when your parents came to visit you?

HH: I felt proud that I hadn't fallen to pieces. I was glad to see them and very sad to see them go in the sense that I didn't know when I would ever see them again, if ever. I wrote to them. It would be interesting if my mother has any of those early letters. Her late letters, if she kept any, wouldn't be of any use because I never told her that I was in combat. I always pretended I was back of the lines in supply work or something, because I didn't want to scare her.

AH: Where did you go from Pennsylvania then, at the end of that week or two weeks, whatever period it was?

HH: We were told to report, and I don't remember how we got down there. Oh, I do remember, we got on a train, troop train of some sort and I was transferred down to Camp Sibert, Alabama. I was told that I was assigned to chemical warfare. I think on the basis of my high school record—not on the basis of my grade in chemistry, because I wasn't a very good chemist. But they put me in chemical warfare, and I thought that meant I would be doing some kind of work in a chemistry laboratory, and I was kind of pleased about the idea until I learned that what I was really being assigned to was a mortar battalion. Then I wasn't so pleased. However, there were some positive things about going down to Camp Sibert, Alabama. First of all, the guys that were in chemical warfare, most of them had been to college. Not all of them, but many of them. Most of them were older than I was; there were some young people who had not been to college, but most people had had some college.

There were people there with advanced degrees even and very bright, some of them were extremely bright.

AH: Now, all these people in chemical warfare were housed together in Camp Sibert?

HH: Camp Sibert, Alabama, was a chemical warfare center.

AH: So what were your first impressions of Camp Sibert?

HH: Ghastly! Ghastly! What a place—oh, boy!

AH: What made it ghastly?

HH: Well, first of all, it was hot down there. Second of all I was in basic training. Basic training was thirteen weeks, and it's thirteen weeks of absolute subjugation to the whim of people above you— sergeants, corporals, mostly the sergeant. And you have no time on your own, no hope of any independence. You might have an hour occasionally in the evening to go over to the PX for a beer, but that was about it! From four or five o'clock in the morning until about eight or nine o'clock at night, they kept you running, and I mean running. You know, under physical control and under mental control. You were constantly regimented; no time for anything.

AH: What were they training you to do?

HH: They were training you to be a soldier.

AH: How? March? Drill?

HH: Yes, march, drill, constant march and drill, cleaning the barracks, policing around the camp, picking up cigarette butts, how to fire your rifle, how to throw grenades, how to shoot phosphorus, how to fire the weapons, how to take apart and clean your rifle, how to use a bayonet. Bayonet drill was very, very difficult, and they did it frequently.

AH: What made bayonet drill so difficult?

HH: What they do is they give you a rifle which weighs about nine or ten pounds and a bayonet on the end of it which adds another pound or two. Then you have to stand and hold the bayonet, for example, in front of you with arms extended and then you have to wait for the command to put it into the next position and then to take the next step. It's a very awkward position to hold something this heavy, and you just have to stand there and stand there and stand there, no matter how fatigued your arms would become. You dare not drop it or let it waver, because the consequence of failing to be able to do anything was usually some kind of punishment, which was even more severe than the thing they were asking you to do. The exercises were the same way. For example, you'd have to lay on your back and do sit-ups and push-ups and do a particular number. I remember that somebody would walk across your stomach while you were doing these things. Of course, your stomach was very tight, because you were using those muscles. We had to go on a ten-mile hike, or a twenty-five mile hike, in the summer, and guys would pass out. It was very, very common for people to pass out. I remember we wore fatigues for one hike and my fatigues and everyone else's were absolutely white from the perspiration—perspiring and then the salt drying in the perspiration and it just made these white lines all over the fatigues, you know, as we'd walk. It was so very, very hot, and you had a full field pack plus a rifle, plus a gas mask, all the equipment, a tent—you were carrying a half shelter usually.

AH: Were you ever subjected to any of these punishments because you weren't able to do it?

HH: No, I don't ever remember being punished for anything. I was able to do everything—not easily. The obstacle course was very hard for me to do, but I managed to do it. I wasn't sure I'd be able to. You had to go on hand bars and ropes, leap up high fences; you've seen these things in the movies. When you face it and someone says "Next," you just do it. There's no real training to do it. You just run and you do it. I was able to do just about everything they asked me to do. But it was absolutely exhausting. When I got in at night, I would hit the bed and be asleep before I even got my head down practically, sometimes I was so tired. I've never been so exhausted as during basic training. Nor have I ever experienced such anonymity as I felt during basic training.

AH: How many men were sleeping in one room with you?

HH: We were in wooden barracks, and there were maybe about fifty.

AH: What were your relationships with the men in those barracks?

HH: Well, I did develop some friendships with some of the younger people there. Not very close; I don't remember being terribly close to anybody in basic training. Again, you didn't have time to get to know them, and often the guys that were with you were like you were, they were just so completely exhausted and dogged. You didn't have time to talk to anybody most of the time. But I do remember going into town with the guys and drinking beer occasionally but very, very rarely. You were told to do something every single minute. Now, if you were cleaning the latrine, you might get to talk to the other guys who were also on that. Or if you were on KP, and I was on KP a couple of times, you would talk to the other guys. But you never had much time. For example, when you were on KP, you'd get up about four o'clock in the morning, way before dawn, and get the breakfasts out, get the tables set, and then you'd clean up after them. It was just constant work. The amount of work you did was just incredible. Then you'd go back at night, when dinner was done and all the dishes were clean, and you'd be done and maybe it was 8:30 or 9:00 o'clock. All you can do is drag yourself to the barracks and fall into bed. Then you'd have to be up again the next morning at six o'clock or five o'clock or whatever and then go on a march or a bivouac or out to the rifle range, then to the lectures on the different kinds of poison gases and then maybe gas-mask drill or a Mickey Mouse movie. Your day was programmed in many ways. The most emotionally difficult time that I ever experienced was during basic training.

AH: Did you have any idea in the morning when you woke up what the day held for you, or did they just tell you as the day went by?

HH: Occasionally you knew. You knew there was going to be an inspection, or there was going to be a march, you were going to have to march a forced march, or there was going to be a parade and you'd have to parade. So sometimes you did know. Often you didn't.

AH: Were these all white men in the barracks?

HH: Yes.

AH: There was no integration in the army at that time at all?

HH: No. They were all white. There were colored companies, but they weren't integrated.

AH: But they were there on the same base?

HH: I seem to recall seeing colored companies on the same base, but that's a little hazy. It could have been somewhere else.

AH: In other words, they were all white men?

HH: Yes.

AH: Were there any kind of ethnic tensions or difficulties between rural southerners and urban boys from New York, or anything like that?

HH: Oh, I'm sure there were, but you didn't experience very much except what they told you to do. You didn't have very much time to talk to anybody. I remember, well, eating at the table. You ate. You were careful not to reach across and take more than your share because you might get a fork in your hand from somebody else. You might be sitting at a table with somebody you knew, but you might just as well not be, too. It was like a lot of individuals who were all being beat down at the same time.

Now, there were guys there who you would single out, or pick out and say, "Well, that guy is trying to get a section 8." Guys who acted like they were crazy, who maybe were retarded or were somewhat disturbed. I remember one guy who used to always appear, and his leggings would not be laced properly and his shirttail would be out and things like that. I believe they eventually did discharge him. He didn't finish basic with us. He was a guy from New York. I was never certain whether he was playing a role or just wanted to get out and that was his way of doing it.

AH: Did playing a role like that occur to you in low moments?

HH: No, I don't think I could have done that. The only time it ever occurred to me was later on in combat, where I thought, boy, I'd like to get a bullet through a foot or something like that. But I don't remember thinking that I could section 8 my way out.

I recall things like officers' houses and noting how officers had so much privilege and how regular soldiers had no privilege at all. I remember thinking I'd like to go to the chaplain and have him do something for me, but I didn't know what to have him do. I remember mail call was important to me; that was the one time of the day that you might get some break from the outside, because this was not a real world. This was an experience that I felt would never end. I couldn't imagine surviving through very much longer of it. But at the same time, I could see that I was getting to be stronger physically, that the physical training was making me much stronger than I had been when I started. And that I was able. I became aware, just as when I was playing tennis in high school, I became aware that I wasn't a great player, but I was a pretty good tennis player, I was a pretty good shot. I wasn't a sharpshooter; I wasn't that good as a marksmen, but I was almost a sharpshooter. In judo, I got to the point where I could throw a guy who was twice my size. And I made those marches. I didn't pass out, although there were times when I thought I was going to.

AH: Or hoped you would!!

HH: No, I didn't really hope I would. I mean that didn't seem like it would solve anything. I remember incidences of learning how to use grenade launchers or learning how to use dynamite, explosives, how to fire the mortar, how to fire a machine gun, how to fire and take apart and clean rifles. How to do KP, how to dig foxholes, how to put up pup tents, how to march and things of this sort. An awful lot of how-to-do things. And I remember feeling that I was pretty competent in a good number of things that I hadn't been before I went into the army.

AH: Supposing I should ask you, "What was the funniest thing that happened at Camp Sibert, Alabama?" Of all the things that happened, what was the funniest?

HH: [Long pause] I'm trying to recall at least one funny thing. I think we must have gotten off once or twice and gone into Gadsden, I sort of remember walking down the street in Gadsden, Alabama, and looking in the jewelry stores at the little souvenirs that they sold, buying a hotdog, going to the USO and getting some doughnuts in Gadsden, and hoping to meet some girls and not meeting any. But it's hard to remember things that were funny. Perhaps there were things that were funny. I know I used to go to the PX on a couple of occasions and drink beer, and I learned to put salt in beer and learned to drink beer there.

AH: Salt in beer! What was the purpose in that?

HH: It just made it taste a little better. People did it. A lot of the guys did it, and I tried it, and I liked it that way.

AH: Didn't you have a special name in the army for the town of Gadsden?

HH: Oh, yes, that was Gonorrhea Gardens! But that wasn't from experience!

AH: Well, all right, what about the saddest thing that happened?

HH: [Long pause] No, I don't have any recollection of [sad] things. I wouldn't think of them in those terms as sad or funny. It was hard. The whole situation had a kind of feeling of sadness for me because of the war we were preparing for. I was sad because I wasn't going to go to college, didn't think I would. I wasn't going to do the things I had hoped to do. But I don't remember any specific incidents. I don't remember very many of the exact incidences that were not part of the routine of getting up in the morning, rushing to eat, rushing from eating to the first condition they had you in, which might be marching or might be exercises, or it might be mail call, or it might be something else. What I remember was that there was no time whatsoever for yourself.

AH: So at the end of basic training, did they send you home?

HH: No. What happened at the end of basic training, was that people were usually shipped out to various places. What happened here was that they came, and I remember this day, they made an announcement. They called us all out, we had to stand out there, and they told us we were finished, and somebody may have complimented us. I don't remember being complimented for anything else throughout basic training. I mean, no matter how well you did it, the best you could ever do was "satisfactory." But maybe at the last day somebody said we'd been a good group.

Anyhow they made an announcement saying that the army had a project at Edgewood Arsenal in Maryland and they were calling for volunteers to be in poison gas experiments. They were testing some gases and that people who did volunteer would be there for, I don't remember, several weeks or maybe a month or two months—I don't think it was that long, though—several weeks and they would get a week's furlough at the end of it. I, and almost everybody else in the company, volunteered to do that. Within a day or so we were shipped up to Edgewood Arsenal, Maryland, in a troop train, as I remember it, of some sort.

Edgewood Arsenal

HH: The barracks at Edgewood Arsenal were stucco, as I recall, and they were two story, and the rooms were very large and the beds were far apart. The bathrooms were clean, and they were real bathrooms, and they were in the same building. You didn't have to go to a latrine. You had clean sheets. It was just great. You had your own bed. It wasn't double-deck bunks. Everybody had a bed of their own. Windows in the barracks and no first sergeant to control you. I mean, you were almost on your own. There was a corporal, one of the people from Edgewood Arsenal was assigned to us as kind of a corporal. He saw to our needs, as it were.

We didn't do anything for the first few days or first week or so. I don't remember doing anything. We had time off, we read, we walked around the camp, we went into Baltimore. We went to burlesque shows at night. We got to know each other. It was really very, very different from what the army had been like before that. It was the first time I began to feel like a person in the army, like an individual.

I remember I met a girl there, a WAC, who was from Kentucky or Arkansas that I liked very much and we went on a couple of dates. I don't remember her name.

AH: Do you remember what you did on the date?

HH: Yes, we went to a movie and did a lot of talking. I might have necked with her a little bit one time. But you know I was very young, very virginal, and destined to remain that way for a while.

AH: What did you like about her?

HH: She was very pretty, very sweet. She was a young girl, eighteen or nineteen, my age. Anyway, I did a lot of reading there. I had a lot of opportunity to just lay in the bunk and read, sit outside and read, walk around. It was like a vacation.

AH: Do you remember what you read?

HH: I think I read mostly pocketbooks; at that time they were just coming out with pocketbooks. I remember one book was the *Keys to the Kingdom*. I may have read that on the boat going over, but it was books of that sort.

AH: Okay, so when did they start the experiment?

HH: Well, I remember what they did with me; they asked for volunteers, and they didn't start doing any experiments right away. They had us doing different things. I got assigned to work with a lieutenant who was developing a new kind of a harness for flame throwers. He was kind of like an engineer. I remember I used to go over to his shop, back in some corner of Edgewood Arsenal. I helped him and gave him my ideas, and you know, actually felt I was really contributing to it—in designing a back frame to hold the flame thrower. We built one and then we took it out and we tested it, tested the flame thrower. I had never seen a flame thrower in operation before, and I got a chance to see what they were like that way. But the thing that I remember is that he had a lot of instruments, very good shop equipment, and he had some very interesting and delicate kinds of instruments that were made from brass that he had made, or other people had made that were in the shop. I recall enjoying doing that very much. Being in the shop and working on this pack for the flame thrower.

The first test they did with us was with nitrogen mustard gas. No . . . yes . . . I guess that's what it was. I think maybe all of these tests were with the nitrogen mustards, which were developed by the Germans. But the Americans had something like them or had some aspect of it, because I know that one of my chemistry teachers when I was at the University of Chicago had been at Edgewood Arsenal, Maryland, and had been working as a chemist on these gases. The first test, in fact, that we did had to do with how well you were protected in these nitrogen mustards. Now, I think I was only in the gas chamber twice. In the first test we put on protective clothing, which basically consisted of fatigues that had been impregnated with a mixture of wax and chlorine—some kind of chlorine chemical, which was supposed to neutralize the burning effect the gas has on your skin—mustard gases will raise huge blisters on your skin, and if you breathe them in what they will do is they burn your lungs, they burn you physically. You'd die from that.

They had us put protective cream on our hands, all over our hands. This was like a cold cream. And on our necks. Then we went into this gas and we wore gas masks and went into the gas chamber, which was a room about ten by ten by ten maybe, made of half-inch thick steel with glass portholes and a big steel door, and it was airtight. I remember going into the room with about maybe ten other guys, all of us having smeared our hands up real good and around our neck. They had just given us the instructions what to do as if we were in the field, and we had done it. I supposed what they were testing was how effective this protection was.

I remember being in there and it was very hot, and I remember perspiring, and I could see the perspiration coming through the cream that was on my hand, and around my ankles I could feel the perspiration dripping off myself and the gas mask only covers you up to here [indicating top of forehead], and you've got all your hair exposed. I don't remember if we wore a little stocking cap or something like that to try to protect the scalp. But I also remember being in there, breathing through the gas mask. There was a fly in there flying around and he didn't seem to be affected at all by the gas; he was just flying around in this mustard gas. Aside from the fact that we knew where we were and what the situation was, there was not anything very particularly frightening to me about it. Although I realized I could get very badly hurt if my gas mask should leak and I should breathe any of this. Anyhow they took us out of there and we went back to the barracks and I guess we washed and took showers and cleaned ourselves off.

Then they examined us the next day or so, and nothing happened to me. I got not a blister, not even a red mark or anything. But some of the guys were very badly burned by it, so badly burned that they had to be hospitalized for a week. One guy had smeared himself up just like I had, but the next day, I guess it was, he got blisters on the backs of his hands and around his ankles and around his forehead, everywhere that the cream had been, there were [blisters] a half inch high and completely full of water. So that if he laid his right hand down and you looked at it, it looked like there were two hands there. One was him and one was just the blister, complete blister. And he was in considerable pain and in danger of infection. He had a big ring around his forehead, I remember, under his chin—it looked like he had a beard—and around his ankles. But I had no reaction to the gas.

AH: Did they explain anything to you about why there would have been a different effect on one person than on another?

HH: No.

AH: Did you speculate about that among yourselves?

HH: Yes. I mean we were very sorry for him and glad that it wasn't us. But we didn't know. Some of the guys got little blisters, a couple of little blisters, but I didn't get anything. No effect I could notice.

AH: Was that because you had done a better job of putting the cream on? Or what?

HH: I don't think so. I don't see how it could be that dramatic. It had to do with the chemistry of the body. I was just not as sensitive to the gas as he was. I'm sure that was the difference.

I think after those tests I went back and worked some more with this engineer. Then for the next test they took us out on the rifle range and they had us fire at the targets from a hundred yards or two hundred yards, whatever. I forget what the distance was; I think it's a hundred yards. I remember making a pretty good record. Then they took us and they marched us from there to another place where they had a gas tank. And this time we went into the gas tank, into the room, again about six or seven of us. And as I remember there was a cat in there and a lieutenant. And the lieutenant had a gas mask, and we had no gas masks. They had us in there and they just had us standing around and they told us to breathe and then just to walk around in a circle in there. The lieutenant was in there with us, watching us. As I say, he had a gas mask and he had it on. We didn't even have gas masks with us. As the gas came in, there was no pain. . . . I don't even remember an odor. All I remember is wanting to breathe more deeply, taking deeper and deeper breaths because apparently we weren't getting all that much oxygen. I remember that the cat—we guys were talking to each other, and we looked at the cat, "My God, the cat is dying!" The cat had fallen over on its side and its eyes had a glazed expression and it may have died. I don't know for sure, but it looked like it was dead. We weren't in there all that long, as I recall, maybe ten minutes. But I was frightened by that. I was frightened by the fact that he had a gas mask on and we didn't and that the cat was so powerfully affected by the gas.

AH: Did they take you out, or did you ask to be taken out?

HH: No, nobody asked to be taken out. They took us out. Because he was in there and I guess he was the one who would have been in command of it. They took us out, and they marched us to the rifle range again and had us fire again. I think we marched at double time. And we fired again. I remember when I came to fire I could hardly see the target. In fact, I couldn't really make out the target at all, but what I could see was, you know, the place where the target was supposed to be, the posts out there. So when I would fire, I fired in between the posts where I thought the target would be, even though I couldn't see it. I'm pretty sure my score was not a helluva lot worse than it was the first time. I think if they'd have had me try to fire at a target that would have popped up out of somewhere that I really would have had to have good acuity to see, I wouldn't do near as well as firing where I was using other cues, other than the pure visual cues beside the target. Well, anyhow, I didn't do badly. I think after we fired at the target they took us over to the medical building and the first thing they did was they drew blood. They drew a syringeful of blood from the right arm. That was the very first thing. Then they took us into another room, and there was an ophthalmologist, and he examined our eyes. One of the things he did, he measured the pressure in the eyeball. In order to do that he had a little thing—it's a plunger that comes down over, there's a little cup and the cup fits right over the iris of the eye and the plunger would be where the pupil is. So what we had to do was hold our eye open while he actually touched our eye with this thing and got a measure of the internal pressure. I remember that was so hard to do, to hold my eye open, even though he had put some kind of drops in them. My eye wouldn't stay open, and I would look away, and I would force myself to look at him, and eventually he got it, got the measure. Once he got it on the eyeball, you know, there was nothing you could do and your eye stayed open and he got the measurement. Then he put drops in one of your eyes and he didn't put drops in the other eye. What he had done, it turns out, is he had given me atropine, which dilates—I believe it's atropine—which dilates the pupil. Or belladonna, I don't remember which. The point is that the gas causes the pupils to constrict to tiny pinpoints, and the stuff he gave us dilated the eye. So I had one eye dilated and the other eye fully constricted. That's when the headaches began, because you couldn't look at anything. When you would try to focus on something to read, what would happen is that both eyes would respond equally and it was something like getting hit on the head with a hammer each time you would look at things. Not only that, but for the first several hours they took blood from us about every half hour. I only remember getting one eye test on the first day, but every half hour they took blood from us for the first six or eight hours at least, it seemed to me. Boy, I was getting sick of having . . . you know, my arm was getting sore. Stick one arm out, then the other arm out, then this arm out, then that arm out. . . .

AH: Did they have you in sick bay or in the infirmary?

HH: No. We were at a medical building, but we weren't patients. We went back to our own dormitories after that. Every day then, it seemed like it was for at least three weeks we gave blood and had our eyes tested. At first they took the blood, I think it was every half hour, then every hour, then maybe twice a day, then once a day. They took blood once a day until the whole thing was over. I got myself a pair of dark glasses, but that didn't help very much. It was these eye tests and the constant having the one pupil dilated and the other pupil completely constricted. We looked weird if you looked at one of us because of the big imbalance between the two pupils. I don't think we could go to a movie, or read, or do very much of anything, except just walk around and try not to look at things too much. Although I think I may have gone into the city once. I may even have taken a weekend trip up to Harrisburg from Baltimore. I think maybe I did go up for a weekend. Well, that lasted for about, as I say, two-three weeks.

Then we were told it was finished. They thanked us. I was to have a week's furlough, and at the end of the week's furlough I was to report to Camp Sibert, Alabama, where I had come from. They gave me money for the train, or they gave me train tickets, I don't remember exactly which they did. Of course, I had money then, because they did pay you, not much. But you know, for a kid who doesn't have any other expenses, that was money. So I did have pocket money.

So I went home. I remember that I still had a little bit of the aftereffects of the experiment. I visited; I remember visiting friends and visiting with my mother and brothers, going out to dinner with them and things like that. But on the last day, when I had to report back to Camp Sibert, Alabama, I started to feel sick. I had a very sore throat and I was starting to lose my voice. I got on the train—I figured I had to go anyhow, as long as I could possibly make it I had to get down there, so I got on the train, said "good-bye" to my family, didn't know what was in store for me. The train pulled out. I remember we may have had a couple of extra hours in Washington, because I seem to remember getting there just . . . you know, stopping in Washington and seeing the place all torn up because an engine had gone through its stop and had crashed through the ceiling in there. I think that's when that occurred, but it may have occurred much later. It may have been a different occasion when I was in Washington. I don't think we stopped in Washington on this occasion, because I was sick, and usually when I stopped in Washington I got out and walked around and went to the National Gallery or something like that. But on this occasion I'm pretty sure we went right on down to Camp Sibert. I think we would go to Birmingham and then take a bus to Gadsden. I don't remember exactly what the train trip was.

What I do remember is that by the time I got down there I was feeling very, very lousy. My throat was just on fire and I could barely talk and I was sure I was running a fever. So when I got in I went to the sergeant and said I didn't feel well, that I wanted to check into the infirmary. He let me go. I went to the infirmary and they checked me in and put me to bed. Well, they kept me in the infirmary for three days, and on the third day they let me out about one o'clock in the afternoon. I went back to my outfit. And when I walked in there was nobody there; it was empty. Nobody! Nobody in the barracks, nobody in the office, nobody anywhere. Finally I found somebody in one of the offices, maybe from another company or something and he said, "Oh, they shipped out." I said, "When did they ship out?"

He said, "This morning." I said, "Well, my God, where did they go?" "I dunno." Finally I went to the main offices of the camp and tried to find out and finally I discovered that yes, they had shipped out, that I had missed my shipment. "Where was I supposed to go?" "You were supposed to go to State College, Pennsylvania." "What for?" "Well, you were going to go to ASTP up at Penn State." A large number of guys in that outfit had apparently been selected for that and I was one of them. So I said, "All right. I'll go right up there." "No, we can't issue you orders. We have to cut new orders for you."

I tried to argue with this guy, a sergeant or somebody. He wouldn't hear anything other than I had to report back to my barracks and they would cut new orders for me. So I went back to the barracks.

AH: All by yourself?

HH: All by myself. Then it turned out that there were two other guys who were delayed coming back from furlough and they were there too. And all three of us had missed our shipments. So there were three of us there that had been through basic training. I didn't know the other guys very well, but I remember that they were in the outfit. They had been in basic with me. I guess they had been up at Edgewood.

What we learned was that in three days a new crew was coming in and that what they had decided to do with us was put us on permanent KP, so they wouldn't have to take any of these new ones and put them on KP except as punishment. That way they could get more time training. So that began I think almost a month of every single day getting up at four in the morning and dragging myself over to that goddamn kitchen and scrubbing pots, cleaning waste traps, peeling potatoes, cleaning [up] greasy pork chops, scrubbing floors, washing dishes—every filthy, hot, difficult job you can think of.

AH: You must have decided it wasn't a just world.

HH: Yes, I had made up my mind by that time that it wasn't a just world. [Laughter] I remember, though, it did have its compensations. I remember there was a guy there who was a pretty bright guy. He'd been to college; he knew calculus. We were both washing pots, and we would make up games. Like I said, "Now, look, when we're scrubbing pots, when we scrub it we're taking metal off of the outside and when we scrub the inside we're taking metal off the inside, so the pot is getting smaller from the outside and bigger from the inside. The question is how big is the pot going to be? Is it going to be half the thickness bigger or what when we're finished with all our scrubbing and before it disappears? We would talk about things like that.

The mess sergeant was sort of sorry for us because he ordinarily had guys in there that were being punished and he joined in the merriment of harassing them. But he didn't try to harass us that much. I mean he would sometimes give us special cuts of food. He understood that he was seeing the same faces over and over and over again and took some mercy on us. But, God, that was a tough business. You know, by the time you were done at night, it was dark, after everybody had gone home, and you dragged yourself back to the barracks and fell into bed and went to sleep and before you knew it you were getting up because you had to be up at 4:00 A.M. to be there to have the breakfast ready for when these guys came in at six. So it was a very, very hard business.

One day orders came. Where was I to report? Well, it was somewhere up north of Harrisburg. Some camp up north, replacement camp. So I get on the train again and up I go. In this replacement camp I'm just hoping—I'm going past Penn State to get up there—I'm just hoping they're going to send me down to Penn State. But you don't know. Finally we were there for several days. Again you're isolated and you don't know anybody; you're just in a big replacement depot. One day the orders came that I was to go to Newport News, Virginia, that I was to go overseas from there. And I guess I got on another train down to Newport News and got on a ship, didn't know anybody. You know, I didn't know any of the other people that were on the ship. I got on the ship, and that was it. That was the beginning of the trip overseas.

AH: Now, the other people who were on the ship had been in basic training together, and consequently it was a group of men who knew each other from basic training?

HH: Many of them. It was a mixed group. There were people who had been in basic training together. There were people from different outfits, they weren't chemical warfare necessarily, they were infantry and artillery and things like that. There was one group of guys who were prisoners who had volunteered for the army to get out of prison, and they kind of hung together in a group. But there was nobody I knew there, although I did make friends after a while with some of the men.

AH: But if you had shipped overseas with your original group you would have been with people you knew.

HH: That's right, except my group didn't ship overseas. My group, mostly, went to college. I'd have been in college with people I knew.

AH: Most of them went to college?

HH: Well, I think a good number of them went to that ASTP. Yes. You see, remember they had taken all these guys who had shown some potential and put them in this chemical warfare outfit that wasn't your ordinary infantry outfit or artillery.

AH: And you were still in chemical warfare?

HH: I was still in chemical warfare, yes.

AH: And you knew that when you got overseas you would be assigned to some kind of chemical warfare outfit?

HH: I expected that I would, yes. Because that's what I was trained in. I mean, I might have been assigned to the infantry or something else, but usually they kept you in the kind of training you'd had and that would determine what you were going to do. I mean, I was a mortar crewman by that time; I could operate a mortar.

AH: Okay, I think we left off with you just having gotten on the ship, and we were going to begin that saga of twenty-eight days at sea.

HH: That's exactly what it was! Twenty-eight days in the number two hold of a Liberty ship. There were five hundred guys in that number two hold, and I understood, although I never saw it, that there was ammunition underneath us. At least that was the rumor. The bunks were next to one another, just barely room enough for you to walk past them. It was just a frame of iron with a canvas strung across it, and you could barely turn over, you were so close to the bunk above you. And they were eleven high, starting perhaps six inches from the floor to maybe a foot from the top of the bulkhead. If you were on the bottom, it was not a very good thing, because the ship rocked and people were very often getting quite seasick. When they got seasick they would sometimes throw up over the edge of their bunk. And when they threw up over the edge of their bunk it would get all over all the guys below his bunk, especially if the ship was at an angle at that point. Almost everybody was seasick on that trip over.

We were allowed to be on deck most of the time, but we were confined to, as I recall, just the hatchways around the number two compartment. We couldn't go fore and we couldn't go aft on the ship. What that meant was that we were always in very, very tight quarters. I remember that there were some guys in one clear space that had been in stockades or prisons in America, and they were now released from the prisons to go in the army overseas. At least that's what I was told. I was on my way to a replacement depot and I was not with an outfit, not with anybody that I knew. I was completely on my own.

AH: How did you feel about being with a group of prisoners?

HH: Well, it didn't bother me particularly. The guys in the army were pretty rough; the training had been pretty rough. They couldn't be any rougher than what I'd been through and what I was expecting to get into.

AH: Did you know where you were going? Where the ship was going to land?

HH: I think we were told it was going to Naples after we left the shore, you know, after we were at sea. When we boarded the ship we had no idea where we were going.

AH: Were you in Newport News for any length of time?

HH: No. Maybe two or three days, at the most. I never got to see anything except the inside of the camp. As I recall we mounted trucks and were driven to the dock, mounted the dock, and there we were on the boat. And immediately put down in the hold. I didn't see the boat leave or anything. We became aware that we were at sea a few hours later when people started to get seasick and you could feel the ship rocking. So I don't remember even seeing us leave harbor.

"Don't ask foolish questions. Th' schedule calls for calisthenics. We'll start with th' left eyelid."

Copyright 1945 by Bill Mauldin

It was a filthy, bad experience. Now, they did have a mess hall of some sort that we would go into. I think it was another level up from the hold, because the hold that we were in was below the water level, I remember that. I remember being very concerned about that, because if they had air raids or drills they would force us to go into the hold rather than to come out on deck.

The latrine was just ghastly on that ship. It was two troughs, the width of a cabin. The cabin was midship, and the troughs ran—I guess they were thirty feet long, and they had seawater running through them, and then planks over them with holes cut in the planks. Then, just in front of you were the sinks and at the ends of the sinks were two urinals. The thing that was so horrible, you know, was that people were sitting on the pot with diarrhea and vomiting into the sinks and with tiny close quarters. You never had any fresh water to wash with; we only washed with saltwater. The soap didn't work; we had something called saltwater soap, but it didn't do a damn bit of good. I remember there were certain times when you could go to the bathroom.

AH: What if you had to go to the bathroom at some other time?

HH: I don't know! I know they had things pretty tight. You see, I think they had to keep the thing organized according to the letters in your name. Maybe you could go to the bathroom, but you couldn't wash, you know, because there just wasn't enough bathroom space for 500 people. [If you] figure twenty toilets, five hundred guys, that would be twenty-five guys per toilet. You had twenty-five guys using one toilet, and you figure each person uses it for a few minutes, and there's only an eight-hour day, there isn't much free time—they were kept pretty warm! Not only that, and this is something that is indelibly etched on my memory—when we had high seas and the ship was rolling a great deal, remember I said it was amidships, and it went across the ship, and it was one large trough? Well, when the ship was rolling, that water that was flowing in that trough would come out of at least the two end toilets, and when the ship would go down, you'd be just sitting there and it would just shoot up two or three feet in the air and onto the floor. Not always, I mean, most of the time it didn't come up, but on the really rough days I remember seeing the damn water spewing out of the ends of the thing and everything that was in the water was spewing out, too. It was like living in a sewer! I really didn't appreciate the way Uncle Sam was treating me! I felt that I deserved better. [Laughter]

They fed us heated C-rations; they didn't feed us any fresh food the whole trip across. It got very rough quite early on the trip, and people got very, very, very sick. I got sick too. I never threw up, but I wanted to a few times. It was just such utter boredom. The seas were heavy, and the ship would move slowly. I think they said the whole trip across we averaged about eight knots, which was eight miles an hour or something like that, a little bit more than eight miles an hour.

AH: You were in a very large convoy?

HH: There were more than, I understand, five hundred ships. There were ships as far as we could see. A convoy like that can't go any faster than the slowest ship in the convoy, and the slowest ships were these landing crafts with these big flat bows that they were sending over there, landing crafts for landing tanks and things. They weren't the infantry-type landing craft but the bigger ones for landing tanks. I think they call them LST.

We were at sea. We had nothing to do. People played cards an awful lot, shot dice. I had a couple of books that I read while I was going over. I remember reading the *Keys to the Kingdom*. That was one of the books I read on the way over there, a book by A.J. Cronin. One incident I do remember: they had an air raid drill one day. It was a bright, sunny day, and the seas weren't really too rough that particular day. I guess we had been at sea two weeks by that time. By that time I was just bored stiff, disgusted by the filth and constantly wishing there were something to do. Guys were sitting around playing cards outdoors. And they were having an air raid drill for some reason. Different ships around were shooting into the air, but we knew it was an air raid drill. Apparently from one of the ships, a 50 millimeter shell—these were explosive shells—maybe it was a 120 millimeter, but I think it was a 50 millimeter shell; it wasn't really very big—landed in the middle of the crap game. It happened to just land on our ship instead of falling in the water. It came about thirty or forty feet from me. I was just standing at the side watching the crap game and all of a sudden I hear this little bump, which was not very loud, and a bunch of guys start screaming. And I see blood. We rushed over and it turned out that one of these shells had landed in the middle of this crap game and had exploded and wounded twenty-one guys. Twenty-one people were wounded. None of them very seriously except one, who was hit in the head by a tiny sixteenth-inch piece of steel from the explosion of the bullet, a fragment.

Now, I didn't get to see these people and have anything to do with it and nobody ever told us what happened. They took these guys that got hit and put them in the infirmary, wherever that was. I never went to the infirmary, so I never saw it. At least I don't recall going. The story I got was that one of them was hurt quite badly and they had to get medical help for him, bring a doctor on board. The seas were very, very bad and the ship was going up and down, you know, huge swells, whitecaps. What I remember happening was that our ship, [although] it didn't come to a stop, it slowed way down—this happened during the day—and a destroyer came right up alongside of our ship. Let me think about this. They made two transfers at sea, one of them was with a breeches buoy. The first one they brought the doctor on board. The seas were very rough, but they just brought the doctor on board.

AH: With the breeches buoy?

HH: No. The destroyer didn't come that close to the ship. It came maybe 200 yards from our ship. they lowered a boat into the sea. The boat came across and brought the doctor over, and [he] was then lifted in a chair or some kind of a sling up onto the deck. But I remember being so impressed by the sailors in that boat, because one of those sailors was standing in the gunwales in the back, steering that boat, and the seas were so high he would literally disappear from view and then come back into view. His boat was just rocking from side to side, and he was just standing up there like it was nothing at all. They transferred him [the doctor] onto the ship, and then two or three days later, the seas were a little bit calmer—they weren't completely calm, but they were much calmer than they had been—then they did this breeches buoy transfer to take the wounded guy and the doctor back to the destroyer where they could work on him. I remember that for the transfer they had all 500 of us on one side of the ship to make it lean to one side. I think it was that we brought the decks down, because the destroyer was lower than we were. We brought the decks down to effect that breeches buoy transfer. And there are these two ships going through the water and transferring. And of course, all this time it's very dangerous because we knew we were in submarine-controlled water, and anything that slows down like that you run the risk of being attacked by a submarine. But I don't ever remember an attack in the Atlantic of any kind, either submarine or air raids. None of those things happened.

We sighted land, I guess, maybe twenty days out, maybe even longer than that.

AH: What time of year was this? Summer? I mean: when you were out on deck, were you warm?

HH: No. It was winter. [Pause] It was February or March. Because I think we made the big attack that we made in May, and that was about a month after I arrived. May is the date that strikes me as being the time when we made the big attack, and I had already been in combat for a while.

AH: So you were saying that you sighted land after about twenty days.

HH: I think it was about twenty days, and I think the land we saw was Gibraltar. We went through the Straits of Gibraltar and into the Mediterranean and along the African coast. We could see land fairly often, and occasionally, I remember, there was an Arab boat that came up. One night while we were in the Mediterrean, which was very smooth, I mean, that was nothing after having been on the Atlantic, we had an air raid at night. I remember being forced to be down in that number two hold—and I'm pretty sure it was on the Mediterranean that the air raid occurred—and that was really my first touch of combat. I remember being rather frightened when our antiaircraft guns on the rear, a 105 or something like that, had fired, I thought we had been hit, because the sound carried through the ship so well. Then I realized it was our own gun firing that was making that noise. That struck me as being terribly dangerous, because if anything happened, there would be no way that the people could get out. There were two four-foot-wide companionways, enough for one, or at the most two people, to go up, and you had 500 people in the hold itself and there were no other exits. So my feeling was that if anything happens, if we catch fire or something like that, we're all doomed. We just couldn't get out. So it was not a pleasant sensation to hear those [guns] and realize we were under air attack and even possibly under submarine attack; we didn't know. We just knew it was a raid of some sort.

AH: What was the morale of the men like, in terms of being so confined and having nothing to do? Were there a lot of fights and quarrels or were people pretty good humored?

HH: No. There were a lot of fights, a lot of quarrels; people were sick; they were very hostile. You had to be very cautious about what you said to people. You know, you didn't shove anybody, or you're likely to get shoved overboard. And nobody really knew each other. I didn't see any real cliques on board the ship. It seemed like everybody was a replacement of some sort. We all went to this replacement depot.

3 Stateside Experiences
Analysis of Memories

The transcription of the tape-recorded interviews of Howard's stateside memories resulted in forty-four typed pages for the initial interview and forty-one typed pages for the interview done four years later. In both sets of interviews, the material generated about each phase of the experience is approximately the same.

Both recall interviews, although conducted four years apart, reveal a remarkably stable memory. Both versions of the incident of the man wounded during an air raid drill are presented side by side (see box). The careful reader will note that while the stories are not identical word for word, and that the information is presented in slightly different sequences, no incident which appears in the first interview is omitted from the second. There are, however, interesting discrepancies of detail. In interview 1 twenty-one people are reported wounded; in interview 2 "five or six guys are wounded." In interview 1 "nobody ever told us what happened," but in interview 2 Howard remembers talking to one of the men who "had some shrapnel somewhere." Aside from these details, however, the narratives, especially as they relate to Howard's direct experiences, are exactly similar. These narratives are so similar that in both interviews the same hesitation is experienced at the same point in the account. Note that in interview 1 Howard starts to describe bringing the doctor from a destroyer to treat the wounded man. Then he starts to visualize the scene and has trouble with it. He says, "Let me think about this. They made two transfers at sea." He then proceeds to describe a scene in very visual terms.

In the second interview at the same point in the narrative when he is describing the transfer, he stops, says, "No, that isn't what happened . . . they put a boat out," and again follows the very detailed description of the sailor in the boat. It is almost as if the image of the sailor in the boat interrupts and corrects the verbal narrative. In fact, as we shall see, there is much evidence to suggest that Howard's memory consists of a number of stored scenes, linked together by verbal constructions to maintain the thread or chronology of the narrative. In this regard, it is interesting to observe that both recall documents contain the same little

Initial Document 1978	Second Document 1982
And they were having an air raid drill for some reason. Different ships around were shooting into the air, but we knew it was an air raid drill. Apparently from one of the ships, a 50 millimeter shell—these were explosive shells—maybe it was a 120 millimeter, but I think it was a 50 millimeter shell; it wasn't really very big—landed in the middle of the crap game. It happened to just land on our ship instead of falling in the water. It came about thirty or forty feet from me. I was just standing at the side watching the crap game and all of a sudden I hear this little bump, which was not very loud, and a bunch of guys start screaming. And I see blood. We rushed over and it turned out that one of these shells had landed in the middle of this crap game and had exploded and wounded twenty-one guys. Twenty-one people were wounded. None of them very seriously except one, who was hit in the head by a tiny sixteenth-inch piece of steel from the explosion of the bullet, a fragment.	They were having this anti-aircraft drill, and we were all up on deck watching, and one bunch of guys was shooting crap on a hatch cover. I was watching the tracers going by in the sky when there was a small explosion—not a large one—and I hear the screaming right behind me, near me, and I go over there, and it turns out that five or six guys have been wounded, because a shell had fallen into the middle of the crap game and exploded and has literally wounded, you know the shrapnel from it, has wounded a bunch of people. It was one of our own shells from the antiaircraft that just happened to fall back on our ship at that particular point.
	I don't know where they went. We didn't see those people again. Well, one of them, I know, I remember talking to, he had some shrapnel somewhere, a little tiny piece of shrapnel it was, but there was one guy that was badly wounded. He was hit in the head. We had no ship's doctor on board. . . . well, there may have been a ship's doctor, but if there was, he didn't feel able to deal with the problem, because what happened was that a day or so later, the next day, as I remember, very bad seas, the seas were very rough, they brought—I don't know if it was a destroyer or a smaller ship, it was a small fast navy ship—came up alongside of us, not twenty feet away. They shot a breeches buoy across and they got themselves so the two of us [ships] were steaming at exactly the same speed. No, that isn't what happened. That isn't how it happened. The first thing that

Now, I didn't get to see these people and have anything to do with it and nobody ever told us what happened. They took these guys that got hit and put them in the infirmary, so I never saw it. At least I don't recall going. The story I got was that one of them was hurt quite badly and they had to get medical help for him, bring a doctor on board. The seas were very, very bad and the ship was going up and down, you know, huge swells, whitecaps. What I remember happening was that our ship, [although] it didn't come to a stop, it slowed way down—this happened during the day—and a destroyer came right up alongside of our ship. Let me think about this. They made two transfers at sea, one of them was with a breeches buoy. The first one they brought the doctor on board. The seas were very rough, but they just brought the doctor on board.

AH: With the breeches buoy?

HH: No. The destroyer didn't come that close to the ship. It came maybe 200 yards from our ship. They lowered a boat into the sea. The boat came across and brought the doctor over, and [he] was then lifted in a chair or some kind of a sling up onto the deck. But I remember being so impressed by the sailors in that boat, because one of those sailors was standing in the gunwales in the back, steering that boat, and the seas were so high he would literally disappear from view and then come back into view. His boat was just rocking from side to side, and he was just standing up there like it was nothing at all. They transferred him [the doctor] onto the ship, and then two or three days later, the seas were a little bit calmer—they weren't completely calm, but they were much calmer than they had been—then they did this breeches buoy transfer to take the wounded guy and the doctor back to the destroyer where they could work on him. I remember that for the transfer they had all 500 of us on one side of the ship to make it lean to one side. I think it was that we brought the decks down, because the destroyer was lower than we were. We brought the decks down to effect that breeches buoy transfer. And there are these two ships going

they did was, they didn't shoot a breeches buoy across, they sent a doctor across. That's what happened. They were off in the distance. I think we stopped in the water. They put a boat out, it was a lifeboat with a motor, a motorized lifeboat with a sailor standing on the back, standing on the gunwales, holding the rudder and steering the boat, but the seas were so heavy that he would disappear from sight every now and then. I don't know how he was able to maintain his balance there, but that boat came alongside and the doctor came on board the ship. Now, two days later they made the transfer, and they made the the the transfer with the breeches buoy. What happened is the destroyer came alongside of us, the two ships went along exactly even. They had everybody on deck go on one side of our boat to kind of cause it to list in a particular way. And I don't remember in which direction they asked us to do it in. I think we were making it list so that the far side was high and the near side was lower in the water. Anyhow, they put a line across, and then they had this breeches buoy, and they took the doctor back and then came back and took the wounded person back. I don't remember exactly how, whether he was in a basket that hung from the breeches buoy or whether I'm mixing it up with scenes that I've seen of people being picked up with helicoptors, so I don't recall if he was actually sitting in the breeches buoy himself or how he went back. But he went back too, and he got transferred to the destroyer, the wounded man who had been hit in the head, along with the doctor. Then they took the breeches through the water and transferring. And of course, all this time it's very dangerous because we knew we were in submarine-controlled water, and anything that slows down like that you run the risk of being attacked by a submarine. But I don't ever remember an attack in the Atlantic of any kind, either submarine or air raids. None of those things happened.

We sighted land, I guess, maybe twenty days out, maybe even longer than that.

AH: What time of year was this? Summer? I mean: when you were out on deck were you warm?

HH: No. It was winter. [Pause] It was February or March.

buoy and disappeared. The destoyer steamed off and, you know, I don't know where they went. They were protecting the convoy, presumably.

AH: What time of year was this, summer? I mean: when you got on deck were you warm?

HH: I'll bet you it was around March or April. It wasn't hot. There were some hot days, but there were a lot of storms. I think it was around March. That's the feeling I have.

interruption at the same point in the rehearsal so that what is stored contains the basis for the interruption as well as for the story.

The accompanying table (next page) shows the numbers of pages devoted to each large episode during the first and second interviews. In general the pacing of the time spent in each phase of each episode and the space devoted to it is uneven. For example, although Howard was in the replacement depot for at least three to four weeks, that episode merits one paragraph in both interviews, while the four weeks of the induction process prior to his arrival at Camp Sibert covers eleven pages in both recall documents.

When the interviews are compared with the available documentation, some interesting conclusions emerge. Howard's discharge papers indicate that he enlisted in the army on May 15, 1943, was sent to basic training on June 15, and was there for four months. The record then states that he left for overseas on March 23 and arrived at the European Theater of Operations (ETO) on April 18. This document further shows that he was in foreign service for one year, eight months, and twenty-two days and that he embarked for home on November 26, 1945, arrived on December 14, and was separated from active service on December 19, 1945. If we calculate the 120 days of basic training and the 186 days that he spent in occupied Germany, however, we found that the ratio of pages of description to the amount of time covered by the description is one to four for basic training and one to forty-six for the occupation. When I asked Howard to account for this, he replied, "Well, you see, when it was over, it was over."

Many historians fervently believe in the kind of documentation

Table 1. Length of Episodes in First and Second Recall Interviews
(pages)

Episode	1978 interview	1982 interview
Induction	11	11
Sibert		
(basic training)	9	7
Edgewood Arsenal	9	8
Sibert 2 (KP)	5	3
Shenango	a	a
Shipboard	10	12
Total	44	41

aOne paragraph.

provided by such documents as the report of separation and honorable
discharge form (WD AGO Form 53-55). They feel that such a document
has a number of advantages: (1) it is contemporary with the events it
records, (2) it is generated by a disinterested party (WAC Lieutenant
M.F. Emerich), (3) it is based upon other government documents, (4) it
can be compared with the artifacts (in this case medals) which it lists,
and (5) it is based not only on documents but also on personal interview. If an Egyptologist discovered a comparable papyrus containing
similar information about a soldier in pharaoh's army, imagine the
treatise he would write based on elaborate extrapolations from such
data.

But the document has a number of problems. First, the alert reader
may have discovered that a rather long gap in the time described
remains absolutely unaccounted for. If Howard entered the service in
May 1943 and was discharged in December 1945, he spent two years,
six months, and four days in the service. If he was in the service for
nine months and twelve days in the United States, then the document
leaves approximately three and a half months unaccounted for.

Where was this soldier from the time he completed basic training,
as this document states, from October to March 23, when the document notes that he embarked for the ETO? Furthermore, when the
medals are compared to the document, it becomes clear that there were
two invasion arrowheads, not one (Howard says these were for the
invasion of southern France and for crossing the Rhine River). He also
now states that he was not in the Appennines, and did not fight Rome
to Arno, but fought Cassino to Rome and then made the invasion of

ENLISTED RECORD AND REPORT OF SEPARATION
HONORABLE DISCHARGE

N 468-20

(left margin, vertical text) Windham Records — page 175   Bk #6, WWII, Sol Dischg   recorded in Sol Dischg   Rec'd for record Oct 31, 1955,

1. LAST NAME - FIRST NAME - MIDDLE INITIAL		2. ARMY SERIAL NO.	3. GRADE	4. ARM OR SERVICE	5. COMPONENT
HOFFMAN HOWARD S		13 158 418	CPL	CWS	AUS

6. ORGANIZATION	7. DATE OF SEPARATION	8. PLACE OF SEPARATION
3RD CHEM MORT BN MTZ	19 DEC 45	UNIT B SEP CTR #45 IGMR PA

9. PERMANENT ADDRESS FOR MAILING PURPOSES	10. DATE OF BIRTH	11. PLACE OF BIRTH
133 W 23 ST MIAMI BEACH FLA	23 MAY 25	NEW YORK N Y

12. ADDRESS FROM WHICH EMPLOYMENT WILL BE SOUGHT	13. COLOR EYES	14. COLOR HAIR	15. HEIGHT	16. WEIGHT	17. NO. DEPEND.
SEE #9	GREY	BROWN	5-10½	165 LBS.	0

18. RACE			19. MARITAL STATUS			20. U.S. CITIZEN		21. CIVILIAN OCCUPATION AND NO.
WHITE X	NEGRO	OTHER (specify)	SINGLE X	MARRIED	OTHER (specify)	YES	NO	STUDENT COLLEGE X-02

MILITARY HISTORY

22. DATE OF INDUCTION	23. DATE OF ENLISTMENT	24. DATE OF ENTRY INTO ACTIVE SERVICE	25. PLACE OF ENTRY INTO SERVICE
	15 MAY 43	15 MAY 43	HARRISBURG PA

26. REGISTERED	SELECTIVE SERVICE DATA	27. LOCAL S.S. BOARD NO.	28. COUNTY AND STATE	29. HOME ADDRESS AT TIME OF ENTRY INTO SERVICE
YES	NO X		DAUPHIN PA	2729 N 5TH ST HARRISBURG PA

30. MILITARY OCCUPATIONAL SPECIALTY AND NO.	31. MILITARY QUALIFICATION AND DATE (i.e., infantry, aviation and marksmanship badges, etc.)
FIELD LINEMAN 641	ENFIELD MKM - JULY '43

32. BATTLES AND CAMPAIGNS
GO 33 & 40 WD 45
ROME-ARNO SOUTHERN FRANCE RHINELAND NOTHERN APPENNINES CENTRAL EUR

33. DECORATIONS AND CITATIONS
GOOD CONDUCT MEDAL
EAME THR SERVICE MEDAL W/5 BRONZE STARS W/1 ARROWHEAD VICTORY MEDAL

34. WOUNDS RECEIVED IN ACTION
NONE

35.		LATEST IMMUNIZATION DATES		36.	SERVICE OUTSIDE CONTINENTAL U. S. AND RETURN		
SMALLPOX	TYPHOID	TETANUS	OTHER (specify)		DATE OF DEPARTURE	DESTINATION	DATE OF ARRIVAL
1 JUL 43	11 SEP 45	18 JAN 45	18 JAN 45 TY*		23 MAR 44	E T O	18 APR 44

37.	TOTAL LENGTH OF SERVICE				38. HIGHEST GRADE HELD			
CONTINENTAL SERVICE			FOREIGN SERVICE					
YEARS	MONTHS	DAYS	YEARS	MONTHS	DAYS		26 NOV 45	U S	14 DEC 45
0	9	12	1	8	22	CPL			

39. PRIOR SERVICE
NONE

40. REASON AND AUTHORITY FOR SEPARATION
AR 615-365 RR 1-1 DEMOBILIZATION

41. SERVICE SCHOOLS ATTENDED	42. EDUCATION (Years)		
	Grammar	High School	College
NONE	8	4	0

PAY DATA

43. LONGEVITY FOR PAY PURPOSES		44. MUSTERING OUT PAY		45. SOLDIER DEPOSITS	46. TRAVEL PAY	47. TOTAL AMOUNT, NAME OF DISBURSING OFFICER
YEARS	MONTHS	DAYS	TOTAL	THIS PAYMENT				
2	7	5	$ 300	$ 100			J J MAHER JR 118.96 MAJOR F D

INSURANCE NOTICE

IMPORTANT — IF PREMIUM IS NOT PAID WHEN DUE OR WITHIN THIRTY-ONE DAYS THEREAFTER, INSURANCE WILL LAPSE. MAKE CHECKS OR MONEY ORDERS PAYABLE TO THE TREASURER OF THE U. S. AND FORWARD TO COLLECTIONS SUBDIVISION, VETERANS ADMINISTRATION, WASHINGTON 25, D. C.

48. KIND OF INSURANCE				49. HOW PAID		50. Effective Date of Allotment Discontinuance	51. Date of Next Premium Due (One month after 50)	52. PREMIUM DUE EACH MONTH	53. INTENTION OF VETERAN TO		
Nat. Serv.	U.S. Govt.	None		Allotment	Direct to V. A.				Continue	Continue Only	Discontinue
X				X		30 NOV 45	31 DEC 45	$ 6.40	X		

54.		55. REMARKS (This space for completion of above items or entry of other items specified in W. D. Directives)
RIGHT THUMB PRINT		LAPEL BUTTON ISSUED ASR SCORE (2 SEP 45) 71 INACT SER ERC FR 15 MAY 43 TO 14 JUN 43 * FLU 9 OCT 45

56. SIGNATURE OF PERSON BEING SEPARATED	57. PERSONNEL OFFICER (Type name, grade and organization - signature)
Howard S Hoffman	M F EMERICH 1ST LT WAC

WD AGO FORM 53-55
1 November 1944
This form supersedes all previous editions of WD AGO Forms 53 and 55 for enlisted persons entitled to an Honorable Discharge, which will not be used after receipt of this revision.

southern France. A great deal of documentation supports this testimony, including the daily log of his company and platoon, which shows unequivocally that Howard's outfit did not fight north of Rome and that instead it was sent to support troops landed on the southern coast of France, to bring a pincers movement on the Germans, and eventually to link up with the forces which had invaded Normandy. When Howard was asked why he did not correct the WAC who generated this document, he says, "Well, by the time I saw what she had typed, I was out of line, and I was so happy to be out of the army I didn't care what she put down."

Thus it must be observed that even a document that seems to have been generated under almost perfect conditions is subject to error. Unfortunately historians will just have to accept the fact that their field of endeavor must necessarily always be an approximation of truth. No document or witness can ever be the whole truth and nothing but the truth that historians and the courts alike seek so earnestly and energetically. This fact ought not to make us cynical and jaundiced about the effort. For the pursuit of the closest approximation of truth that can be achieved leads to greater assurance of the usefulness of extrapolation and moral judgments based upon it. Therefore any means to achieve this goal ought not be dismissed because of a doctrinaire approach which insists that one form of data is inherently superior to another. Data from many sources must be carefully preserved and subjected to the most rigorous canons and applications of analysis. As the successful detective knows, the entire ability to divine "who done it" may rest on a single hair in the carpet coupled with a myriad other small events which at first blush may seem to be trivial and unrelated.

The analyses of the descriptions of the events remembered prior to Howard's arrival overseas are more problematic than the analyses of the fighting in Europe. First of all, it is difficult, if not impossible, to find corroborating documentation. Very little has been written about the research and training programs of the chemical warfare battalions of the U.S. Army.

This Is Camp Sibert, a pamphlet in the National Archives Record Group 338, describes the training that was offered at Camp Sibert.[1] *The Chemical Warfare Service Organizing for War*, a volume by Leo P. Brophy and George J.B. Fisher, is part of a series on the history of World War II published by the Department of the Army.[2] Neither of these sources proved very useful. For the most part they described the officers' view of boot camp and of Edgewood Arsenal and did not deal with the recruit's actual experience. The focus was army training, described as it is supposed to be on the charts and in the prospectus. Howard recognized and was able to relate to precious little of it.

These documents did, however, provide a useful supplement to

Howard's oral testimony as a means of corroborating it or of defining problematic areas and occasionally of providing a means to correct the oral documentation provided both by Howard and by John Berzellini, who was at both Camp Sibert and Edgewood Arsenal at the same time that Howard was there. We met Berzellini at the reunion of the Third Chemical Battalion held in Baltimore in July 1986. By analyzing his tape-recorded testimony along with the documents I was able to resolve the confusion at several points resulting from Howard's tendency to compress certain segments of the story and virtually to eliminate others.

As Bartlett's work revealed, memory tends to extract the gist of an experience and to eliminate a great deal of detail. In responding to the Freudian notion that all experience is hidden somewhere in the recesses of the mind, William James, the pioneer American psychologist and philosopher, observed, "If we remembered everything, we should on most occasions be as ill off as if we remembered nothing. It would take as long for us to recall a space of time as it took the original time to elapse."[3]

Howard's memory provides us with the following time line for the events from mid-May 1943 to April 18, 1944, when he disembarked in Italy. He remembered that he entered the army within a few days of his eighteenth birthday and went to some receiving center variously remembered as Mechanicsburg, Indiantown Gap, or Cumberland for an indeterminate but short period of testing. He then went by train to Camp Sibert in Gadsden, Alabama, for basic training. After the completion of basic training, he volunteered to go to Edgewood Arsenal to be a subject in chemical warfare experiments. He was unsure of how long he remained at Edgewood Arsenal but remembered having been there in late summer, and he thought his furlough home had occurred near Thanksgiving time, so that on the basis of a reconstructive memory search, he concluded that he was at Edgewood Arsenal from late August until late November.

After the furlough, he returned to Camp Sibert, where he was hospitalized for perhaps a week with a strep throat, and then, since he had missed the shipment of his outfit to the Pennsylvania State University for the Army Specialized Training Program, he was assigned to thirty days of KP (a number of days about which he is quite definite). He was then shipped to a replacement depot for a few weeks and was then sent to Newport News for a twenty-eight-day sea voyage (another number of days about which he is quite positive). Here his enlistment record is in sync with his memory, as it states that he left for the European Theater of Operations on March 23, 1944, and arrived on April 18, 1944. That is an elapsed time of twenty-seven days, and since it is entirely possible that he was either loaded into the ship one day before departure or held on board for one day after arrival in the depot, his oft-repeated comment of "twenty-eight days in the number two hold of a Liberty ship" must be accepted as essentially accurate.

This perfect match between his memory and the record does not continue to hold up, however. The records variously indicate that he entered active service on June 15 and May 15 and spent four months in basic training and was at Edgewood Arsenal in September and October. Thereafter the record is absolutely silent as to where this soldier might have been from the end of October until March 23, when he embarked for Europe.

Since his memory tells us that the he enlisted within a few days of his eighteenth birthday and one of the documents has the date of enlistment as May 15 and active service as commencing June 15, it seems reasonable to accept these dates as probable for the following reasons: (1) the memory of an eighteenth birthday and of enlistment in the army records such a cataclysmic change from the previous experience of being a teenage high school student that it is likely to be potent, (2) an interview with his mother reveals that she does not remember his high school graduation but does remember that he enlisted within a few days of his birthday and that he was sent to Indiantown Gap, where she visited "a skinny kid in a toy soldier's uniform." From there she stated that he went to Alabama and came home from Edgewood Arsenal, "where they did something to his eyes and thank God his eyes are all right now" in the late fall. Then she said he was at Mechanicsburg, where she visited him several times, and from there he was shipped overseas.

Thus the available evidence does not permit us to say with certainty exactly when he might have arrived at Camp Sibert to begin basic training. What can be stated positively is that between May 15 and July 1, 1944, Howard Hoffman left high school before his graduation, enlisted, went for induction (probably to Indiantown Gap), and arrived at Camp Sibert in Gadsden, Alabama, for basic training.

While Howard was not absolutely certain that he was inducted at Indiantown Gap, the location is verified by his mother and by John Berzellini and is the place name that always comes first in any rehearsal of the story.

Howard was slated to receive training in chemical warfare. The army tended to send recruits who were candidates for a college education or who had some college experience into that service. At any rate, both Berzellini and Howard remember being told that they were a high-caliber group, and both of them felt that this was confirmed by their assessment of the ability and experience of the men who were in basic training with them.

In February 1942 General George Marshall ordered the activation of four chemical battalions. Almost as soon as these battalions were created there ensued a high-level debate within the army command as to whether they would in fact be required in this war. Some argued that they should be abolished, as gas warfare would play a less important role in this war than it had in World War I. Others argued that the best way to prevent a gas war was to be prepared to fight one. The latter view prevailed. Moreover, sometime in 1943, General Porter, chief of the Chemical Warfare Service, urged that these battalions remain in service because the British reported from the field experience in North Africa that the 4.2 mortar was highly effective in supporting infantry as a mechanism for delivering high explosives and not just as a vehicle for firing gas or white phosphorous or for laying down smoke. Thereafter, the training of chemical battalions emphasized the delivery of high explosives.

In response to this change in direction in August 1943, the basic training given to chemical soldiers was increased from eight weeks to seventeen weeks. In the initial interview Howard states that he had thirteen weeks of basic training, but this figure is not corroborated by a careful review of the literature. Initially the training consisted of thirteen weeks; when pressure for troops in the field increased, the training was cut back to eight weeks and then in the late summer of 1943 was increased again to seventeen weeks when complaints were registered about inadequately trained and undertrained recruits. Furthermore, the desire to have troops who could, if required, both fight a gas war and in the meantime use their artillery to deliver high explosives suggested increased training in order to produce a soldier competent to respond to either need as the occasion might arise.[4]

Eight weeks of training is the only amount of time that is consistent with Howard's having been at Edgewood Arsenal during the months of September and October as stated on a commendation for meritorious service which he received. Furthermore, it is the only amount of time consistent with John Berzellini's memory that he celebrated his twenty-first birthday at Edgewood Arsenal on September 10, 1943. And finally, Howard arrived at Camp Sibert sometime between June 15 and July 1, several weeks before the new extended seventeen-week training began to be implemented in August. Therefore, one is forced to conclude that the separation qualification record, which describes four months of basic training, is in error and that in fact he had two months of basic training followed by two or more months at Edgewood Arsenal, where he participated in chemical exposure experiments as a human guinea pig.

In an effort to enhance Howard's memories of basic training, I first conducted an interview with him based on my own research on Camp Sibert, on the training of chemical warfare battalions, and on the history of Edgewood Arsenal. Next we read together descriptions of basic training at Camp Sibert and looked at pictures of the camp itself and the various training activities which were carried out there. These activities did not elicit any new memories but did evoke considerable recognition. That is, when I gave him information or showed him a picture, he would in some instances say, "Oh, yes. I remember that" or "Yes, it looks familiar," but the sight did not stimulate any additional information. But subsequent and repeated exposure to these recognition items would occasionally elicit additional recognition responses. The only exception to this statement is the occasion when I showed him a picture of troops entering a tent where there was gas.[5] He responded as follows:

> HH: No. No, that was not the way it was.
> AH: Tell me about how it was different.
> HH: The main difference was that we were in a real house. This is a kind of a cabin, kind of a tent. But this does remind me that we did go into a house with the gas masks probably on and then were told to take it off to experience some of the tear gas. That does seem like one of the things that would have happened to us. And I remember it being in a house, just a regular house like a shack or farmhouse. That's not the place. It was a clapboard white house. That's not what we did, and it wasn't called gas chambers.

Thus as we shall observe frequently, before cue items can enhance recall, they must be specific to the encoding or tagging of their organization in memory if they are to provide additional information from the memory store beyond simple recognition.

At the conclusion of basic training, the men in Howard's outfit were given the opportunity to "volunteer" for chemical exposure at Edgewood Arsenal.

> AH: Tell me, how did you get to Edgewood Arsenal?
> JOHN B: They asked for volunteers. You see we were all college people or had an IQ over 117. We figured anything was better than Camp Sibert, I guess. The whole outfit volunteered. We were scheduled, all of us, to go to college when we came back.
> [Tape-recorded interview with John Berzellini, July 25, 1986]

In an attempt to assess the effect of returning to the place where the remembered events had taken place, Howard and I made a trip to Edgewood Arsenal in the summer of 1985. We drove over the base. Howard recognized some of the barracks, and they were as described in the recall interviews. We also visited the archives at the arsenal. The archivists were helpful but explained that the material which might describe the experiments in which Howard had been a subject had been destroyed. We were both appalled to make this discovery. Howard and the men in his outfit had voluntarily taken great risks to participate in these experiments. They had done so, of course, with mixed motives. True, he and the others in his group had thought that "anything was better than Sibert" (Berzellini interview) and that the work was likely to be less hazardous than going overseas into combat. But the men had also volunteered to be useful to their country during wartime and to participate in an effort to obtain scientific information that might have medical application if the enemy used gas. Howard's participation in these experiments and his intense interest in the methodology employed influenced him in his later decision to devote his life to scientific inquiry. Therefore, he was shocked to discover that these data had been destroyed. In Howard's lexicon of values, few crimes are more serious than the destruction or distortion of experimental data. We were also disappointed to find that this potential means of confirming his memories had been cut off.

Perhaps the destruction of the records was part of a bureaucratic cleanup, but little imagination is needed to suggest another reason why documents might have been destroyed. We were after all making our inquires in the post-Vietnam Agent Orange era. The long-term toxic effects of exposure to hazardous chemicals had only recently begun to be widely appreciated. It may have seemed better to the bureaucratic mind to avoid potential liability by simply destroying the evidence. We make no accusations here, particularly not as regards the personnel in the archives. The decision to destroy the documents had obviously been made elsewhere. The work of future historians is certainly not made easier by a government which increasingly requires the use of paper shredders in order to "protect" the people from the need to grapple with difficult questions of ethics and morality.

The archives did contain maps of the Edgewood Arsenal area during World War II and newsletters that had been distributed at the base as well as pictures and various other types of documents. The missing material was confined to the notebooks or data sheets on the experiments themselves. From the maps in the archives we learned of the presence of an old armory that had been used as a gym in the 1940s. Another feature on the map was a landing strip for aircraft. Unfortunately neither of these geographic features helped in our effort to corroborate or validate Howard's memory, as neither he nor John Berzellini recalled them. These maps dating to the period when Howard had been at Edgewood led to the most serious altercation caused by the project. A joint undertaking of this sort was bound to create tensions. Some of our friends had cautioned us against it from the first, recognizing that it might harm our marriage inasmuch as it involved dredging up a painful past. Who knew what repressed de- mons long quiescent might be awakened from their slumbers. But we had persisted in taking the risk. And now at Edgewood we had a big fight. When we looked at the map, the tributary of Chesapeake Bay was a prominent feature. I found it difficult to imagine spending any length of time there without being aware of it. Certainly we discovered it in the first hour we were there. But we were exploring by car, not on foot. Howard insisted that he had not experienced it and then forgot it. He was adamant. He asserted that he had never seen water while he was at Edgewood Arsenal.

We went back a second time in an effort to find barracks like those Howard remembered, placed in a location that might explain his failure to experience the water. We could not locate such barracks. More puzzling still, the only building that seemed at all familiar was the theater, which was less than two blocks from the water. Still Howard insisted that he could not have forgotten the water.

When we went to the first minireunion in September 1985, several of the veterans stated that they had been back to Edgewood but had been unable to find any familiar landmarks. For some reason, however, we did not pursue the issue of their awareness of being near the water. Howard expressed great glee and a sense of vindication when in an interview his buddy Berzellini was as surprised as Howard had been to learn that the arsenal was anywhere near water: "No, I never saw any water." We hooted with laughter, and Howard especially enjoyed the joke.

A map of the arsenal taken from a descriptive brochure written shortly after 1983 shows that the Gunpowder River, which is an arm of the Chesapeake Bay, is a stone's throw from the PX complex, which contained a theater that Howard felt he recognized. The Officer's Club just beyond these structures is actually on the water. If it bore the same relationship to these buildings forty years ago that it does today, then perhaps the area by the water was restricted to enlisted men.

Berzellini, like Howard, had no memory of an airfield. He remem- bered the chemical tests, their effects, and also trips into Baltimore with Howard to see the burlesque shows. Moreover, he remembered the pretty WAC that Howard dated, asserted that she was from either Arkansas or Kansas, and recalled that her name resembled that of a movie star, which is more than Howard can remember of her—and she was Howard's girl! But then part of the clue to this memory phe- nomenon may be explained by Berzellini's revealing statement that "I couldn't understand how she picked him!"

While the WAC's name was on the tip of his tongue ("I'll remember it as soon as I leave this room"), he did not recall the structure and purpose of the exposure experiments as readily as Howard. But when

Howard describes those experiments to him, he recognized them and provided additional information: "Oh, yes, our eyes got like little beads."

This result is similar to those obtained by Marigold Linton and suggests that events important in one's future life, or, as she puts it, salient events, are retained longer and more perfectly than less salient events. In this case, the fact that Howard subsequently became a scientist would explain why he remembered the experiments more vividly than Berzellini, who became a manager in a steel mill in his postwar career. Furthermore, numerous memory studies show that facts related to one's career are more likely to be vividly recalled. For example, carpenters will recall the details of building structure more accurately than the general population.

Sometime in the late fall the volunteers from Sibert were furloughed. Howard remembers going home. A picture of Howard on the porch of his home in Harrisburg (see photo section) shows Howard without a coat, but the fact that he has a winter cap on suggests that the picture was taken on a warm day in late fall or early winter.

Both Howard and Berzellini remember returning to Sibert. They had both missed the shipment to the Army Specialized Training Program. Berzellini remembered that Howard missed the shipment because he was sick, a report which corroborates Howard's own memory of having gotten sick on the train from Harrisburg to Gadsden, Alabama. They both report having spent a month or more on KP at Sibert, but at that point both the validity documents that we were able to find and the recall documents go blank. No document or clear memory exists to explain Howard's activity in February and until March 23, when he set sail on the Liberty ship for Naples, Italy.

There are vague hints. His mother seems to think he was in Mechanicsburg, Pennsylvania. We have a snapshot labeled Mechanicsburg, 1943, in his mother's handwriting (see photo section). But it seems to have been taken in warmer weather than January or February; in the background men can be seen taking an outdoor shower. Such a picture might have been taken overseas. Since Howard never told his mother that he was in combat but wrote all his letters to her in such a way as to maintain the fiction that he was well behind the lines and hence not in great danger, information from her on this point is likely to be confused and garbled.

Howard remembers going to a replacement depot in Sharon, Pennsylvania. A picture of him taken there, which was sent to his mother, is in the photo section. But about this army camp Howard remembers only that he thinks he went there by train and that there might have been snow on the ground.

In a further effort to enhance his recall, I read to him sections from

Studs Terkel's oral history with World War II veterans and the book *V-Mail* by Keith Winston.[6] Both books deal with situations similar to those described in Howard's recall documents. One of Studs Terkel's interviewees had been at the army base in Sharon. He described a racial incident that occurred about a year before Howard's arrival in which military police, in an effort to quell what they mistook for a race riot, shot and killed or wounded several black soldiers. The interview is a bitter and powerful document of attitudes that were prevalent at the time. And although it evoked memories of how isolated the white troops were from black soldiers in all phases of training, living quarters, and recreational and even religious activities, it did not evoke any further memories about Sharon, Pennsylvania, itself.

Similarly, the experiences of Private Winston, which were based directly on letters he wrote at the time to his wife, evoked considerable recognition for Howard but did not stimulate additional memories.

We shall discover another, similar blank period in Howard's memory just before the invasion of southern France. These blanks are characterized by subsequent experiences that may have prevented rehearsal of any experience that might have occurred during the blank. In this instance Howard was in a replacement depot, separated from everyone he had known at Sibert and Edgewood Arsenal. He was perhaps preoccupied with thoughts of where he might be sent next. Furthermore, when he was on board the ship, he was once again isolated, not with buddies he might have developed at Sharon or elsewhere. He was with a group of men, including ex-convicts who neither knew nor cared what this fresh young recruit had to say about anything. They all were preoccupied with how to exist in extraordinarily crowded conditions and with the need to deal with seasickness, boredom, and their fears for the future, if indeed they were to have much of a future. They all knew that they were in submarine-infested waters, and the hold was rumored to be full of ammunition. This was hardly the occasion or the circumstance for the rehearsal of stories about the replacement depot in western Pennsylvania or the army base in Mechanicsburg. Thus it seems likely that events from this period were not rehearsed. No thought at all was given to them until Howard attempted forty years later to provide a coherent, chronological description of his army service. By that time the events of the late winter and early spring of 1944 were simply not in memory, and no strategy we could devise enabled us to access them.

4 The Italian Campaign

First Recall Document

After landing in Naples, Howard joined the Third Chemical Mortar Battalion and participated in the drive for Rome.

HH: I remember landing in Naples. I don't remember how we got to the replacement depot. I think we went on some kind of a weird little train, you know, over the Italian countryside. Maybe we were in boxcars. I just don't remember very well. But we went to this very big tent city which was a replacement depot. I wasn't there very long; I was there maybe a week as best as I can remember, and the next thing I knew I had orders. Every day some people would be leaving. I don't remember very well if we slept on cots or on the ground or how we slept, but the next thing I knew I was assigned to my outfit, which was 4.2 mortars. I do remember going into the outfit on the very first day, arriving—it seems like maybe I arrived in the evening, or I may have arrived in the afternoon and had lunch or something, or dinner. I do remember the tent and meeting people in this tent, [being shown] the squad that I was assigned to [and] the tent where I was to sleep. They had pulled back from the lines, so they weren't in combat, but they were close enough that, I believe, you could hear shooting in the distance. But it was not front line. We really weren't in danger. We introduced ourselves to each other; the guys were showing me their guns and what they carried, what they did.

AH: These were combat veterans, now, that you're being introduced to?

HH: Right. They were reasonable with me; they didn't ride me or anything like that. Just as I don't think I ever rode any replacements that came in, unless they did something that called for it. Otherwise they treated you as a poor bastard who was in for the same kind of thing.

AH: All right. So now you arrived in Naples, and you were there for a few days, and you got orders to report to some particular place on the line. Where was that?

HH: I have no idea! Outside of Naples somewhere, but I don't remember how far away it was.

AH: Who was the commander there?

HH: I don't know. I have this thing in the back of my mind that we had somebody named Captain Cook. He was from Louisiana; he was fairly short, blonde, not very old, and very stable, as I recall. But I don't remember him very well. That's it.

AH: All right.

HH: I'm getting closer to combat, and I'm starting to blank out.

AH: Really?

HH: Well, it's hard to remember exactly what happened there.

AH: Well, was this before the Battle of Cassino or after?

HH: The Battle of Cassino was going on now. Cassino had not fallen yet.

AH: When did you first get into combat?

HH: Well, not too long after that. But I don't remember exactly what happened in the first days of combat. I remember digging in and getting started. But I don't remember exactly where we were or what we were doing, you know.

AH: What kind of perceptions did you have of what the battles were about? Did any of the officers come to you to tell you that you were to take this strategic place and the reason that it was important was because this, that, or the other? Or were you just sort of blindly told to dig a hole here and dig a hole there?

HH: The latter, the latter.

AH: So you had no sense of whether you were engaged in what was critical or not?

HH: Right. We really had no idea of what, exactly, we were doing.

AH: Did the men develop their own ways of figuring out what the situation was that they were in?

HH: Well, as you got more and more experience you came to be able to sense what you were doing and whether it was important to do or not. But not at first. At first, you had no idea what the hell was going on. You were just taking orders; you were a body that was being told to do various things. And you did what you were told to do.

HH: One of the earliest things I remember is . . . the early parts of combat. I don't even remember the guns being set up so much as being on the line, if you know what I mean. Being in places where we were moving from one place to another. Like I say, I don't remember setting up the guns, the mortars, and I was a mortar crewman. It was as if we spent two weeks going from one place to another, but always where we were under fire, where we could be shelled. Because I do remember getting shelled a couple of times. That was my first experience at combat.

I remember digging foxholes, jumping into the foxholes, and hearing shells [whistles like a shell]—boom! That kind of sound, and shells landing—nothing landing very close to me. By "very close" I mean within a hurting distance—but certainly within sight and within sound things were landing. But nothing in those first weeks ever landed where I felt that I was really in danger from shrapnel. Although you didn't know. You were in the hole, and a shell could land right on you. In fact, I do remember one night—at [one of] these places where we would stop we would try to dig in. We were on the side of a mountain for some reason, a kind of pasture sort of halfway up some mountain, and we had gotten to it by going along this little dirt road. I remember that the soil was so full of rocks, it was just sort of like it was just rock with some soil that just happened to be there. Little scraggly trees that had grown in there, kind of pastureland, but you simply couldn't dig a hole there. So what I did, instead of trying to dig in, I went and gathered rocks about a foot across and I built a little cairn about a foot and a half high, three feet or four feet across and six or seven feet long. I got into the cairn and laid a shelter half across the top of it in case it rained. Also you felt more protected if you had that shelter half over you. You really weren't, but it made you feel at least that you were covered from the sky.

I remember that I had a friend; I don't remember his name. But he didn't dig a foxhole. He just laid his shelter half down and then he laid two blankets doubled up on top of it and he was lying on top of that. I recall that evening there was an air raid. We were lying there; we couldn't see any airplanes because it was nighttime, but we could see the tracers shooting up. The Germans were making an air raid on us. We could see the tracers shooting up and I remember lying there in my thing, with the shelter half pulled back, watching these tracers going into the sky from all around us, because apparently there were antiaircraft guns at various points around us, a quarter of a mile away maybe. That guy, who was twenty feet from me all of a sudden jumps up, and he says, "Something just missed me! Just missed me. I can't stay here. Can I stay in your foxhole?" I said, "Sure." So he came in, there was room for him, and he slept in the foxhole that night. After an hour or so, or a half hour, the thing was over, then there was nothing else happened.

The next morning, he says, "Jesus Christ, Howard, come over here and look!" And he showed me, and there, not two inches from where his head must have been, there was a hole in the blanket. You could see it, it was just sort of like punched through. We pulled back the two blankets and the shelter half and he dug down with a spoon and he kept digging and digging and digging and after a while he came across a 30 caliber or 50 caliber solid bullet from one of the antiaircraft machine guns. It was brand new, but it was bent in half where it had hit a rock down there. Now, if that had been three inches to the left, he'd have been dead. It would have gone right through his brain. As it was it missed him by a couple of inches. So that, I guess, was one of the first of the events.

Now, I remember also in that period passing orchards, and everywhere we would go there would be mine fields. It would say "Achtung, Minen." The Germans had been there recently, and there was white tape there from our engineers, indicating that the fields were still mined. I remember not seeing it but being told that the Goumier would go into those mine fields to pick the oranges anyhow. They didn't give a damn about it. These were the troops we were fighting with. And you could see these guys; they were big, rough-looking French foreign troops. Well, they were Arabs of some sort, but Goumier, actually. They wore robes. The guys in my outfit had fought with them before, and they told me stories, which I believe, that these guys had been paid by the ear for killing Germans until they started to find Americans with their ears missing. So they stopped paying them in that fashion. But they looted everything that was lootable, and you would see them walking along the road, a troop of them moving. They had horses, they had old rifles—old, Springfield-type rifles—and they would be carrying all kinds of things, pots and pans and chairs. I even saw a guy once walking along, and he had a goat around his neck, a live goat. The goat had its feet lashed together around his neck, along with blankets and whatever else he had managed to steal.

The first time I remember our guns firing was the attack on Castelforte, which was a town that we were to attack. It was just on the other side of the hill that we were dug into. We had come to that hill, and I remember carrying ammunition up the side of the hill. Each box weighed fifty pounds. It had two shells. Each shell weighed twenty-five pounds. Two shells to a box. And then, of course, there was the mortar to be lugged up this hill. The mortar weighed—a barrel weighed a hundred pounds, the tripod, I think, weighed seventy-five pounds, and the baseplate weighed two hundred and fifty pounds, so it usually took at least two guys to carry the baseplate. There were two handles that came out. There were only the three parts to it plus the sighting instruments, the gunsights, which you put on the top and look through and then take off when you fired. We carried hundreds and hundreds of rounds of ammunition up this hill. I remember carrying it at night and in the daytime. But we never fired anything. What we did was got everything lined up and sighted and so forth, and the idea apparently was that at a particular time this major attack was going to start. You must have read about it back home, you know, big major attack. It seemed to me like it was at eleven o'clock in the morning on May 11. Things had been worked out so that the great big guns way in the back would fire first, and then the 105s would fire and then the, I guess, howitzers or what have you, and then the 4.2 mortars and then, if there were any other guns in front of us, which I doubt, they would fire. But the idea was to try to have all the shells land on the village at the same time. I remember that it was timed like to the second and that when the attack actually started, when we started firing, I remember hearing shells. You know, we were supposed to fire as rapidly as we could. We fired hundreds and hundreds and hundreds of rounds on that. It was just incredible. I've never seen so much firing go on at one time and hearing all these other guns going. It was just massive firing into this town. Off and on during the rest of that day, we would fire.

AH: Were there civilians in the town?

HH: Yes, I think there were.

AH: Did you think about that?

HH: Yes, but I didn't know whether there were or not. I knew there wasn't going to be much of a town left. Now, you have to understand I had seen Naples, which was pretty well flattened, the parts where I saw it. And I had passed many small Italian towns that were just wiped out, nothing there, just rubble. So by that time I knew what happened to the people. I had met very few Italians, as I recall, because there just weren't very many of them around. It was mostly GIs, and that's who you had contact with. People got away from the front lines and wouldn't come back until the fighting was over, and then they'd come back into the area. So you didn't have that much contact with civilians. It was rare in combat to encounter one unless they couldn't get away, at least in the places where I was fighting.

Now, I remember shortly after, we moved—the next day, I guess— we moved into Castelforte. It had already fallen. I guess the infantry had taken it. But it couldn't have been very far in front of us. If the infantry had gone in there, they had gone in maybe twenty minutes or an hour before we got in. So anyway, into Castelforte, and there was nothing there. I just remember seeing that everything was . . . I saw one old woman who didn't know who she was or where she was. I remember hearing that there were some children that were kind of like that, too. But there was nobody else there, and I don't remember seeing any bodies or anything. I just think the town had been emptied beforehand.

What happened was that we didn't stay in Castelforte. I remember they took us to a ravine [about] three stories high. There was a little stream that ran down at the bottom of it. I remember digging in. But there was a foxhole the Germans had used across the ravine from me and down the ravine. And apparently the Germans had fleas. I didn't even go in the foxhole over there, or at least maybe if I went in I only went in for a minute, cause some other guys were staying in there, but all of us got terribly infested with fleas. Boy, you would just lift your belt and there would be like a half dozen of them around your waist or go to your socks to pull your socks up and there'd be a half dozen of them around there biting all the time. They brought up some DDT for us and eventually, I guess, some powder. We eventually got rid of them, but I remember for a week or two I had very bad fleas.

I also have some remembrance that it was kind of attractive there. Somehow it reminds me a little bit of Sullivan County [Pennsylvania], that little ravine that we were in. I also remember one night they had an air raid, and I remember I was lying in the ravine, and a German plane came by and it was very low and it was dropping bombs, and I remember seeing that big black swastika—not the swastika, but the black cross on the bottom of it, two crosses, and being scared shitless he was going to come back. I mean, he was almost directly overhead and he was like 300 yards in the air. He wasn't very high, and there were some bombs dropped. I don't remember seeing any bombs dropping toward me, but I could see bombs dropping in front of me, and he must have dropped some before he got to me. And there were people shooting at him. I remember that was a very frightening kind of thing and I figured how open I was. But I also figured that, unless his bomb landed directly in the ravine, I was safe because I was below the level. The bomb would explode up above me, so all the shrapnel would go up that way, so I felt less frightened for my own safety at that particular point.

My other memories of that period are quite blurry. I don't really remember exactly where we were. I remember there were many times that we would go someplace in a truck or in a jeep. We would stop, we would unload everything, we would dig foxholes, set up the guns, fire them, stop, sit down and cook ourselves some supper. In the middle of it we would be told we were going to move. We'd load everything up and start moving, stop, dig foxholes, set up the guns. This was just over and over and over again. Every now and then there'd be a shell come in. You know, we'd be walking around and all of a sudden [HH makes sound like shells dropping]. We'd be under fire and we'd be diving for the foxholes.

AH: Were you advancing?

HH: Yes, we were advancing. What we were doing was we were going around Cassino up to Rome. And at some point in there we heard that Cassino had fallen, that the Polish troops had gone in and finally taken it. That's who took Cassino. I remember one experience near Pico.

It was in the middle of a big plain, and we suddenly came across— could see in the distance—this one big mountain, like a big anthill in the middle of the plain. We got closer and closer and closer to it, and finally we were at it. But by now it's dark. Okay? Night. And we were told to get out of the jeeps and to go across the field and then kind of like 200 or 300 feet up on the edge of the mountain set up our guns there. So I started walking down the road—I'm the first one—and I see all these clumps of dirt in the road, big clumps of dirt. I thought to myself, "I have the eerie feeling that these are bodies, but no, it can't be; it must be that a bomb landed in the field here and these are clumps of sod from the field." I remember feeling one of them with my foot and it felt like sod. Anyway we walked past them over there and then came back. We kept walking by them the whole time until we had all the equipment and stuff. Of course, you could never make a light at night because of the danger, but I remember that there were some British troops near us somewhere nearby. We went to bed. We were supposed to fire in the morning up above, over the top of the mountain, and I think we were there because our mortars could have that kind of high trajectory to come down on the other side, and yet we were protected, because apparently the Germans had the other side of the mountain.

Morning came, and it was a bright, sunny day, and it was the most ghastly smell I have experienced in my entire life. Apparently the wind had shifted. I just about vomited just from taking that first breath in the morning. It was sort of like a glue factory might smell. It was just absolutely ghastly! I said, "God, what's that?" The other guys said, "I don't know. There must be some dead bodies around here."

Well, we went to see what the hell was making this odor that was so impossible. It turned out that what we had thought were clumps of sod were, in fact, pieces of German bodies. Apparently a German truck had been hit and there were at least a dozen dead bodies lying around there, and pieces of bodies—arms and legs and stuff. But they must have been there for a couple of weeks, because there was one that was a whole body, I remember. It was a complete body, but it looked like his face was a balloon. There were just sort of holes where his eyes were; there was no nose. It was just like a big melon; the skin was all cracked and black. The thing had swelled up and the uniform was filled like pumped up with air. You could see that the guy had a ring on of some sort; you could see a little piece of ring. And you know, the next day I happened to pass by and some son of a bitch had cut that guy's finger off and taken the ring.

But the thing was that a truck had been hit or strafed or something and nobody had ever buried any of them; they just left them there, and that's what it was. The odor was so bad that we moved out of there; we just couldn't stay there. The captain—the captain was the highest ranking officer that would be with us, nobody higher than that I don't ever remember seeing at the front, despite anything you may have heard. Colonels and people like that are usually back where there's no danger of being hit by any shells.

Well, I remember we moved out of there, we never did fire our guns from that position. We moved, maybe a half mile away, to the side somewhere, to a small Italian cemetery. They had a bone pit, and they had the slab where they laid people out. I remember seeing these little caskets that had bones in them and jewels. I didn't think they were real jewels; they looked like pearls, but they might have been real, I don't know. And flowers, dried-up roses, stuff like that. And caskets everywhere in the walls, some of them broken open, some of them not, and this bone pit in this one gatehouse. I remember I spent one night in the gatehouse with a couple of other guys. I slept on the slab and the other guys slept around, you know, on the floor. But it was very uncomfortable, and I didn't really care for it.

So the next night I went out to where the trucks and stuff were parked, the ammo trucks, and I dug a foxhole. It was kind of like a drainage ditch, and I remember digging into the ditch itself, because there was no sign of rain, and it was already partly dug because it was a little ditch. I remember that a bunch of my friends had dug foxholes near by, in a kind of star-shaped pattern. One guy had dug a hole in the middle, and then four guys had dug their holes around it about four or five feet away from the center one. These were pretty deep foxholes, maybe four or five feet deep, because we were very exposed at that place, in that cemetery, which was sort of out in the middle of a field, you know, with a road coming by. There was a little hill right next to the cemetery, a ravine or something, and there was a German dugout there. I remember thinking maybe I ought to go spend the night in the dugout, but I remembered that episode with the fleas, and I decided I didn't want to take another chance on getting fleas, so I wouldn't go there.

So I'm sleeping away in the morning, dawn had come up and gone, and the sun is up, and all of a sudden this officer is shaking me and saying, "Come on, Hoffman. We just got a direct hit. We've got to dig up some bodies." I thought, "Oh, Jesus, I didn't even hear it!" And here a shell had come in—just one shell—had come in, landed in that middle foxhole of those five foxholes, and exploded. It was a pretty big shell. It had just missed, by maybe five feet, hitting the ammo truck. Had it hit the ammo truck, I wouldn't be telling this story. Had it exploded on the surface instead of down underground, I wouldn't be telling this story. I don't understand why I didn't hear it explode. I was digging away with an entrenching tool, positive that we were going to be digging up dead people but we weren't sure. We knew that the guy in the middle was dead, but the ones around the edges, there was a chance that the concussion went up above it. But you couldn't see any foxholes there. They were covered over completely with dirt. We were digging with our hands, with the entrenching tools for the first half foot or so and then with our hands. And by God, we pulled one of the guys out, and he's completely okay. Before we even can get to the other ones, we see this earth moving and this guy manages to free himself.

[Then we were digging for the guy in the middle foxhole,] looking for the parts of the guy who would fit the bill. We knew that he was dead, and what we had to do was to find something to identify him. A piece of uniform, or something, anything. We couldn't find a god-damned thing. We couldn't find anything; nothing could we find. This had been a direct hit, the shell had landed right in the foxhole. So I remember a couple of hours later, or an hour later, standing there, I had a mess kit; they had brought a hot breakfast. I knew who had been in there. At least as I remember, it had been Frank Iotse, was the guy's name, a little short guy. I'm eating my eggs, and I look up, and there comes Iotse, walking down the hill. I nearly shit a brick, I was so flabbergasted. It turned out that he had decided to go and spend the night in that German dugout, so there hadn't been anybody in that center foxhole.

AH: Did he get fleas?

HH: I don't think so. [Laughter] Boy, oh, boy! That was really incredible. You know I was just astounded, and I'll never forget it.

AH: By this time, had you developed considerable camaraderie with these men?

HH: Yes, yes. You felt like they depended on you and you depended on them. There were a couple of young fellows in the outfit that I got to be very friendly with. I can't remember a single name. Anyhow the rest of my experiences in Italy were very much like that first few days that I told you about. It was constantly moving and digging in and occasionally being shot at, as I recall, but not often. The biggest problem was that you never knew what was going to happen. It must be much like what it is to be a policeman, you know, in rough areas. It isn't that he's under attack all the time, but at any moment he could be.

AH: This must have been going on when you had your birthday? Do you remember that?

HH: No.

AH: You don't remember your birthday at all?

HH: No. Not that one. I remember the next one. Or at least I remember the package that came for the next one.

AH: Okay. Well, so finally they took Rome?

HH: I don't remember any fighting around Rome. I remember simply riding into Rome on the Via Appia, just riding into the city, and people screaming and shouting and throwing flowers at us; seeing the Coliseum, those buildings, you know, St. Peter's, places like that.

AH: Very exciting.

HH: Very exciting. And the streets lined with people, giving us wine and flowers, I remember. We would occasionally get beer, I remember. Not too much to drink over there, no hard liquor, or rarely. But the rest of the fighting in Italy was of the sort I was describing. We'd move to a place and dig in and then pull out and move to another place and dig in and then pull out. Maybe fire a gun but more often than not not even firing the guns.

AH: How long were you in Rome?

HH: We were outside of Rome. We stopped at this place outside of Rome; I think it was a big dairy farm and estate. We set up pup tents there. We had a week or two there, okay? Now, I remember going into Rome and meeting this very attractive girl. She showed me around the gardens, the statues and the gardens. And while I was in Rome I went to the opera, the Teatro de Real.

AH: By yourself or with this girl?

HH: No, all by myself. One incident I remember when we were camped on the outskirts of Rome is, I was sitting in my pup tent one night, and this friend of mine came up to me, and he had a bottle of champagne, a full bottle of champagne. He said, "I just got word that I'm going back." He had very bad eyes; he wore thick glasses, and apparently they had decided to send him back to the States. He said, "I want to celebrate with you." We sat there in my pup tent and each of us drank half a bottle of wine, champagne. Here I was nineteen, just turned nineteen. We got so drunk and we both had to go to the bathroom and neither of us could walk; we had to crawl out of the tent and crawl back in and go to sleep. We were so drunk. I guess a day or two later he left. And I never saw him again.

About the end of that week, I began to feel terrible; I felt awful. I started running a fever. They sent me to a GI hospital in Rome. It was a Roman hospital, but they had GI doctors there and Roman nurses. I figured I was only going to be there for a day or two until they'd get my fever down. I was really very sick, chilled and shaking. The fever was very high. [I was] almost delirious but not quite. Or if I was, I don't remember it. I didn't get better and they transferred me, and I remember being put in an ambulance and being driven to, of all places, Anzio.

Now, Anzio had fallen by that time, so there were no Germans around there. I think I spent a week at Anzio. They treated me with quinine, and they diagnosed it as malaria; I had contracted malaria. That was the place where I got friendly with this orderly and he brought me, one day, a can of orange juice, and a little medicine dropper and two glasses. He poured two glasses of orange juice, and then he took the medicine dropper, and he put three or four drops of this stuff and he put it into each glass and stirred it up. I said, "What the hell is that?" He says, "Ether." I said, "You can't drink ether." He said, "Yes, you can. It's great." So we drank it and we got very, very high, and I got a very, very bad hangover and headache from it. But we drank it.

When I finally started to get better and wasn't so feverish and able to move around . . . See, we were in tents then, and they did have a couple of air raids while I was there, but nothing came real close by. I remember going up and walking up the hill around there and seeing what it was like up there on the hill looking down at *and my God!!*

AH: At the beach?

HH: What those guys must have been through! Because that's where those 88s were. They could shoot anywhere. Just like when we were at the Golan Heights. That's exactly what it was like.

Finally I got released from the hospital and went back to that place. I think maybe I had one or two days in Rome. In the meantime everybody else had had a couple of weeks in Rome, got to know it, and met people and had all these good meals and everything, and I hadn't even had one goddamn plate of spaghetti. Here I was sick during the time when we weren't in combat. All the combat was now up north. Well, they took us from Rome, they put us in trucks and they took the whole outfit down to some beach near Bari, which is near Naples, I believe. [Bari is on the east coast of Italy, however, and Naples is on the west coast, almost directly across the peninsula—AH] Now, that's a beach resort area, but we were just sort of in like a vacant . . . near the edge of the beach, but we weren't in the beach itself. But I remember there was a big, kind of a, not a castle, but a fortress hewn out of rock right near there. I walked over there; I spent some time walking around it and looking at it. I also remember doing some target practice there. Not target practice, but shooting. We had grenade launchers that they wanted us to learn to use properly. I remember firing a grenade launcher from my shoulder, because I knew how to shoot very well by that time, and the guys were very surprised that I would even be willing to try it, because you're supposed to break your shoulder, there's so much kick. You're supposed to brace it on the ground, but I felt, you know, I had seen other guys do it and thought I could do it if you need to do it and I did. It didn't break my shoulder. I felt very good that I could do that.

But anyhow, we stayed there, I think we were there for a month. I remember going swimming in the Mediterranean there, a half a mile or a mile away we could go swimming. I also remember we had mortar fire practice a couple of times, and one of the [places] was sort of by a beach, and I remember on one of the mortar crews, one guy either lit a cigarette, or something, when he shouldn't have, and a whole bunch of the powder caught fire and made a big flash and burned quite a few of the crew, one of the other crews that I was with.

AH: How many men were in a mortar crew?

HH: I think there were about eight.

AH: And you stayed in that crew? Those eight people worked together all the time?

HH: Yes. They tended to. It may have been fewer; it may have been four.

AH: So where did you go from Bari, then?

HH: We were in pup tents there and we were allowed to go into Naples occasionally and Bari and around there occasionally. Some guys went to Capri and places like that, but I never got to go to any real neat places like that. I don't know why; I should have.

What we were doing there was we were getting ready for the invasion in southern France, and we were going to go in on gliders. I thought to myself, "Oh, Jesus!" About that time they asked me to be a forward observer, because we had already had some casualties, but I don't remember very many casualties, nor anybody close to me being wounded. But we had some replacements anyhow, so there were some new people and I had a little bit of seniority. I think it was around then that they asked me if I would be a forward observer, and I had agreed that I would.

Then I found out they were going to make these glider landings, and there was some talk about the forward observers going over and dropping by parachute. I thought, "No, no, no. No way." [Laughter] I didn't want to go in by glider to begin with. Then it turned out that some other outfit, it was decided, would make it by glider, and we would go in on the second wave on a landing craft.

Well, after that month or whatever—it seemed like a long period we were there—we . . . were on the boat. We had a hammock to sleep in, which was not terribly comfortable. The boat that we were on was a British boat. It wasn't big enough to be a cruise ship; I don't know what the hell it was! It wasn't a navy boat. It was like maybe one of these island boats they have in the Greek waters. It was bigger than the Liberty ship. It wasn't particularly fancy, although there was one kind of a room that was pretty nice. It was old, fairly old, and it was painted white. I remember guys getting haircuts from these little short Indian guys who would give haircuts.

On that boat is when I started to smoke. Because I started to think about the idea of making an invasion, and I knew how difficult the invasion of northern France had been. There was no reason to believe it wasn't going to be as difficult in southern France. Although there was some talk that the resistance might not be as strong.

5 The Italian Campaign
Analysis of Memories

As revealed in the initial recall document, Howard had virtually no appreciation of the broader dimensions of the drama in which he was a bit player. Therefore the reader may find it useful to have some historical context in which to place these memories.

The Italian campaign was the result of the dogged determination of Winston Churchill to maintain the Allied presence in the Mediterranean. The American hopes were more concentrated on the invasion of France and a direct drive to the heart of Nazi Germany. In January 1943 it was decided to invade Sicily and to make further plans as the situation developed. The successful conquest of Sicily in August 1943 placed the Allied troops only two miles across the Straits of Messina from the mainland of Italy. Meanwhile the government of Benito Mussolini collapsed, he was placed under house arrest, and King Victor Emmanuel asked Marshall Badoglio to form a new government, which began to sue the Allies for peace. These events might have taken Italy out of the war but for the fact that Hitler also appreciated the psychological significance of the surrender of Rome to the Allies. He moved quickly. On September 12, 1943, Mussolini was captured by German commandos and was installed in a sham government in northern Italy completely under the control of the Third Reich.

All of these events argued strongly for an invasion of the Italian mainland with the goal of a quick capture of Rome. At the least an invasion would draw German strength away from the defense of France and away from the Eastern Front. Albert Kesselring, Hitler's commander in Italy, constructed a strong series of defenses of Rome with the high ground at Cassino as its center point. The front known as the Gustav Line consisted of concrete bunkers, barbed wire, mine fields, and, most formidable of all, the naturally mountainous and virtually impassable terrain.

The Allied forces were brought to a standstill below the monastery of Cassino. Throughout the winter of 1944, the Allies had thrown themselves against this barrier in futile and bloody frustration. The attempt at Anzio to make an end run around the line had resulted in a precarious toehold on the beachhead from which it had proven impossible to break out. Those troops spent a miserable winter under German guns placed on the heights and trained on the beach.

As the miseries of the Italian cold and muddy winter abated, the spring offensive was planned. A polyglot assemblage of Allied forces was massed before Cassino. British, Americans, Canadians, Free French, New Zealanders, Free Poles, and an amazing mixture of colonial troops including Senegalese from West Africa, Moroccan Goumier, and Nepalese Gurkhas represented, as it turned out, the last of the colonial mercenaries ready to give their lives for their European masters.

The plan was to make once again a frontal assault across the Garigliano and Rapido rivers and into the Liri Valley to link up with the forces pinned down at Anzio. Fortunately there was also another plan. General Alphonse Juin, commander in Italy of the Free French Expeditionary Forces, argued persuasively that he should be allowed to try to go in behind the Gustav Line by taking his colonial troops, the Goumier, through the mountains at Castelforte to Pico and thus to open the road to Rome. While the British and American troops were once again stymied beneath Cassino's heights, Juin's troops accomplished this miracle of hazardous mountain fighting and erected a huge French tricolor on the top of Monte Majo which Juin hoped could be seen at Cassino.

By May 18 after a week of intense fighting, the French drive toward Pico weakened German resistance to the point where the free Polish forces were able to take Cassino and the Germans were forced to withdraw north to less fortified defenses before Rome. The Third Chemical Mortar Battalion was attached to the troops under the command of General Juin which had broken out of the beachhead on May 24, and together they drove north to Rome, which fell on June 5, the day before the invasion of Normandy.

While Private Hoffman was most assuredly a part of these momentous events, he never, until very recently, understood the historical context of his experience. He thought the tremendous convoy of ships, men, and materiel was routine. He imagined that similar convoys were crossing the Atlantic every week or so. He did not realize that this was the preparation for the big push against the German defensive lines known as Operation Diadem. In fact, he had no name for the line of defenses at Cassino, now called the Gustav Line in the history books. The name Winter Line, as the Allied commanders at the time called it, he only vaguely remembered as a term "I might have heard sometime."

When Howard arrived at the front in early May, he found himself attached to a group many of whose members had been fighting together since the African campaign. From their stories of the previous winter before Cassino, he understood that now he was to be a part of a major spring offensive. He was impressed by the synchronization of the artillery bombardment that began the offensive, and while he remembered the zero hour as eleven o'clock, he mistakenly placed the hour in the morning, when in fact it was at night. He did remember moving the ammunition up to the guns in the darkness, and this memory is corroborated in the *Battle for Rome* by W.G.F. Jackson. Jackson describes the men moving forward in the dark. "At eleven o'clock . . . the combined artillery of the Fifth and Eighth Armies opened fire. . . . The flashes lit up the black shapes of the mountains from Minturno on the coast to Monte Cifalco north of Cassino. . . . Juin's Frenchmen started their assault within minutes of the beginning of the artillery programme."[1]

Howard's memories of the event from the second set of interviews appear below.

AH: When did you first get into combat?

HH: May 11, I think, was the day. At eleven o'clock in the morning on the eleventh day of May somehow is what I remember. At Castelforte was the first place that I experienced any combat. They brought us up to Castelforte in trucks, and we unloaded hundreds and hundreds of rounds of ammunition, carried it up the mountainside to a place sort of a quarter of the way up the mountain, set up the guns and then we were told that we were to start firing at a particular time. Now, I think that we had set up the day before, and it was the next morning that we were to start firing, and the officer was there with a stopwatch and he told us when to exactly drop the shells in. And the interesting thing is that just before we fired I could see the guns behind us firing, that is, hear the guns way, way back like the long toms, the 240-millimeter cannons which could fire for miles. The impression I got was that they had tried to time things so that all the shells would land at the same time even though the ones further away would fire sooner. That was the opening of my first experience of combat. [Second recall interview]

In the first interview he emphasized how heavy the mortar was and how many men it took to lug it up the steep hillsides. He says, "I remember carrying it [the mortar and ammunition] at night and in the daytime." He again emphasized the synchronization, but interestingly enough, when he describes the hour at which the firing began, he qualifies it in both interviews with the phrases, "It seemed to me like it was eleven o'clock in the morning" and "I think it was the next morning when we began to fire." In both interviews he emphasized the massive character of the bombardment. Historians have described the bom-

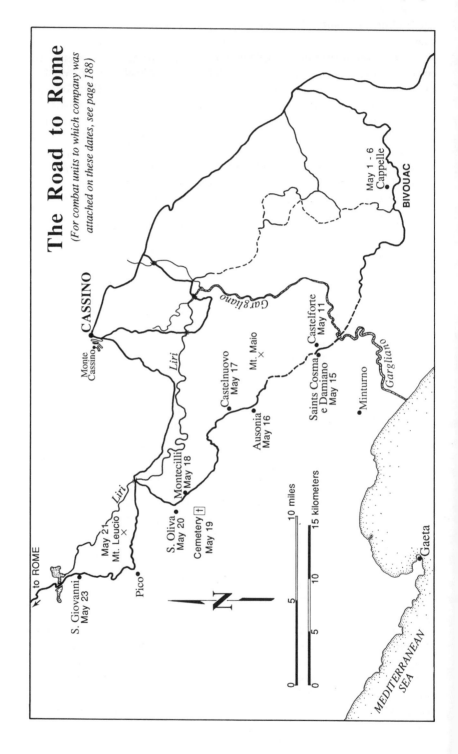

The Road to Rome

(For combat units to which company was
attached on these dates, see page 188)

CASSINO

Monte
Cassino

Garigliano

Liri

CASTELFORTE
Castelforte
May 11

Castelnuovo
May 17

Mt. Maio ×

Saints Cosma
e Damiano
May 15

Ausonia
May 16

Minturno

Gargliano

Montecilli
May 18

S. Oliva
May 20

Cemetery †
May 19

Pico

Mt. Leucio ×
May 21

S. Giovanni
May 23

to ROME

May 1 - 6
Cappelle

BIVOUAC

Gaeta

MEDITERRANEAN
SEA

N

10 miles

15 kilometers

0   5   10

0   5   10

bardment as rivaled only by the barrage at El Alamein in the annals of war.

In the first interview in response to the question, "Who was your commander?" Howard replied that he did not know but that he thought his name was Captain Cook. He did remember that he was young, blond, a stable leader, and from Louisiana. In the second interview in response to the same question, he again states that he doesn't know but that

> we had somebody who—I keep thinking his name was Cooper, and I think he was from Louisiana, and he was a fairly young man, a captain. But I remember him from much later, from during the Bulge. In fact, it was during the Bulge that he was sent home on a furlough and came back again. And the name Cooper—I'm not sure it's Cooper, because Frank Cooper was the head of Haskins Lab, and I may have the names mixed up, but somehow the name Cooper seems appropriate for Captain Cooper, Captain Something.

This time Howard changed the name to Cooper but sensed that this may not be correct and volunteers that Frank Cooper was a figure from a later period in his life. He also now remembers more about the captain from the Battle of the Bulge and, as we shall see, recounts a story about the captain at the point where he discusses this battle. In searching through the records of Company C, we find that the captain was John Moore, that he was much admired by his troops, and that he was from Louisiana. Furthermore, in September 1985, after our research at the War College in Carlisle, Pennsylvania, had disclosed that the Third Chemical Battalion held occasional reunions, we attended our first of these gatherings in York, Pennsylvania, at the home of Corporal Ralph Worley. While Captain Moore was unable to attend this particular meeting, he called from Louisiana and talked to each of the veterans at the reunion. That conversation caused Howard to recall that this officer had shared his liquor with his men on at least one occasion, an act of generosity remembered because it was unusual. Now Captain Moore's name was brought back to what might be described as its rightful place in Howard's memory. Thus we can conclude that memories which seem to be unavailable can be redintegrated, given the appropriate stimulus.

These events also provide some evidence for the hypothesis that memories are not only chained but also cataloged under certain headings. For example, in the first instance where Howard attempted to retrieve the name, he said Cook probably because of its association with the captain in the Peter Pan story. Furthermore, since Howard's self-perception about his memory is that he cannot remember names, he didn't search very hard, figuring that the effort would not be worthwhile. In the second interview, when he was asked the same question, he did engage in a search and retrieved the name of Frank Cooper, a respected authority figure. It's as if he had a subject file in his memory labeled "respected authority figures." While he sensed that this name was not correct and even offered an explanation of why it had emerged, he still was unable to produce the correct name.

Another possible storage category might be names with "oo" following the first consonant. But when he found the correct name in the records, he recognized it instantly, and furthermore, when he spoke to the man on the phone, an entire series of memories and stories about him emerged which are linked to his name and to conversation with him, all of which had previously been inaccessible. This incident suggests that there may be a great deal of information and experience in memory's storehouse which, at any particular time that is called for, may not be available but is not necessarily erased. I mean to say not that all experience is retained, however, but merely that more experience may be retained than can be elicited by mere free recall and that a great deal more may be retrieved, given appropriate cues.

All of the stories or vignettes are contained in both interviews with considerable reliability. In both documents the stories are told in the same order and in the same way, often in virtually the same words. For instance, in describing the incident of coming upon the German dead in the dark, Howard says in interview 1, "I see all these clumps of dirt in the road, big clumps of dirt. I thought to myself, 'I have this eerie feeling that these are bodies, but no it can't be.'" In interview 2, he says, "There were these big clumps of dirt lying in the road. And I just had the funniest feeling about those clods of dirt, as if they were maybe people. But I didn't think it was people."

The main difference between the two interviews is that in the first interview the initial stories are grouped under topic headings such as "incidents which were frightening" or "incidents when we were shelled." He then turned to a more chronological treatment of the incidents. In the second interview he states that his form of organization will be chronological and then proceeds to put the stories into that kind of sequence, "I'll just describe things as I recall them . . . with some kind of temporal organization." There are, however, discrepancies between the two interviews. For instance, in the second interview he describes the Italian children begging for food, and that description is not in the first interview. Moreover, neither interview contains a story that he has repeatedly told the family over the years about the Italians greeting the GI as follows: "Niente scarpe, niente mangiare, multi bambini, alles kaputt." [no shoes, nothing to eat, many babies, everything is broken] Another incident described in the second interview but not in the first is also a story which he has occasionally told before about "short-arm inspection." "Short-arm inspection" was the soldiers' term for an inspection of the genitals to discover signs of venereal disease. This particular inspection was held in an open field with a lot of Italian women looking on. The women found the GIs' discomfort and embarrassment hilarious as they pointed, laughed, and hooted.

One hypothesis to explain these discrepancies is that Howard had a very limited number of stories about the war which he regarded as acceptable fare for close friends and intimates. These stories were usually amusing in some way. But for the most part, he had never discussed his war experiences. In fact he felt some disdain for those who talked about the war, a sense that it was somehow unmanly to burden others with the true stories of the horrors of war and that most of the talkers had not really been there at the front where the fighting was. It was only after he decided to engage in this project that he told most of these stories. Hence it was as if he was telling those stories not told before, so that stories which had previously been a part of his repertoire of war stories were now culled out.

The memories of the Italian campaign can be submitted to a more rigorous validity analysis than Howard's previous descriptions because the events of the Italian campaign have been the focus, of course, of a great deal of historical attention. Howard's descriptions of the terrain can be verified in many other accounts and in photographs. The facts that he was fighting with the free French forces and that the Goumier mountain troops opened the road to Rome are a matter of record. Furthermore, now for the first time in the narrative it has become possible to compare and contrast Howard's memories with the diary of events kept in the company headquarters on a daily basis.[2]

These entries corroborate much of Howard's memory, but of course, they offer no information at all about many of his stories. They are unemotional and are sometimes designed to put the actions of the officers in the best possible light, with the minimum distortion of fact. The entry from 10 May 1944 will perhaps illustrate their character. "The Company spent the day in preparation for the move to the forward area. The Company departed from battalion bivouac area at 2100B hours. There was much traffic on the road. The last truck was unloaded at the gun position 0230B hours, May 11th. The night was quiet and no enemy shelling. Casualties: None." Throughout the month of May, these records corroborate Howard's memory of moving, setting up the guns, and moving again. In fact, they serve to explain that memory by commenting that "Jerries were on the run and it was almost difficult to keep up with them" (22 May 1944).

On the 19th of May the following incident is reported:

The Co. was awakened at 0520B by a heavy enemy shell burst close by that sounded like a delayed action bomb. Several men called for help about 20 feet away. Sgt Edmondson was lying with a lump of dirt the size of a bedroll on his chest and with a cut on his face. Capt Moore found no severe cuts on him so ran to the other calls and found Pvts Ryan and McGrady, the two first aid men, and Pvts Depresco and Childress buried in their slit trenches with only their heads exposed. Sgt Toscano's squad was summoned for help and the two First Aid men were soon on their feet and uninjured. Pvts Depresco and Childress, however, were deeply buried and Pvt Aciz worked some 15 or 20 minutes digging them out. Pvt Childress was lifted onto a stretcher but Pvt Depresco, who was underneath and somewhat protected, scrambled out and onto his feet. Sgt Edmondson, Pvts Childress and Depresco were sent back to Bn Forward Aid Station. [Daily Log, 19 May 1944]

Obviously this story is the same as that reported by Howard. While it provides considerable corroboration, however, it also reveals some discrepancies. Howard, in the first interview, had described moving up to a small Italian cemetery where he slept one night with several other guys. Not finding it too comfortable, the next night he went to where the trucks were parked and dug a foxhole in a drainage ditch. In the morning he was awakened by an officer telling him that he was needed to help dig out some bodies. They dug furiously and pulled one man out. Another managed to free himself, but the one in the middle hole, which would have taken the direct hit, could not be found—no part of him. Later the guy who had been supposed to be sleeping in the middle foxhole came down the hill from the German dugout in which he had gone to sleep. The middle foxhole had in fact been unoccupied.

In the second interview Howard says that he did not sleep in the cemetery. He remembered lying down in the crypt but found it eerie and uncomfortable, and so he went below and dug into a ditch. He tells the same story about being awakened in the morning to dig the men out. He states that there were four men buried in their slit trenches, a figure which is corroborated by the company history, which names four men. He again repeats the story about looking for the guy in the middle foxhole, not being able to find any part of him, and then later seeing him come wandering into the breakfast chow line, much to Howard's amazement. The company history makes it clear that the second interview is the correct one with respect to whether or not he slept in the cemetery, since they were not in this area for two nights but only for one. The second interview also contains a more obvious effort to get the memory right and in so doing provides a very interesting insight into the memory process.

We started digging, mostly with our hands and we dug up, as I remember, four guys and not one of them was hurt. Now I can't picture it any more. I seemed to think that last time I was able to say that I, you know, helped them up. But now I'm not able to picture reaching down and grabbing them. . . . They had been buried alive but loosely by the dirt—but now I can't picture it any more. That's a memory that's . . . I can remember sort of standing there, I can remember . . . I seem to think I have a shovel in my hand, I seem to think I'm pulling, but I can't picture lifting somebody up, coming across a person. The other thing is that the story, I can remember telling the story from four years ago, and I remember . . . This is what I remember about it, that the shell landed, it had just missed the truck coming in. If it had hit the truck which was loaded with ammo, we'd all be dead. It just missed the truck and landed in the middle foxhole. And the concussion apparently went up above all the other guys and covered them without killing them. Now, maybe they had been removed from the hole before I came along, but I remember the lieutenant telling, I do remember him physically waking me and saying that I had to come along and help dig these guys out. And the one who was in the middle, we couldn't find anything. And I remember digging and looking and there was no trace of him. And we assumed that he had just [been] completely disintegrated by the shell. Well, about an hour or two later, he comes walking down the hill. [Second recall interview]

In the first interview he had stated that after digging one guy out, before they could get to the next one, "we see this earth moving, and this guy manages to free himself." This statement is corroborated in the company history: "Pvt. Childress was lifted onto a stretcher but Pvt. Depresco, who was underneath and somewhat protected, scrambled out and onto his feet." For whatever reason, there seems to have been a greater effort toward accuracy in the second interview than in the first, at least at this point in the narrative. The story about sleeping in the cemetery Howard had told over the years to entertain friends, and presumably he judged actually sleeping in the cemetery more interesting and entertaining than just thinking about sleeping there. In the second interview, however, Howard drew several blanks when he attempted to image the scene and thus became unsure about what in fact had happened. Note that after he states that he "can't picture it anymore" there are several false starts and points of verbal confusion, followed by a clear effort to reconstruct the events from the logic of what "must have happened." Whether Howard actually dug the men out cannot be stated with any certainty. The history of Company C mentions only Private Aciz but does also note the fact that Sergeant Toscano's squad was summoned to help.

In any case, it is clear that here we have an event witnessed by

Howard, which he has described in both interviews and the substance of which is corroborated by the archival record. Moreover, the effort to recover the incident reveals interesting information about the basic strategies employed by Howard. When he makes an effort to provide accurate information from memory, he tends to do so by calling up the image and then describing it. As noted in a previous chapter, Elizabeth Loftus, who has done many experiments on the accuracy of human memory, describes two kinds of rememberers: verbal and image makers. We see that Howard falls quite definitely into the latter category, which is perhaps consistent with his effort to become a professional artist later in life and with the fact that throughout his life he had been interested in drawing and painting and conveying his perceptions of the world via an effort to reproduce them visually.

Of course, we can't know how much error, distortion, and/or corroboration there may be in stories which are not in the company history or in other historical treatments of the Italian campaign and are not corroborated by information from other veterans in the same unit. But on the basis of the portions that can be validated, one can feel confident that these stories contain a central core of fact even though certain details are missing or have been reconstructed in order to make sense of the memory as the effort is made to share it with others.

Another characteristic of rememberers who rely on images rather than on verbally stored stories is that they tend to place more confidence in their memories than do those who rely on verbal stories. After all, such rememberers are simply calling up the scene and describing it. Likewise, if they cannot recall an event, there is a strong tendency to feel that it could not have happened. This characteristic is illustrated by the description of events when the Third Chemical was bivouacked on the Italian coast after Rome had been taken and while preparations were being made for the invasion of southern France known as Operation Anvil.

After Rome fell, Howard had precious little time to enjoy the spoils of victory because he contracted malaria and was hospitalized, first in Rome and then at Anzio. As he began to recover, he was allowed to walk around a little bit. In the second interview, he described this period.

> HH: "Eventually I was free to walk around a little bit, and I walked around Anzio, went up and climbed the mountain next to it and saw where they were, and Christ Almighty! you know, the Germans were looking right down their throats. You couldn't go out to take a pee that they wouldn't see you and shoot off your pecker if they wanted to.
> AH: At the beach?

HH: Yes, at the beach. We were on the beach. That's where the hospital was, at the beach at Anzio. It was a ghastly place. I'm very glad I wasn't there." [Second recall interview]

But the most compelling memory from this period, after the taking of Rome, was of a fire on the beach north of Naples which ignited the nitrocellulose rings on the ammunition and caused a flash fire that burned five or six guys very badly. Ralph Worley also remembered this incident and described it even more vividly than Howard. He said, "One guy just had the flesh hanging off his chest in strings, like hot cheese." But Worley went on to say that Howard had gone out in an amphibious vehicle to drag a target out into the sea for target practice. Howard did not believe that that could have happened. He felt that he would have had a great interest in such a vehicle and could not possibly forget having ridden in one. We taped the following exchange between Ralph Worley and Howard Hoffman at the reunion in September of 1985.

"WORLEY: Well, I know you were there because I have a picture of you on that amphibious vehicle coming in. You went out with . . .

HOFFMAN: I don't believe I did!

WORLEY: I know you did! Because I have a picture of you coming back.

HOFFMAN: You've got to show it to me. I've got to see that one.

WORLEY: It was Lieutenant Meshany and our warrant officer and you and I believe Z.J. Hatcher, it might have been.

HOFFMAN: Well, if it's a picture of me, it will be the first thing that's clear that's happened to me that I don't remember.

WORLEY: They made a raft out of wood and then they put some kind of cloth on it and they took it out and set it out there and then they fired mortars at that target out on the Mediterranean and you were on the vehicle, one of those like a truck that you can go on land or sea.

HOFFMAN: I've got to see this picture, because I don't remember.

WORLEY: Yeah, I have it in there. I'll show it to you. I've got a colored slide.[3]

When the slide was shown (see photo section) Howard still felt that it was not he, even though there was a chorus from the veterans of "That's you, all right, Hoffman." Howard went up close to the picture, denying all the way that it was in fact a picture of him until he saw a ring on the finger that he knew to have been his and that he had subsequently given to a French girl. But even after he had been forced to acknowledge that this was indeed a picture of himself and hence a valid record of an experience from his own past, he had no memory of the event—and has none to this day. He feels that this picture is unrelated to his own experience although he knows otherwise.

How can this phenomenon be accounted for? Is this the only example of repression that we have found in this study? There is some evidence that this might be the case. In the first interview, as he begins to describe the events which took place when they were bivouacked on the beach, Howard says, "I also remember doing some target practice there. Not target practice, but shooting." Thus there is a denial of the target practice. In the second interview, when he reaches the same point in the narration, he says, "There are several incidents on the beach I ought to tell you about. Can I do it later, though?" I said no and added that we were almost through the story of the Italian campaign, and so we should continue to the end of that chapter. He then gave a big sigh and proceeded with the story of the flash fire.

There are also some reasons to reject the notion of repression, however. For one thing, it is difficult to hypothesize repression in the absence of any reason for it. Worley states that Howard was not near the fire when it happened; he could not, therefore, feel responsible for it in any way. Moreover, the material unavailable for either recall or recognition is not the story of the fire but rather the story of what looks like a pleasant interlude involving a boating excursion. One theory about memory is that it requires rehearsal in order to go into long-term store. In this case, it may be that the horror of the fire and his subsequent preoccupation with the fears attendant on invading southern France, prevented the rehearsal of this event in the amphibious vehicle. At any rate, Howard does describe considerable preoccupation with thoughts of the invasion. In the second interview he says that they had picked him to be a forward observer and that forward observers were slated to go onto the coast of France in gliders. "That scared the beJesus out of me. I really didn't want to do that because I thought that's one helluva way to go. You don't know what you're landing in, who's going to be there to greet you, what it's going to be like. I sweated that out for, I think, maybe weeks." Whatever the cause of Howard's inability to remember the ride in the duck, one thing about it seems certain. It is absolutely unavailable for retrieval even with the most cogent of cues, namely a picture of himself in the boat!

In summary, what do these episodic accounts of the Mediterranean Theater of Operations contribute to an understanding of this phase of the war, if anything? Well, for one thing, they give a definite picture of its smell, its taste, the hurt of it, the fear, and the humor. Such elements are missing for the most part from the records and the histories of these battles. While historians have debated whether Churchill was correct in his insistance on slogging northward from

Salerno to Rome or whether the American generals and Roosevelt were more correct in going for the heart of Nazi Germany through an invasion at Normandy can (and will, I suspect) be debated endlessly in various geopolitical treaties for quite some time to come. Historians have tended on the whole to sum up the issue in the following way: "The question has often been raised whether the Italian campaign, forced pretty much by the British, was necessary for the Allied victory. Without Allied presence in Italy, the bombardment of Germany and of southeastern Europe would have been less effective; the support of Tito's forces in Yugoslavia would have been less efficient; and the German strength on the Western and Eastern Fronts would have been more formidable. The Allied Italian campaign was a necessary component of the giant ring that squeezed the life out of the Nazi state."[4]

What these stories may contribute to an understanding of memory is a more complex issue and one best saved for later, when we have analyzed the full range of Howard's memories of World War II. For now, it may be enough to point to the obvious importance of primacy in retaining memory, to the demonstrated necessity for rehearsal to ensure storage and the indications that storage is both chained and categorized. It is apparent, furthermore, that some memories are simply not effectively available for recall or recognition no matter how cogent the cues to enhance them might be.

6 From Southern France to the Elbe

First Recall Document

In August 1944, Howard participated in the invasion of southern France. The Allied forces drove north through the Vosges Mountains into Germany. In December of that year, the Third Chemical Battalion was attached to Patton's Third Army when it rushed to the relief of Bastogne. Later this force crossed the Rhine River and eventually met the Russians at the Elbe River in April.

HH: There were airplanes flying over, strafing the beach and strafing the pillboxes out there, cannons going off, shooting at the pillboxes. We went down the side of the boat on a rope ladder and got into these landing craft and the landing craft came up on the beach and dropped their front and out we ran into the water and up the beach. Nobody ever fired a shot at us. There wasn't a single casualty in the whole goddamn invasion from what I understand. But we didn't know it was going to be that way, of course. We landed on the French Riviera, but I don't know where it was exactly. Later they brought in the trucks, and then they brought in the equipment.

AH: How much later? Within the day?

HH: Yes, that afternoon or evening, I guess. But first they landed us.

AH: Did the officers know there wasn't going to be much resistance?

HH: No, I don't think so.

AH: There must have been rather poor information.

HH: Well, what was clear was that there was very massive preparations for it by way of bombing and strafing and shooting. But the officers may have known.

AH: Who was there? The Vichy forces or were there Germans there?

HH: There were Germans there. There had been. At least that's what we assumed. There was no resistance, none at all.

AH: Why don't you just describe in your own words what happens next?

HH: The next thing that happened was that we started moving north in trucks. We passed through the fields where gliders had landed. What the Germans had done was they had planted in these fields stakes, sharpened stakes, pointing at an angle, two or three different angles—they looked like just grape fields—but they were really kind of booby-trapped to destroy the gliders. No explosives, just these sharpened stakes and many crashed gliders. And I thought, "My God, how lucky that I didn't go in by glider," because "there, but for the grace of God, go I."

Anyhow I don't remember a great deal of . . . In fact, I don't remember any fighting in that area. I remember shortly after we landed we were in a large baronial-type farm that had a stable and horses, and a bunch of the guys had got horses and were riding horses. I don't remember seeing any civilians at this point. I remember it was a nice day, the day of the invasion. But anyhow I don't really recall very much combat in that region. In fact, none at all. What I remember doing is moving up near Arles. Now somehow we got from where we landed up into the vicinity of Arles, because I remember the name.

AH: Did you associate it with Van Gogh?

HH: No. I didn't know anything about painting then. I hadn't started to study painting at all. I had been to the Vatican, because I wanted to see it, and I had been impressed. But I had no idea of modern painting. I don't think I even knew who Van Gogh was. I remember riding in a truck full of ammunition, riding up a mountain, and then looking across the mountain, and now I do recall there was some enemy fire, some shells were landing, and then seeing that the mountain was on fire—a forest fire. Watching it from a distance and then suddenly realizing it was coming our way. Now, we had unloaded four or five truckloads of ammunition, and the forest fire was maybe a half mile away when I first became conscious of it.

AH: How long after the invasion was this? One or two days, or a week, or . . . ?

HH: You know, I don't know. It could have been a week, and it could have been two days. It could have been a month. I just don't remember how I got there. I don't have any recollection whatsoever of going to this place. All I know is that it was in southern France, and see, I'm going to jump from there over to the border of Italy, because that's the next place I remember being. So it must have been within a few days of having landed. As I say, I don't remember a great deal about it except being on this mountain and watching this fire at a distance and saying to the officer, "You know, that thing could move very fast; it could be on us in just a few minutes if the wind should shift" and his kind of scoffing at this. When the wind shifted and I saw the fire starting to move toward us, I pointed this out to the officer and he said, "Well, it will take a while." He wasn't really terribly concerned, but all of a sudden, I looked out, and running past me are rabbits, snakes, just going like lightning, as fast as they can, running away from the fire. Rabbits, snakes, I think I saw a badger, squirrels, all kinds of animals, just fleeing. Within fifteen seconds of seeing these animals go by, everybody was mobilized, and we were taking the ammunition and trying to get it back onto the truck. Now, the thing I remember about this ammunition is that we had pulled the pin off of a lot of it. Now, when you pull the pin on the ammunition, what that means is that you're ready to fire. The safety pin, when a mortar shell comes out of the barrel, it has to make two and a quarter turns or two and a half turns and then that throws out a tumbler of some sort that's held in by that safety pin, so when you pull the pin, it makes it possible for that tumbler to fly out. When that tumbler flies out, then the plunger on the detonator flies forward, and then anything that presses that plunger in is going to cause it to detonate, to fire and cause the shell to explode. So if you pull the pin that doesn't mean the shell is going to explode, but it does mean that it could; it's in a much more dangerous situation because it's possible to drop it or twist it and then the plunger would fly forward and then it would be very, very dangerous.

Anyway what we had to do was to take these shells, and we made these human lines and we were throwing them from one person to another down the hill to get them away from the fire, because if the fire got to where those shells were, there would be hell to pay. We got, I guess, all of them out, as I recall. But the fire was within, I remember seeing the flames, maybe a hundred feet away from where we were. You know, sparks coming, and thinking, "My God, are we going to get out of here?" So the next thing I remember is riding out of that place, sitting on top of the ammunition, and now the ammunition doesn't have any firing pins in it, and I'm thinking to myself, "Boy, if this goes, they'll find half my ass in North Carolina and the rest of it will be in Dallas." Because that was a lot of TNT there, and I was very much afraid, not so much for the shells to explode as for that material that you use, nitrocellulose that you use, to fire it. That is terribly inflammable and if you light it it goes THWWWWWWWWWWWWWWWW. You know, a big burst of fire. Anyway, that was the experience on the mountain in Arles. The thing I remember is riding on this truck over lots of bumps and thinking to myself, "Goddammit, none of these shells have pins in them!"

The next thing that happened, or the next thing I remember, [is that] I remember we must have camped somewhere there for a couple of days, because I got word there that a guy I knew had been killed

during an inspection. Somebody had pulled an inspection and somebody had a live round in the barrel and the thing went off and killed the
guy. One guy killed his friend this way and I knew both of them and I
was very horrified to hear about that. The next thing that happened is
that we pulled into this little town on the border of Switzerland and
France and Italy, right on the corner there. There was a little tiny—it
wasn't really a town—it was maybe like a restaurant on a road.

It was a beautiful place and the weather was very much like it is
today, a beautiful kind of an autumn day. The whole battalion was
there: battalion headquarters, the supply sergeant, other companies. I
remember that the first day we were there, we had been sent to this
particular spot at the border of Switzerland, France, and Italy to keep
the Germans from leaving Italy and coming into France. The idea was
that there was only one pass that they could go through, and we were to
set our mortars up down here at the foot of this mountain, or at the foot
of this range of mountains. Actually, we were kind of in a pass; I recall
there were mountains on either side of us, and there was a beautiful
stream just two hundred yards away from where I was, and on the
other side of that stream, if you climbed up, you would be climbing
toward Italy in these very high mountains. The idea was that there was
only this one pass that the Germans could escape through, and we
were to keep that pass under cover, under mortar fire. That would
presumably prevent them from getting out of Italy. I don't know
exactly who we were supposed to prevent. Somehow I had the impression at that time that it was the entire German army, which seemed a
bit ludicrous to me, that we could hope to prevent them from getting
by.

AH: It seemed ludicrous to you at the time or looking back on it?

HH: At the time. I mean I realized that it's difficult to move when
there's mortar fire, but we were just one battalion and we had a fixed
amount of ammunition that could be fired for only a fixed amount of
time. And I saw no other support; there were no infantry with us.
There was nobody else there except us, this one battalion. It seemed to
me that anybody that wanted to get by us could just wait until we were
finished firing everything and then come through. They'd have to wait
three or four days; we didn't have that much ammunition. But as a foot
soldier you don't have any idea what's really going on.

I remember the feeling that it was a very quiet, beautiful place.
There was a bar and a kind of restaurant. In addition, I do remember
going over to the stream and thinking, "Gee, I wish I had my fishing
equipment to fish in that stream." We set up a pup tent and piled in a
lot of ammunition. As I recall the first day nothing happened. The second
day, suddenly, in the morning, ten o'clock perhaps, there was an
explosion and then another and another, and they were very close by—

right in the camp. Of course, I hit the dirt immediately. I remember that I had been over to the stream and bathed in the stream and I just had on a pair of pants and no shirt. What I recall doing was quickly throwing on a shirt and a field jacket even though it was kind of warm.

What happened was that apparently the Germans had sent some mountain troops that they had up to the top of the mountain. They had carried pack howitzers up there. These are 75 millimeter guns and they were shooting point-blank down from the top of the mountain down on us. Now, I wouldn't swear that it was point-blank. For all I know, it may not have been; it may have been they were lobbing them over. But somehow they had gotten these howitzers in, and the shells were coming into the camp, shells were going down to the road, and everybody was in a tremendous panic. Officers were running around, telling guys that had never been under fire before what to do. Many of them, like the supply sergeant, had never been under fire before.

So the supply sergeant, the major, the battalion commandant, all of these people had to leave or did leave. And the way out, there was only one way out, and this was along a very narrow road, a paved road, a winding road, and there was one place along this road where you were in the open. That is, where you were exposed to artillery fire and where the Germans had the shells coming in. There was a field there and I remember there was a kind of bluff, or cliff, on the far side of the road from the Germans, the side toward France, and you had to drive along the foot of this cliff. There was a field to your right—and the shells were falling in the field and hitting above on the cliff and all around. There hadn't been any shells that had hit the road itself, nor had I seen any jeeps or trucks get hit.

The orders were to evacuate and pull back about five to ten miles, but in order to evacuate you had to ride a jeep out of there, or a truck, past this one spot. When they did evacuate, the evacuation, took perhaps two or three hours. . . .

AH: Now, wait a minute, they evacuated all of you or just the personnel like the supply sergeant and . . . ?

HH: No. Everybody. Everybody was evacuated.

AH: But you meant to say these other people went out first?

HH: They went out first. I was one of the last out. There were very few people left when I went out. I stayed there with my gun, and I helped load up one load after another of guys going out. I say, it took a couple of hours. It took like . . .

AH: You weren't returning the German fire with your mortar shells?

HH: No. No. No return fire. What we did do was . . . the sergeant picked up a bunch of people, and luckily he didn't pick me, to go on a patrol up into the mountains to see what was going on. This happened as soon as the firing started, and those guys went. I watched them go up the side of the mountain. I guess there were maybe twenty guys in this patrol, and up they went, and we never saw them again. Never! I assume they were captured by the Germans, because they never came back. Not any of them. And there never was any word from any of them that I ever heard of or that I can recall hearing. I may have heard that they were captured, because I do have a kind of vague tweaking in my memory that something, that there was some time that I talked about them at some point, and the word "capture" keeps coming up. But that was the last I saw of them. I don't recall ever seeing any of them again.

In the meantime, what happened is that a jeep and an ammo carrier would go out, and they usually put in some ammo, some weapons, the guys would take some clothing, some blankets and stuff. Each guy would take just what he could carry on his back and then climb onto the jeep or onto the ammo carrier, and then they would make the dash out of there and go five to ten miles upstream, and then somebody else would take them from there and go even further up toward Grenoble, along the border of Switzerland and France, away from this corner where Italy jutted in.

One after another of these trucks would go out, and then they'd come back and drive back that road, and then drive out again. And it was one helluva dangerous thing for the drivers. Every time they went out, they were taking a chance of getting killed. We didn't get too much more firing in the camp after that, after that initial onslaught. Then almost all the firing was on that road, which was maybe a mile away from where I was. I could hear it.

AH: Did they kill anybody in the first onslaught?

HH: No. Not that I know of; I don't know of anybody who was hurt.

AH: Did any of the drivers get killed in this run they had to make?

HH: No. No, I don't think so. I just don't remember seeing any blood. All I remember is being scared, and hearing the firing on that thing and knowing that I had to go through it. It wasn't continuous firing. They'd fire maybe five minutes and then nothing for ten, and then they'd fire for five and then nothing for ten and then BOOOOM, BOOM, BOOM, BOOMMMMM, BOOMMMMMM. You just never knew when a shell was going to land there. And what they would do is they would drive up to the point where they then had to go past this place where the firing was and then zoom past it when they thought that maybe the last shell had dropped for some period.

Now, you understand that a shell doesn't have to hit you to kill you. A shell could land 200 yards away and it would throw shrapnel out. Shrapnel consists of whirling pieces of the shell itself that has exploded, a jagged piece of metal maybe an inch long and a quarter of an inch wide, like a piece of a pencil, but it's steel and it's spinning, and if that were to hit you . . . For example, if it were to hit your leg it could take your whole leg off because of the momentum and the speed with which it's spinning. The fragments from shrapnel are terribly, terribly dangerous, and they go for a long distance. Actually, I guess if a shell landed 200 yards away, the odds would be very small that you'd be hit, because you've got to picture the shrapnel as being spread out and the distance between successive pieces is larger and larger the further away you are. So the actual odds of being hit get smaller and smaller the further away you get, but even so, the odds are pretty good. Similarly, if you shoot a bullet into the air, when it comes down, it's traveling almost as fast as it was when it went up, only it loses its momentum gradually, but then it picks it up coming down. If something is ricocheted off something else, it will be spent, but most of the time when there's an explosion nearby if it was shrapnel, not just heavy explosive, it's very dangerous. And your helmet doesn't really stop it; nothing stops that stuff, except being underground.

Anyhow, eventually my turn came. I remember I had a field jacket, one blanket, my spoon, knife, my carbine, some ammunition, and a couple of hand grenades. That's all I took out. That's all I could take out. I left behind every personal effect I may have had. I don't know what I might have had! Any souvenirs I might have bought in Italy, things like that I might have been carrying with me. So I made the trip, and I remember we came up to this place and waited, and they were firing as we approached it. The firing stopped, and we made the dash, and on the trip I was on, there must have been a dozen guys on the jeep itself— guys sitting on the hood, you know, all around, everywhere. Maybe it was a dozen or so riding in the ammo carrier, which is as many people as could possibly fit on it. And out we went that way.

AH: How many had to be moved that way?

HH: Well, there were 500, or something like that, maybe more, maybe 600. It was a whole battalion that had to be moved out of there. First went the cooks and the bakers and the officers. We were the last ones out, the foot soldiers, the mortar crewmen. I remember how beautiful it was. We went through a big, long tunnel, and I remember you'd be driving along and the mountains, there'd be a waterfall like from a thousand feet, a little, narrow waterfall falling down the mountains, just like pictures of the Alps in the spring or fall. You'd look over the edge of the mountain and way, way down at the bottom, you'd see a little stream down there, a thousand feet down below. And if you looked up, there'd be a thousand feet up above you still to go before you'd be to the top of the mountain, and you were just on a little road that was kind of cut into the edge of the mountain, and at one point it came to a tunnel. The tunnel was maybe 300 or 400 yards long, as I remember—a big, long tunnel. It was cut right through the mountain. We went along that tunnel, and on the other side of the tunnel we kept on going, and we came to a chalet, a beautiful ski chalet, I recall. We were like five miles from where we had been originally.

They let us out; the weapons carrier stayed there. The weapons carrier is like a slightly armored vehicle. It's got tires instead of tracks, but it does have a 50 caliber machine gun on it. I don't know who else was there, but there was somebody from a reconnaissance patrol; I don't know how they got there. But it was somebody from another outfit besides ours—a reconnaissance outfit. Our task was to be the first line of resistance in case the Germans came up. Now, we had gone through the tunnel, and somebody told me that they had set up dynamite, in the tunnel, so they were going to blow up the tunnel if the Germans made a break for it.

Well, we stayed there for about two or three days, as I remember, and I remember there were four of us, four guys from my company who were there and knew each other, and we had two blankets between the four of us, to share. We had half a can of C-rations apiece per day, I think. We had all the water we could drink, but the food was very scarce because we had left a lot of the food behind when we ran out. We froze our butts off during the night. During the day it was very comfortable, but at night it was just as miserably cold as could be, very high altitude, and we just didn't have the clothing, or equipment, blankets, or sleeping bags, or anything to keep warm. And you couldn't make fires because we didn't know where the Germans were, and we couldn't eat any hot food because we couldn't make hot food, couldn't make coffee, except during the day. We didn't have very much in the way of rifles or equipment or anything. So that was one of the coldest nights I ever recall spending, sleeping between two other guys, three of us sleeping under one blanket and on one blanket. And each having an hour in the middle and then having to shift and be on one of the ends, trying to keep warm. When we weren't doing that we had to be out, actually standing guard and watching.

Anyway after a couple of days of that, I remember an officer came and took all of us on a patrol, formed a patrol with us to go down toward the villages, toward where we had come from. We went through one or two little tiny villages. I remember, it would just be a street with houses on both sides. I remember going through these villages and being terrified, because you hear the least little thing move and you're ready to shoot at it. But you don't want to shoot at it because it might be a civilian, on the one hand, or a child. On the other hand, it could be a German with a grenade or a machine pistol.

Anyhow, I remember going through one or two of these little

villages, and then the officer said that he felt that the rest of the men should go back and that he wanted one person to go with him on a reconnaissance patrol to make contact with the Germans. He thought they might be pretty far away from the fact that we hadn't encountered any so far. I don't know why, but I volunteered to go with him. He told me to collect some grenades that I carried in my pockets. I had my carbine. I think I had a carbine; I may have had a tommy gun at that time. I don't remember which I had. I think it was a carbine I was carrying. Yes, it was a carbine. I may have also had a pistol. I had a knife, I had grenades, as I say, hanging from my pockets. He was a paratrooper who had been dropped into that area. He was an officer; I think he was a lieutenant. He was at least a lieutenant. He had been dropped into that area before the invasion and had made contact with the French underground in that area. But he was wearing an American army uniform, paratrooper's outfit, actually. I just did what he told me to do, went where he said to go. I remember we came up, and there was this barn, and we kind of sneaked through the barn. I kept thinking how absolutely like cops and robbers this is. This is exactly what I used to do when I was a kid. I couldn't get over that feeling that there was no difference, none whatsoever. I remember we went into this one house, and there was a couple of Frenchmen and he talked French to them, and they said there had not been any Germans there. Anyway we kept going and going from one little kind of village to the next—not village, from one farmhouse to the next.

I remember at one point there was a village down the road; we could see it maybe a mile away. He decided we should approach the village from the back, so we went off the road and through these fields and up over meadows and fields up behind the village so we were coming in behind the village. We were coming in the back of one of these rows of houses. I remember each of them had a kind of a backyard, extending about the same distance back to where the mountain kind of started. We were down there at that point in the back. He went up to the house and had me cover for him. I in the back, with my rifle or carbine, and he's up in the front. He went through the yard, and he was now on the back porch of this house. When I look down the street, I see coming down the street a girl. I thought to myself, what am I going to do? I better warn him since I don't want him to shoot the girl. So I slap on my rifle and he looks up at me like that and I point to the road, whereupon he gets his gun at ready and he puts his back up against the wall like he's just going to leap out and start firing. I slap on my rifle again and go like this—shaking my head from right to left meaning "no"—and he lifts his hands in the air, indicating "What do you mean?" and finally I made the sign for a girl, which was kind of waving my hands in a sort of a figure eight or hourglass to indicate that it's a girl and not a German, at which point he nodded his head. When she came within hailing distance, he called her and she came up to him, and he was able to talk to her, and it was clear that the Germans were not there. Anyhow, that was kind of interesting, because it could have been a tragedy if the signals hadn't been interpreted properly.

Anyhow up the back of the village we went, back into the meadows, and kept on going until we came across the crest of a pretty high hill, and he had binoculars and I didn't. I remember all of a sudden, we were kind of crawling over the crest of the hill and looking down the other side, and there on the other side of the hill are the Germans and there's a whole battalion of them, I guess. I don't know, there were trucks there and they had made it out of Italy and had stopped there. That was what he wanted to see, but they weren't attacking. It looked like they were just settling in and making camp. So we turned around and went back. By now it was just getting to be dark, and by the time we got back to where the other guys were it was already nightfall, and it was quite late. I guess we had been gone eight hours maybe—six to eight hours, something like that. Anyhow we were gone long enough that I was told I was considered missing in action by my outfit. They knew I had gone on patrol with this guy, but they assumed I had been missing in action.

I seem to recall that I don't remember spending any more nights there. I think they took us from there back to the chalet and we got onto trucks, and we went on, started north, and from there we went, as I remember, through Grenoble, or near Grenoble and there was another big French city, Metz. Actually Metz is a French city, but very north, near the German border. And I don't remember whether that was then or later, but from there the next place that I remember any real action was in the Vosges Mountains, which is where we moved to next.

AH: This is the beginning of our third session, I think, and where we left off, Howard, was that you had just finished describing going on patrol with an officer who was some kind of scout. You stated that when you went back they took you in trucks to Grenoble, and from there you went to another place.

HH: It may not have been Metz, but it was a large—I'm pretty sure—a large French city.

AH: The transcriber, Mae Smith, looked it up and she found that Metz is a French city, but she says that it's very north, near the German border.

HH: Well, I'm not sure.

AH: I think that gets us into the beginnings of correction, and I don't think we want to take that up now. On a subsequent cut we'll start looking at maps.

HH: Okay.

AH: We broke off where you were about to describe the action that you saw in the Vosges Mountains.

HH: All right. We were with the Nisei in the Vosges Mountains.

AH: Now, the Nisei were Japanese-American troops.

HH: Japanese-American troops.

AH: How did you happen to be with the Nisei?

HH: We were a battalion that would be attached to whoever needed us at the time, a mortar battalion. Apparently the Nisei were the ones we were attached to at that time. We had fought with all kinds, the Senegalese, Goumier. . . .

AH: By this time?

HH: Oh, yes, we fought with the Senegalese and the Goumier in that push up to Rome from Castelforte. I think I mentioned some of that earlier. So at this point we were attached to the Nisei. It was in the Vosges Mountains. The Vosges Mountains were, at this point, largely, as I remember, very large trees. It was a wooded area, and it was a lumbering-type area that we were moving through, as I recall it. I don't ever remember setting up our guns, so much as I remember being in a couple of different places in the mountains. It was very much like Colorado. I was reminded of the Colorado mountains with tall, very large trees, and I remember being shelled there. I also remember that there were troops along who had saws and were cutting the trees at one point, but I don't remember why.

It was in the Vosges Mountains that all of us got word that Roosevelt had died. I recall that. It was also in the Vosges Mountains that I had this experience in which I was—we had dug into the side of a mountain, and it was raining, and night had fallen, and I had dug a foxhole, and there were two of us sitting in this darkened foxhole. Pitch black, actually, with a shelter half coming down over the top of it. The rain was seeping in from underneath the ground, so that there was maybe an inch or two of water on the bottom of the foxhole, and we were sitting on boxes, as I recall, either ammunition boxes or our helmets or something like that. This fellow and I got into this conversation about foods, the different kinds of foods we especially missed from not being in the States. I told him that I missed artichokes, and I think he was a Southerner, and he asked me, "What's an artichoke?" I proceeded to try to explain what an artichoke was and discovered that it's virtually impossible to do so without some kind of a visual aid. Since it was pitch black and we couldn't see each other or anything else, I broke into gales of laughter at the effort of trying to explain. "You know," I'd said, "Well, it's sort of like a pinecone." And he'd said, "You're crazy, man, pinecone?" "Well, it's not exactly like a pinecone, but you peel the leaves off and you dip them in butter." He said, "You're pulling my leg. You can't possibly be telling the truth." I said, "No, I really mean it; that's how you eat the damn things!"

Anyhow, the other amusing incident there was that they brought up in the jeep a mail call, and I had received a package from home. This must have been in . . . did Roosevelt die in November?

AH: No, he died in April.

HH: In April?

AH: Yes.

HH: Then it was pretty early. Much earlier than I suspect, you know, than I feel it was. In any event, I received a package from my mother around that time and as I recall she included in it a yo-yo and my fishing cap from when I was in high school and went fishing with a gang of guys. All of us wore the same kind of fishing cap; my mother had gone out and bought us each one of those old-fashioned sleeping caps, that kind of looks like a triangle made out of cloth or a funnel made out of cloth and you just kind of put it on your head and it hangs down the side.

AH: Like a nightcap?

HH: A nightcap! Right! That's what we used to wear when we went fishing for some silly adolescent reason. Anyhow she sent me that, and she also sent me a pair of mittens, leather, fleece-lined mittens which ultimately were going to prove to be very important to me, because it was going to become pretty cold in not too long.

The curious thing is that I don't remember a great deal of what we did in that period. I know that we were shelled several times. I know that we did a lot of moving; we moved out of one place and into another. But my next recollection is either going into a big city somewhere along the border of France, and I would believe that this is a border that was near Germany. We were told about the Bulge and the counterattack, and we had to move up into the Bulge. I thought the Bulge was much later than that. But in any event I remember going north. . . . I remember one incident, in fact, when we pulled into this place and we had to carry . . . Let me think about this a little bit more. We must have done some fighting going up there, because I recall one place that we came into, and there was no snow on the ground, although it was cold. I don't recall very much resistance going into it. It was a French town, and we were the first Americans into it. It had been very heavily shelled previously and the first thing that I noticed was that there were dogs and pigs in the streets. The next thing I saw was that there were quite a few civilian bodies lying around, and to my horror, the pigs and the dogs were eating them. We chased them away, but I don't know whether anybody came in to bury these people. We didn't shoot the pigs or the dogs; we just chased them away.

I remember going into a room, one room of a house that had been shelled quite a bit, and there was a two- or three-year-old child in a crib, and it had been shot in the head. There was also a baby that couldn't have been more than a few months old, lying kind of by the edge of the floor where the floor and the wall were joined. It was dead. You could see that it had been killed simply by being flung against the wall. Its head was pushed in. Somebody called me—I was standing there, horrified, looking at these things and considering what kind of people would do this, thinking of the Germans—I remember being called to come out back into the barn. I went around there, and back in the barn was a ladder up against a rafter, and there was a man who was also dead, who was tied to the ladder hands and feet with baling wire that had been wrapped, you know, tied very, very tightly around his wrists and ankles. He, too, had been shot. I don't think he was shot in the head, though. It was just a horrible place, and I think that was the first time that I ever really felt that I hated the Germans. Up to that point my feeling was that they were kind of a distant enemy who were probably very much like myself, and most of the people I was fighting were people who probably didn't want to fight but had to, as I had to. But that was a change point in my entire war experience. Because at that point I felt that I hated the enemy, that I hated all of them, the men, the women, and the children. That anybody that could do anything like this—there was no room for compassion in my feelings at that point.

I guess it was around that time too that the Bulge started to be a serious problem and we were moving up into it. There were probably a lot of experiences that happened there that I just can't even dredge up. I do recall . . . well, for example, I remember one night when we were moving along a road—it wasn't a road, it was woods, and we had to move, the whole company had to move, jeeps and trucks and every- thing else. But we were in combat and under the view of the enemy, except it was very, very dark. It was again a very cloudy night and probably pitch black. Well, it was pitch black; it was so dark that we couldn't see but maybe four or five feet in front of us if we didn't have something white, that is, the ambient light was so dim. And I remem- ber walking with one hand on the hood of the jeep and holding a white handkerchief up and the jeep driver simply trying to follow the hand- kerchief because he couldn't see the road. He couldn't see the trees, he couldn't see anything. And I was literally guiding the jeep along. We must have gone half a mile or maybe even a mile this way. I also remember that it was in this region—we were now coming out of the Vosges Mountains, probably the northern end of them by this time.

Again, I have very little sense of what the geography of the situation was.

I remember another incident near there where again there was a captain, and I think his name was Cooper. He had been sent home to the United States on a furlough and had come back. He was not terribly old; I guess he was in his thirties, maybe mid-thirties. But of course, I was still nineteen going on twenty. I recall there was a tall kind of a bluff, again much like that bluff that I described earlier where the road had to go around a place where the Germans were shelling. I wasn't hurt. I remember also somewhere in there beginning to feel that I had had enough close calls, that I was not likely to survive the war if it continued.

I recall a house in the middle of a field, the house wasn't in the middle of the field, the house was on the edge of the field, along a road. There were no other houses around, a couple of barns, maybe. There were eight or ten of us sitting in a room when suddenly the Germans started to shell that particular house. One of the shells hit either the wall of the room that we were in or burst just outside; I don't recall exactly which it was, but I know there was a huge amount of plaster fell on the floor from the ceiling and from the walls, there was a hole where the window was, the window was blown out, and glass flew all over the place. Miraculously, nobody in the room was hit. I was very surprised by that.

I remember often the feelings that you have when you hear the shells coming in and you know that you're not protected, and there was nothing you can do except hope that this one didn't land on top of you. Or if it did that it landed right on top of you, and it would be quick.

I recall a point where we were walking along and it was necessary to go through a field and the field said that it was mined. But we had to go through it anyhow.

AH: You mean there was a sign that it was mined?

HH: Yes. They had told us that there were several kinds of mines. There was the "bouncing Betty"; if you step on it, it doesn't go off immediately. What happens is that a second or so later something flies into the air and explodes about three feet or so above the ground. That's the most dangerous kind because it will have a wide dispersion of shrapnel. Another kind was a "shoe mine," and it was a wooden box, actually, and if you stepped on it it just blew your foot off. A guy stepped on one of those shoe mines maybe not more than five or ten feet from me and I immediately, but gingerly and carefully watching where I stepped, went over and helped him. He was knocked down and his foot was hanging by the Achilles tendon. That's all. His boot and his foot in it. I remember debating in my mind whether we ought to cut his foot off or leave it there and send him back with it and deciding that we should send him back with it. And the medic came pretty quickly. Although what we did was we carried him over to the road and we didn't go in there any more, because often the Germans would put signs saying "mines" in places where there weren't any mines. And we hadn't seen any mines and we had been very gingerly about going in there. But in any event, I remember when we were back standing on the road itself, I can picture the scene, and standing there looking down at him, and he's already had some morphine so he's not feeling too bad, and thinking, I wish it was me. Because he was for sure out of the war and that was a wound that one could certainly live the rest of their life with. Whereas the Lord knew what was going to happen to me.

I remember a lot of incredible filth, places that we would sometimes have to stay in, would be stone barns that were full of dung and lice and all kinds of garbage laying around everywhere. I remember one night—this was just before the captain was wounded—I don't recall what the occasion was, but he pulled out a bottle of scotch and shared it with us privates, which was very surprising, because officers didn't fraternize very much with enlisted men. Although in combat they did more than anywhere else. But I was still a PFC [private first class]—I think I had made PFC by that time. . . . No, I guess not, I didn't make PFC until the Bulge.

The next occasion that I remember is that it is now getting very cold, and the snow has started to fall and we were moved up into Belgium somewhere, near Bastogne. What I remember about this was having to ride on the trailer of a jeep, sitting on top of the ammunition and being about as cold as one could be, and the wind starting to blow and the snow falling and then shortly being in the middle of the woods and not being able to make a fire, because the smoke would attract shelling. And having dug a foxhole in the snow and having stood guard the night before, sleeping in the snow and being as cold as possible and not having taken off my shoes for several weeks, because I had never been anywhere but outside, and becoming very, very edgy about the possibilities of surviving. The sign that I was edgy, the thing that told me I was edgy was one time when we were in the forests up north, and again this is somewhere in Belgium or the edge of Belgium, in the Bulge, and I was standing about twenty or thirty feet from my foxhole, and I heard a shell come in. Instead of hitting the ground, which is what you do when a shell comes in, I ran to my foxhole and jumped into it, and I felt like a complete ass for having done that. First of all, because I had really exposed myself to much more danger than if I had hit the ground and I said to myself, Goddammit, I must be really scared because I've never broken in that way and not done what was appropriate for the situation. And that let me know that my nerves were pretty well shattered or getting shattered.

I also remember at one point . . . I don't know what the occasion was, how I got back of the lines. I was only there for . . . , I might have gone to carry a message or something like that with somebody else, but I remember going back and giving the supply sergeant—I seem to remember that his name was Shipper, big, tall, heavyset guy who always stayed in the back lines, of course—giving him a letter, not a letter to anybody, but telling him that in case I was killed, this is what he was supposed to do with my equipment. You know, whatever I had, the stuff in my barracks bag or footlocker or whatever was stored back there, because I became convinced about that time that I was not going to survive. I've only described a couple of the shellings and close calls, but there were so many of them that I just can't remember them all. You know, some of them are starting to come back, and it takes me back in time to before the snow and I think we were fighting at that point with either the Third Division or the Thirty-sixth Division, and I remember fighting in the woods, and there was a mill—not a windmill—but some kind of a mill near there. And I remember carrying a carbine and wishing that I had an M-1 and thinking that these were good soldiers, they really knew how to fight, working with them. When I say "know how to fight" I don't really mean in hand-to-hand combat, because I never saw any of that, never saw it happen, but being a good soldier meant you could hold your fire until it was appropriate to shoot. Even when you did shoot, you didn't see what you were shooting at, but you could tell the general direction to shoot in. You'd shoot usually where you heard the shots coming from.

That was when we were either with the Third or the Thirty-sixth Division. I just don't recall which one it was at this point. But as I say, they were damn good soldiers, very seasoned. They'd had a lot of experience in Italy and Africa, and I guess in southern France too, some. But there was not too much resistance down there.

Well, you [Alice] and I have talked a little bit about how cold that winter was, and you always said that it never gets very cold in Europe, but I'll swear that it was down near zero on many occasions. Your breath would come out like a puff of steam, and there was wind and there was snow on the ground and many, many cloudy days. In fact there were so many cloudy days that I recall that was one of the problems that they had, that you couldn't get air cover for the things we were doing.

Now, we were taken up near Bastogne and assigned to Patton's outfit. Patton was driving in to relieve McAuliffe, who was the general that sent the message "Nuts!" when asked to surrender. That was his one-word message to the Germans. We went with the troops that were going into Bastogne and I recall that the lines were terribly, terribly fluid. It was not clear, when you saw another set of American vehicles and people dressed in American uniforms, it wasn't necessarily true that they were Americans, because the Germans had overrun so much and had captured so much that it was always possible that they were Germans in American uniforms with American equipment. So you had to be very careful, and passwords were used all the time. That was the place where one evening I was separated from my outfit and I was trying to get over to them and I got stopped by a GI with a rifle loaded and pointed at my guts. He asked me for the password and I'll be damned if I could remember it. I told him, "Look, don't do anything rash, because I'm an American. I was born in Brooklyn." Actually I was born in Manhattan. He says, "Yeah? Well then who did the Dodgers play in nineteen whatever?" And I said, "Now, wait a minute I don't know a damn thing about baseball. I've never been interested in baseball, but take a look at my dog tags. The name is Hoffman. I can tell you the type of blood I have; I can tell you my serial number, and so forth and so on." Anyway he finally was convinced that I was an American and let me through and didn't shoot. But it's a very uncomfortable feeling when somebody's got a loaded rifle pointed at you and all they have to do is squeeze that trigger.

It was also in that area, I remember, being on a road, this was a road, I'm pretty sure it was *the* road that went into Bastogne. We might have been twenty miles away from there at that point, and it was one of the first clear days and I look up and I see these P-47s, American planes, coming in from off in the distance, and I'm thinking, "Boy, they're going to hammer some bastards pretty hard with that," when all of a sudden the son of a bitches come in and they start strafing us, and I'm diving for foxholes and I even—I was going to say "shot at them" but I didn't. That was just one of the several occasions that we were strafed by our own planes in this area. And the problem—it wasn't really the pilots' fault—the lines were so fluid there that they would have a strike mission and they would see trucks and they would say, "Well, those trucks are over the line where the Americans are supposed to be, they must be Germans in American uniforms," so they would attack us. There wasn't a goddamn thing we could do about it. Some of the guys shot back at them; I never did. But there was nothing you could do. I was mad as hell at them, though, I can tell you that. And I was mad as hell at the whole system that would allow something like that to happen. I was also lucky that they were such lousy shots.

Anyhow, there was another experience that I had there. It was very cold. I remember spending the night inside of a house. In fact, I remember there was heat in the house, and not only that, I slept in a bed, a big feather bed. It was fantastic. We were not at the front of the wedge that came into Bastogne. We were back maybe seven or eight miles from it. So we were really in the rear at this point, although we were on combat status. Our assignment was to keep that road into Bastogne open. We had our machine gun out there on the edge of the road or overlooking the road. There was a house and then a very large field. It had been a farmhouse, and this was part of the farm. Then, maybe 200 or a 100 yards of woods and then the road, and then more woods and then there was a field on the other side. Now, I believe the Germans were on the other side, but they were supposed to be pretty far away on the other side. We were down there on the edge of the woods on our side. I was about fifty yards from the trees with another guy, and there were two guys up there, right at the edge of the woods, with a machine gun, and we were kind of off to the side with our rifles. We were going to try to dig a couple of foxholes over there because we figured we'd be able to have some cross fire with the machine guns if anything happened. All of a sudden I hear this sound that sounds like a lion roaring, from the other side of the road. I said, "Jesus Christ, what's that?" The other guy said, "I don't know." It literally sounded like lions roaring, just huge loud noise. And the next thing I know, it gets louder very rapidly and all of a sudden there's explosions all around us and I get literally lifted off of the ground. One of these shells lands about—I don't think it was more than ten feet from me and not more than six feet from this other guy I was with. It lifts us both off the ground, the concussion, and it felt like it threw us, I don't know, a foot or so forward. We were lying down at the time, both facing toward that road and it went over us and landed behind us. And shells also landed everywhere else, half a dozen of them landed everywhere else. These shells were actually rockets. The Germans called them Nebelwerfers. They were fired from some kind of a mobile unit that's on the back of a truck. It has a ring of six of them in a circle, and it fires them all off, you know, ZZZZZZFRRRRF, like that, and that roaring noise is, I think, part of the built-in effect to produce fear. The reason we weren't hurt by them was because most of the structure is fuel for the rocket. Each one is about six inches in diameter and about five feet long, I would imagine—four or five feet long, and the head of it is high explosive, but the casing for the head of it, as I recall, was pretty thin metal, so there wasn't a lot of shrapnel from it, and whatever shrapnel there was from it seemed to have gone mostly straight up. Because behind us there was a smoking hole about four feet across, four or five feet across and maybe six inches deep or less. As I said, it lifted us and shoved us forward. I thought for sure I had been hit. I was afraid to look at my feet, and so was the other guy. We both thought we had probably been hit and weren't feeling anything because we were in shock, which is typically what happens. I said to him, "I'll look at your feet if you'll look at mine," and he said, "Okay." So we both sneaked over our shoulders and took a peek, lying there in the snow. I said, "Yours are okay." He said, "So are yours." I said, "Christ, I need a cigarette." So I pulled out a cigarette and gave him one, and I took one, and then I remember trying to light it. My hands were shaking so bad that I couldn't light it and his hands were shaking so bad that he had to finally take my hands, and between the two of us we were able to get his cigarette lit and then light mine. But it was really a very, very close call. What we did was we went over to where the machine gun was. We were under the trees there. We went over there to see how those guys were, and they were okay. The shells hadn't landed as close to them as they had to us. I remember thinking to myself, "They're going to fire off another one of those, I wish to Christ they'd call us back. We can't do anything here if they're really going to make an attack."

Well, while I'm sitting there wishing they'd call us back, we hear those lions roar again. And all of just . . . there were about four of us, I guess, maybe five, we just hit the snow and just lay there thinking, "Oh, Christ, what's going to happen?" Well, I did more than that. That was the only time I can ever remember in the whole time I was in combat that I prayed. Because I was dead certain that I was going to be killed by the next round of these, because they obviously had us zeroed in. You had time to think while those things were coming, and I remember thinking how sad my mother was going to be when she heard about my death and thinking, you know, sort of, "If you let me through this"—I was kind of praying to the big man in the sky—"If You let me through this, I'm going to make something of myself." And then the shells hit and they hit all around us and one of them hit the tree above us. When the explosions were over I looked around and I hadn't been hit at all, nor had anybody else. But you could see where the kind of whatever shrapnel there was had peppered the snow all around the tree, and branches had fallen down and things like that.

But in any event, we stayed there. We still couldn't leave. But within about five minutes, somebody came running up and said that they had called us back, had called us to come back to the house, because they could see that we were being shelled there. I remember grabbing part of the machine gun, the barrel or whatever part it was, you know each of us grabbing a piece of it and running like hell back to that house. Because at least back there you'd have a little bit of protection and they hadn't zeroed in on the house yet, obviously. And I don't remember if we got any more shelling there or not. But that was one of the really significant events for me.

Around that time I lost Jerry Farnsworth. I wasn't with him when it happened. What was happening was that our outfit, there were quite a few guys in my platoon and company and battalion that had been wounded, though none that I can recall when I was actually with them. But somebody would go out to fire a gun, and a shell would land nearby and would catch somebody. I was just always lucky, [the shells] just never, never hit right. . . . Nobody right next to me ever got hit that I can remember, other than the event on the boat, and the guy who stepped on the mine. I can't recall anybody getting wounded directly. Jerry Farnsworth was somewhere else when this happened. I mean he was maybe half a mile away or so. He was not where my guns were. Around this time we started to get bad ammunition from the United States. Bad ammunition is ammunition that explodes prematurely.

AH: Is that what killed Jerry Farnsworth?

HH: Yes. He had a barrel burst. When you fire a 4.2 mortar you drop the shell—the shell is about as big as a 150 millimeter howitzer shell—it's 4.2 inches in diameter and about a foot and a half long, and it looks like a bullet with a powder charge on the bottom, and what you do is you drop it into the barrel, and it slides down the barrel and hits a firing pin on the bottom of the barrel, and that explodes a shotgun shell. I think I described this once before. That fires off a powder charge, strikes a brass or steel plate that then presses a copper plate out that catches in the rifling, and then it twists, comes spinning out of the barrel. After you've pulled the firing pin, there's a centrifugal device that the shell has to spin two and a half times before that device pops out. Then the firing pin on the shell itself pops forward so that whatever it hits will then cause the shell to explode. Now, if something goes wrong there, for example, if the safety device that requires two and a half turns isn't properly constructed, the shell could explode just after it leaves the muzzle of the mortar, or it could explode inside the barrel. That's what happened to Jerry Farnsworth.

You know, memories come back. I remember one time firing shells so fast out of the mortar, and I had a raincoat on, and it was raining. This must have been in the Vosges Mountains period, and I remember that the baseplate, which is about three by three feet and weighs 250 pounds and takes two men to carry it, I remember, you know, you have the baseplate, you have a bipod that holds the barrel up, and then the barrel and the sight—those were the four parts of the mortar itself. And every time you fire the mortar, it kicks the baseplate down toward the ground. And this was kind of in soggy ground, and I remember firing it and having to keep firing it and firing it over and over again, and you'd have a line of guys that would hand you a shell. I was doing the firing at this point, and I remember I had a raincoat on, and I'd drop the shell into the barrel and then put my head down as close to the base of the barrel as I could. We always did this to get our head out of the cone of concussion. I remember firing shell after shell, and then at one point my raincoat went over the end of the barrel after the shell was dropped, and the shell came out and went right through my raincoat, kind of gave it a little tug. We couldn't even stop then, we'd have to just keep readjusting the mortar as best we could. I remember that eventually the baseplate dug itself so deep into the ground that I had to lie down on the ground to drop the shell in, because there was only about two feet of the barrel sticking up above the ground.

What happened in the Bulge was that our outfit got very, very decimated. I remember that we should have had . . . now these numbers are not exactly correct, but the numbers that come to me is that we should have had had something like twenty-four men or so in the platoon and that we were down to eight, including the officers in this period. And the reason we were down to eight was not so much from losses from the enemy but from barrel bursts, from bad ammunition. I remember one night—it must have been not too far from Christmastime—it was very cold but I don't recall that there was snow. Every time there would be a barrel burst—there were two mortar battalions that I knew about there, the Third Battalion and another one, but I don't remember what number it was. But anytime either one of them would get a barrel burst, a piece of bad ammunition, that automatically meant that the guy who dropped the shell in was killed. And probably a couple of other people were either killed or seriously injured.

We were so decimated by this, from this bad ammunition, that as I say we were down to eight people in our outfit. Every time we'd get a barrel burst, when the fighting was over, we'd check the number of the ammunition lot that the shell came from and we had a list of bad lots.

Now, I don't know what the occasion was, but I had to go to the ammunition depot with somebody else and pick up the ammunition to bring it back to where we were. We went in a truck. There was nothing but bad lots there, so we had to take ammunition that we knew from the list, and I had actually gone through checking it myself, that we knew had shells in it that had burst.

When we got back to the company it was decided that rather than fire these, since we knew that they were bad lots, we would use a lanyard. Now, there is a method of firing the mortar with a lanyard. What you do is you have a yoke, kind of a Y-shaped piece that fits over the shell, and the base of the shell goes into the barrel, and then this Y-piece keeps it from dropping. Then you have about a hundred feet of rope, and you go and dig yourself a foxhole a hundred feet away. You put the shell in the mortar, and you get in the foxhole, and you pull the lanyard and it drops the shell in, and if the shell explodes you have some protection. I mean, these are big shells, and they can do a hell of a lot of damage; they're high-explosive shells. It's the only way you can protect yourself against it.

There were two guns, I think, that we had going there, and we had maybe fifty shells, all of which we knew were bad, and we had our lanyards and we were all set to fire them with the lanyard.

AH: All of which you knew were from bad lots.

HH: Were from bad lots. And we got an order that there was a counterattack coming in, and they needed heavy cover. Well, I was a forward observer part of the time, but at this point I was firing the mortar. I remember dropping the shells—we couldn't use the lanyards because we had to fire them so fast. I remember dropping the shells in, and what we did to minimize the chances of the number of people that would be killed if anything went bad, we put all the shells next to the mortar, and that meant if the mortar shell went off all those shells would go off and everybody else just went away, as far as they could get. They went behind the building or barn or whatever it was that was near there.

I remember spending about a half hour firing off fifteen or twenty shells all by myself. And every single time I'd drop a shell down the barrel and listen to it slide down, I'd say, "Is this the last sound I'll ever hear?" That was a very, very nerve-racking experience. Well, I'm shaking now as I talk about it. It was so . . . it was very much like playing Russian roulette.

Then when I heard, later after the war, about the Garsson Munitions scandal, I'm not certain, but I'm willing to bet that Garsson Munitions must have been the people that were making these 4.2 shells, because, as I say, we were really decimated by these things. We lost more people from that than from combat. Our outfit was replaced—I heard some statistics at the end of the war—that our outfit was replaced three times. That doesn't mean that everybody, you know . . . Most of it was for wounded, I would imagine, but we had a lot of casualties from that. I can pretty distinctly recall hearing about at least five or six barrel bursts.

This reminds me of the counterattack that I was describing earlier—the one with the Nebelwerfers. I remember reading about it in the *Stars and Stripes*, so I assume it was in the newspapers at home later on. It was reported that the road into Bastogne had been opened and then cut for a few hours. The place where it was cut was where I was. But the Germans didn't come across there where we were. We didn't see them, although we were back now, you know, a thousand yards or so in the farmhouse, and they may very well have occupied the road itself. Because there was that couple hundred yards of woods there, so we wouldn't have seen them if they were on the road.

AH: After Bastogne?

HH: After Bastogne, I remember being pulled off the lines and getting a week's, or maybe even a little bit longer, rest in a small Belgian town somewhere. It might have been a French town. I don't know which. I think it was French. I remember we were sleeping in a gymnasium and I was up in the bleachers of the thing. I was sleeping on the floor up there or on the benches up there, on the bleachers of this . . . not bleachers, you know, like the balcony. Down below was a large kind of a hall. The thing I remember about it is that that was the first time that I came off the line from the invasion of southern France, and it was 154 days after the invasion of southern France that we came off the line, so I had 154 days of straight combat there, which is a very long time for anybody to be in combat without a break. It wasn't fighting all the time, but there was never a break when you weren't in some kind of danger, whether real or imagined.

Now, we went from there north up near Aachen. Aachen is either in Holland or on the edge of Holland near the Ruhr River (on some maps spelled "Roer."), and we were going to cross the river. The town where we crossed was right on the river. I remember the thing that was scary about this area was that in Aachen all of the houses had holes all the way through them. I think there had been very heavy fighting there and they had literally blasted their way from room to room through each house. I wasn't involved in that fighting.

AH: You mean before you crossed the Ruhr River there was some fighting?

HH: Yes, there had been fighting there, but it was by the British, I think. Maybe the Americans, I don't know. I didn't fight there with them. I don't remember doing any fighting with a rifle there, is what I'm saying. Or firing mortars there. The thing I remember was being in a basement with a vaulted ceiling, vaulted bricks. The room was maybe ten feet across and fifteen feet long, and it was pretty solid and pretty far underground. I also remember having something to do with telephone lines and communications at that point, but I don't recall exactly what it was. I remember being shelled there a number of times and feeling very safe in that vaulted basement, except for one time, and that one time that I didn't feel safe was when the buzz bombs—occasionally you could hear these buzz bombs coming over that were on their way to England, but one time I remember we heard one coming and all of a sudden it stopped buzzing. I was very, very concerned. I don't think it landed very close to us, but the impact was very large and there was a lot of mortar dust fell from it. But we really were underground and no windows or anything like that, but you could still hear the buzz bombs even down there.

I also remember hearing one of my buddies tell me about having been up at the observation post, which was on the river, and having seen a new British artillery shell. The typical artillery shell like for a 105 travels at a . . . I don't remember what the muzzle velocity is, but it's fairly slow compared to, say, a rifle bullet. But this particular shell was made for antitank purposes, and it consisted of something like a pencil of some kind of special hardened steel in a plastic casing that would be where the shell was. This had some incredible muzzle velocity like that of a rifle, 30,000 feet a second or something of that sort. And he told me that they fired it at a haystack on the other side of the river and the haystack just exploded. You know, even though it was just one dart kind of going through it.

We weren't in that town for too long.

AH: This was Aachen?

HH: No. It was on the edge of the Ruhr River, near Aachen. It couldn't have been too far from Aachen. The next thing I knew we had crossed the river. I think we crossed the river and I think they had some kind of a ferry to take us across, but it's possible that we crossed it on a pontoon bridge. I don't remember exactly. I remember we crossed the Rhine River on some kind of a bridge, I recall, but I'm not even sure of that either. Anyway, that's the beginning; that's where we jumped off into Germany. And I guess on the next tape I'll try to recall what happened in Germany.

AH: This is the next installment, being done on the evening of March 9.

HH: 1979.

AH: We had left off where Howard was just crossing into Germany.

HH: The German campaign, like all of the others, was for me a series of vignettes rather than a sequence of unified events.

AH: In your memory, that is?

HH: That's right. And I'm not sure how much of it I can actually recover with any degree of accuracy. I know that I . . . The first landmark for me was an airfield that we took. That was near Hannover. Now, I know that we went through some industrialized cities on the Ruhr, but I can't remember very much about them. I can't even recall them with any degree of precision. The second landmark was Gardelegen, which was, as I remember, north of Hannover and further to the west perhaps. The third landmark would be Münster and what happened there. And the fourth landmark would be the Elbe River and what happened there. So we'll go back now to the first of those landmarks.

AH: Hannover?

HH: No, it's the airfield before Hannover. I have only the dimmest of recollections of either passing very nearby or possibly being at the edge of an airfield. But I don't remember seeing any airplanes. And I don't even remember any hangars. I just have this very strong impression that we were by an airfield that had been abandoned by the Germans because of our advance.

Now, in that region there was an incident that did happen that was of considerable relevance, I think. Somewhere in the region we were . . . Well, I recall two instances. The first of these was that at one point we were advancing with our rifles at the ready—through some woods very close to a road, and we came upon a field, and I looked up and I see a small reconnaissance Piper Cub painted brown, of the sort that we used. He came down to within fifty feet of the ground and circled. It was like a field with woods all around the edges of it, and he made about two circles around the edge of the woods, and then he threw out a monkey wrench with a streamer attached to it and a note tied to the monkey wrench. I remember getting it and reading it and taking it to the lieutenant, who was some distance from me. It had a message indicating that there were Germans in the woods either to the front of us or to the left of us, somewhere fairly close by, and warning us that he had spotted Germans very close to us. But I don't remember ever encountering them and I don't remember what we did at that point. But that is one recollection from that particular time.

Now some of the incidents are starting to come back. Another one . . . We had just moved into and taken . . . Gee, as I think about it even another one is coming back. One of them is the time we were strafed, the second one is the time that I captured my two prisoners, and the third one was the time that I was standing guard and we were being infiltrated and I saved our company from an attack of a rabbit!

AH: Of a rabbit? [laughs]

HH: Yes, of a rabbit! These are stories of which I am the hero. The first of these incidents, we moved into a little town—this is how I captured my two Germans—we had just moved into this little town. We had driven.

AH: Excuse me, you said the first of them was when you were strafed.

HH: No, I was strafed after I captured the two Germans.

AH: Okay, all right.

HH: Because I remember it was immediately after that that this happened. The first one was how I captured my two Germans, and this is how it all happened. We had moved into this very small town, and the incident that I remember was going down into the basement of this one house where we were settled in, and it was clear that the Germans had been there very, very recently, because you could smell the acety-

Clockwise, beginning top left: (1) "A skinny kid in a toy soldier's uniform" at Indiantown Gap. (2) This snapshot, labeled "Mechanicsburg 43," may actually have been taken elsewhere. (3) Howard on the porch of his home in Harrisburg, Pennsylvania. (4) At Sharon, Pennsylvania, site of a replacement depot of which Howard has little recollection.

Returning in the duck from towing a target to sea. Howard is at far right.
Below, Goumier soldier, near Cassino, Italy. *Photographs by Ralph Worley.*

Setting up a mortar near Münster, Germany. *Photograph by Ralph Worley.*

At Gardelegen, Germany, Nazis herded hundreds of prisoners into a barn and burned them to death to prevent their liberation by Allied forces. Any prisoners who managed to claw their way out of the burning barn were systematically shot by the Nazis. "There were bodies that were just burned terribly. Some of them had on striped clothes, as I recall." *Photographs by Ralph Worley.*

lene from their lamps. The Germans had acetylene lamps, and we never did, and that has a very distinctive smell. This was just a few houses, kind of in a little square. We weren't there more than fifteen or twenty minutes when I. . . . It wasn't dark yet, but it was getting to be evening, and there were only just a few of us now, because you remember our outfit had not had any replacements that I could remember, or if we had, they were very few and we had been pretty decimated during the Bulge. I had to go out to the jeep to get something. I went upstairs and went outside. There was nobody else out there; everybody else was inside, and the jeeps were all around the corner. I remember that there was a body, a body of a German, very close near the road there that had been apparently run over by a tank. He was dead as hell. You know, flattened. There had been fighting there, but I hadn't been involved in that fighting. But I knew that the Germans had been there very recently. I turned the corner and as I turned the corner I physically—what I mean is that I bumped physically—into two Germans that were coming back from a patrol. One of them had, as I remember, a rifle, and it was slung over his shoulder on his back, you know, with the barrel pointing upwards. And the other one had a machine pistol, and that was slung over his back, too. Because they didn't know there were any Americans in there. And I had on my hip a .45 which I always carried, but I never carried a shell in the barrel because I felt that was too dangerous. There were shells in it, but to use it you had to cock it and put a shell into the chamber. But it was just too dangerous, I thought, to carry a shell in the chamber.

We physically bumped into each other and all three of us jumped back and threw our hands into the air. And I quickly saw that their guns were behind them, and I quickly grabbed the .45 out of my holster and pointed it at them. Of course, I couldn't have done anything because I didn't have a shell in the chamber, but in any event, they didn't put their hands down; they just gave up very meekly and with no argument at all. I took their guns from them and directed them—you know, said, "Hand hee ho," but they already had their hands up, and I took them in, and somebody else stood guard over them until the . . . I don't know how they were disposed of eventually. I think they were taken back to some MPs that were further, you know, in the back. Because there weren't MPs up close where we were. Anyway, that's how I captured my two Germans.

The next incident was, as I remember, I was in a truck and I was sitting in the cab of the truck, and we were driving along a road, our whole convoy, when I looked straight in front of me, and I see a plane coming down to make a strafing run, and it's a German plane, and it's coming down very, very low, just exactly like what you always see in the movies. The convoy immediately stopped. As I recall it was coming from our right, and it was up above it, and I saw it after it had passed into our front vision. It was going in the same direction we were. But I could see it was going way down the road and then making a turn to come back. Everybody stopped. The whole convoy stopped and everybody piled out of the trucks and some of us got on the side of the road and shot at it with our guns. I had, at that time, that tommy gun that there's a picture of me with. I only shot at it once. It made two runs, and between the first and the second run a lot of the guys ran into a house that was right by the side of the road. I was planning to run to the house, but for some reason I didn't, and the plane made a second run and this time I just maybe took one shot at it when it was pretty far in front of me and then I could see the bullets coming down, you know, tat-tat-tat, and I just hit the ground. I saw a puff of smoke six inches from my foot. I actually saw it hit there, but I wasn't hit, wasn't hurt at all. It made that run and then disappeared, and I went on into the house and the guys in there had been watching through the window, and they said, "Jesus Christ, I thought you were hit. I saw those shells coming down right next to you and I thought I saw one hit you." That's how close it was, but I hadn't been hit. But I remember that very clearly, I remember lying there and seeing that puff of explosion right by where my foot was. It was a bullet, and it wasn't an explosive shell that had hit there. But it was very close.

The incident when I saved my company from an attack by a rabbit was shortly after that. We had again taken a small place, and this was a farmhouse, and the thing that I remember about it was that there was a field and then a little ridge that you went down, and the field was like six feet higher than the house, if you can picture it. The road was in a kind of a cut so that the house was up against this . . . , and it had a lawn, it was up against this cut. We had parked our jeeps there along the edge. Now, this was at night. I went out to stand guard duty, and I'm standing out there and I hear something in the jeep, a sound of something. And I know there are Germans nearby, because, you know, they had been there recently and we were right at the front. I assumed that there's something in that jeep, because every now and then I hear this [taps] you know some kinds of sounds, life-type sounds coming from the jeep. I didn't know exactly what to do about it. There was another guy on guard duty and I said, "Go back and get the rest. There's somebody in that goddamned jeep over there." It was fifty feet away. What I had envisioned was that the Germans had infiltrated through the fields and had just come down the embankment and were either sitting in the jeep and I didn't know whether they had guns or what the hell was going on. I was very, very quiet because I didn't want to draw any fire on myself. So he went and got a bunch of the guys and they came crawling out of the house, because it was night, pitch black. I don't remember there being an officer around, for some reason, but anyway I was the one who was on guard duty, and so what I did was, when everybody was out there, I said, "You be back-up and I'll call for a password. If I don't get it, I'll fire." At this point I remember I had a carbine. I remember what the password was. The password was "ness" and the countersign was "dress." So I said, "Ness." Nothing happened. Then I heard that sound again. I said, "Ness." This time out loud and as I said it I rolled over so that if they fired back to where the voice was they wouldn't hit me. Nothing. I said, "Ness." No response. And this time I fired two shots or three shots and rolled over. Whereupon some guy runs out of the house who was in a different room of the house. He says, "What the hell's going on out here?" By this time I realized there couldn't be anybody in there or if there was I must have hit him. But I didn't hear anything and then I heard the sounds again. And that was really puzzling to me because I couldn't understand how the hell that could be, you know. I said, "There's somebody in that jeep." He says, "Oh, shit. I've got a rabbit in there in a box!" [laughter] And that's what it was. We were all laughing about it. We really thought it was funny. But you just never know. I mean you're in combat, you don't know what the hell is going to be there. Incidentally I had not hit the rabbit. I didn't even hit the jeep! So anyhow that was the incident of how I protected us from a rabbit.

I recall going past Hannover. I don't remember fighting in Hannover. I remember looking out from a hilltop one night and seeing a burning building maybe a mile away. We didn't actually go there; we went past where it was and then I heard about what it was and went back and saw it. What I saw when I went back there was that the Germans had taken 1,054 or 64—the exact number escapes me, but it was more than 1,000—civilians, and these were people who were forced laborers and were being marched from, I believe, Berlin to Hannover, and when they saw that Hannover had fallen, rather than let them go, they herded them into this large, like a factory, building, but actually it was more like a barn, and they had spread straw on the floor and perhaps gasoline too, and they set it on fire. They had buried about 800 of the bodies but there were about 300 or 400 or 200 bodies still left in there of these burned, charred remains. They had dug big trenches and buried the bodies in the trenches.

AH: Outside the building?

HH: Just outside the building, yes. There were people who had clawed their way under the door, and you could see a person with his arm and his head out under a door and a bullet hole in his head. The Germans had systematically shot anybody that escaped. Even so, I heard there that there were one or two people who had actually escaped. After all some of this was at night, if not all of it, and they apparently had gotten into the woods and had made it out of there.

What I understand happened was that the soldiers who were there, the Americans—not people from my outfit, but there were other troops near there, infantry, I think—went into the town and rounded up every man, woman, and child, you know, above the age of fourteen or thirteen or so and brought them up there and made them dig individual graves and bury each of the corpses from the trench and from the barn in an individual grave. That was the only kind of systematic atrocity that I ever saw, but it only reinforced my feeling about the nature of the Germans. I heard that they weren't even SS men that did that, that they were people from the airfield, some nearby airfield.

The next serious incident that I remember occurred . . . going into Münster. I was fighting with, I believe it was the 101st Airborne. It's either the 101st or the Seventeenth. I don't think it was the Seventeenth. I think it was the 101st Airborne, and I think this may have been their first combat experience. These are paratroopers. By now I think we must have crossed the Rhine. But the point is that there were two rows of us and I was like the third or second guy from the very head of the column. There was a tank that was right along with us, and these paratroopers were walking along and acting like it was a big game. This was a pretty much beat-up city that we were going through, with lots of apartment houses and destroyed, bombed-out areas, but there were pockets of places that had hardly been touched. There was a church nearby with a big tower that didn't seem to have been touched. There was a kind of a center square of the city, and the far wall of it was a whole row of stores. And they didn't seem to have been too beat up. We went for a number of blocks, I remember, fairly slowly. At one point the guys in the tank who were Coldstream Guards would just sit out there with their berets and no helmets, and at one point they stopped and had some tea. We stopped too at the time they did. The paratroopers were making a game of it. They would hold a gun, their rifle, with one hand up at arm's length and without even looking where they were shooting just be kind of shooting the gun to be making noise and shooting up, not in the air, but up toward the buildings. Nothing systematic about it. I was horrified by this. And the reason I was horrified was because I knew that if there were any snipers around and we got shot at, we wouldn't know where the firing was coming from, these guys were making so much noise.

We were sure enough, after we were moving on, and I think this was after the tea, I remember just kind of passing a lot of rubble and stepping over boards and things like that and having this radio on my—I'm pretty sure I had my radio on my back—when one of the guys very close to me was shot. I don't remember if he was hit in the chest or the back or the arm or somewhere. I don't believe he was killed, but he was knocked down, and lots of blood. We had no idea of where the shot came from. And I knew that if these had been more seasoned soldiers they wouldn't have done that. They wouldn't have allowed that to happen. Now I knew there were snipers around, but we had to be in the open, and we had to keep on going.

And the other incident that happened there was when that shot was fired most of the tankers went into the tank, but one guy with a beret stood up there and didn't even put on a helmet anyhow, just stood with his head and shoulders out of the tank, sort of standing out there directing the tank, and the tank was at this point firing straight ahead of it. No, it wasn't, it was firing up at the tower to the right. That's what was happening. It was firing up to the tower to the right when all of a sudden out of the doorway of one of those stores about two hundred yards in front of us comes lobbing one of these Panzerfausts. It's a thing about as big as a football, and it's fired by propping a rocket kind of a device against the ground, and it shoots the head of it off, and it goes lobbing through the air. It's an antitank weapon, but it's usually used by propping it up against the side of the tank, but it can be fired this way. It comes lobbing through the air, and it landed maybe twenty yards in front of the tank and to the right of me. I was on the other side of the tank from where it landed. Well, you know, that explosion happened, and within like five seconds that tank had brought its gun down and fired three or four shots into the store where that thing had come from. Those guys had seen it coming, and while it was really in the air they were already bringing the gun down. They were really good! I don't remember exactly how that ended. I remember that we moved from there to . . .

AH: Well, do you think they destroyed the gunners in the store?

HH: Yes, I'm pretty sure of that. But I don't remember what I did after that. Whether I went forward or backward or where I went. But that wasn't so atypical. I mean my memories of these thing are really rather truncated, it seems.

AH: That was coming into Münster?

HH: Yes. Now, the next thing I recall was being in some barracks on the edge of Münster. Münster had fallen; we had taken it, and we weren't under attack. We weren't at the rear, but we weren't at the very front lines. I don't remember. . . . That's curious now. Wait a minute. We weren't in the barracks. We set the guns up by some farmhouses, and then I was sent with a brand new fresh lieutenant—it was his first combat, a replacement that we got for a lieutenant we had lost—I was sent with him to go with these paratroopers because a bunch of

German kids, fourteen through sixteen or so, were manning some antiaircraft guns led by an SS trooper out on the edge of town somewhere, and we were supposed to go and clean them out. As I say, these were troops that had no experience, and I'd already experienced how they fought in town and I knew they didn't know what the hell they were doing. When I joined them we were in the edge of a woods and the woods butted onto a field, and on the other side of the field—the field was maybe 200 yards wide, twice as long as a football field, I think—and then down about 100 yards to our right were three or four antiaircraft guns. And the antiaircraft guns were shooting into the woods to their left, so that they were shooting very, very far to our right, maybe a 1,000 yards or so further to our right. Now we were under cover; we were in the woods. So they should not properly be able to see us. Directly in front of us, 200 yards on the other side of the woods, is a tank, a German tank, and it, too, is shooting into the woods at the place where those antiaircraft guns are shooting, way over to our right.

The woods where we're at is about 100 yards wide, and there's a road, a road, woods, then the field, a fairly typical kind of pattern. There, in the front of the woods, and it wasn't very thick by the way, there wasn't much underbrush there, but there was some bushes, a few bushes along the edge, so that they probably could not see us. There was a paratrooper colonel, and he's looking over at the tank, and he says to his captain or somebody there—there were several officers there—he says, "This is what we're going to do. We're going to knock the tank out and then we're going to make a frontal attack directly through the field." And I say to myself, "He's crazy. You can't get across that field. First of all, you can't knock the tank out. How's he going to knock the tank out? Secondly, if he does knock the tank out, what's he going to use, a bazooka? You know, a bazooka can just barely fire that far. And it will have no accuracy. And if he misses, they'll be right on top of us."

So I said to my lieutenant, "Tell him that we'll put mortar fire in on top of them. We'll bring in mortars on there, and we'll put in phosphorous and burn it up." He says, "No, he knows what he's doing." I said, "He doesn't know what he's doing. He's going to knock that tank out, he thinks. He can't do that." He (the lieutenant) says, "He's a colonel; I can't tell him." I said, "Goddamnit, you've got to tell him. They're going to kill us." He says, "No." And he wouldn't say a word to the guy. I couldn't, as an enlisted man, say anything that would oppose what his plan was. And they brought up what they called a recoilless rifle. Now, this was a new invention that I had never seen, and it fires something like a shell. The shell had a lot of holes in it, I remember, and I'd never seen one of these before. They put it in there and lined it up, unlike a bazooka, which you just line up with a plain, ordinary sheet-metal sight. This thing had cross hairs, a telescope, everything. And they lined it up, and I thought, "Jesus, I don't know what this weapon is, but it better be damn good, because we've had it." And he fires it, and I'm standing right beside the guy, and he fires it, and son of a bitch if he doesn't hit the tank, and out of the tank jump three or four Germans and run into the woods over there. He knocked it out with one shot.

The next thing I knew, the lieutenant says, "All right. Now we're going to prepare for the attack." And I'm thinking, this is crazy. We can't possibly be going to make an attack. In the meantime the 88s are over there to the right of us, and they haven't realized that the tank has been knocked out, because it was a couple hundred yards away from them. In the meantime, this colonel is kind of walking up in front, getting everybody up there, getting ready to make this attack across this wheat field. The field is about two feet high in wheat, as I remember. But I'm not sure, it may have been lower. Somebody spotted him, and all four of those 88s come around like this [gesturing] and come pointing at us, and then all of a sudden, boom! boom! boom! boom! boom! And those 88s are shooting directly at us from, as I say, it's what? 200, 300, 400 yards away. Well, Jesus Christ, it was like you were in the middle of a lightning bolt. Trees started falling down; there were just these tremendous explosions. The colonel was the first one out of there. He said, "Pull back to the road." And he was the first son of a bitch out of that place. That's the only time in the whole career that I've been in the army when I saw guys leave their rifles. Anything that wasn't nailed down they dropped and ran. I've never seen troops do that before, but these guys did.

I'm running through the woods with a radio on my back, wishing I didn't have it. I had a pistol on my side, so I didn't have anything to drop, really. But I remember I was running, and I remember trees just crashing all around. These were big, tall trees. And the only son-of-a-bitch thing that saved us was that they were using armor-piercing shells, so that they were solid shells and that's why it was knocking the trees down so much. They weren't exploding, it was just that they were just going through the woods.

We got back to the road, and I remember that what we did was we waited until nightfall before the attack was made on the actual encampment. The lieutenant took me, and we went back to where our outfit was dug in. We didn't stay with them there. And they, I remember, captured some of the kids, and I remember seeing a couple of these kids that they had captured, and they were just kids, you know, sixteen, fifteen, fourteen years old. But that was a very hairy experience, very harrowing.

The last incident that I can remember from combat occurred at the Elbe River. By now we all know that the war is almost over. We moved, my outfit, just the platoon of us, maybe twenty guys by now, because we had some replacements, including that dumb lieutenant that I told you about. We moved into a small, tiny town, Again, when I say "a town," that's really not describing it right, because there were no stores or any services or anything like that. It was really a cluster of houses, maybe six or seven houses in the middle of some fields, and then there would be woods, and beyond the woods was the Elbe River. I recall talking to some of the guys, and what we were discussing was mail. One guy showed me a picture of his wife and his wife had sent him a picture of a baby, but it wasn't her own, and she had said, "I can't wait for you to get home and when you get home, we'll have a baby just like this one." There were many of the guys there—not many but several— that had been in combat since North Africa. They'd had maybe almost a year more of combat than I had, although I was one of the old-timers by now, too.

We set up a machine gun at the corner of the house covering that field, and we set the mortars in the yard, surrounded by these houses. I also remember something about talking about photography or planning to do some photography. I had liberated a camera from somewhere. I'd found it in a house or something, an abandoned house or something like this. That reminds me that we found a warehouse full of booze and eggs somewhere back there. This just reminds me of that incident. And I remember having my first fresh eggs for so long. I mean really fresh eggs, and as much as I wanted of them. Because there were cases and cases of eggs. It was a German supply depot. And cases and cases of liquor, including scotch and bourbon and stuff like that and all of us getting drunk and getting sick from eating eggs.

But at this point, anyhow, we were in the house, I remember sitting in there with a bunch of other guys, and we get a call on the radio that there's an attack going on up in the woods near the river.

AH: Did you know you were going to meet the Russians at the Elbe?

HH: No, we didn't know whether we were going to cross the Elbe or what. We knew that the Russians were very close to us, but we didn't know what was going to happen there. It was getting to be evening now; it was quite dark. So what was happening was that I remember going outside, and we were getting ready to fire our guns. They were calling for fire, and I was out there, listening to what the coordinates were from somebody else. I don't know who was observing for that, but they were calling for fire when all of a sudden, not more than fifty-sixty feet away, I see machine-gun fire, I see pistol fire, shooting, you know, it's just the edge of darkness, a bunch of Germans over there, shooting at us. What had happened is that a bunch of SS troopers had crossed the Elbe River in rubber boats, and I think they were high on drugs, because they didn't act normal. I don't know that they were all SS troopers, but I think there was a fairly sizable number of them that were SS troopers. And they had attacked us, the mortars, and my response—I grabbed the radio, it wasn't on my back, but I grabbed it— and I ran. I couldn't run back to the house, because that's where they were, so there was a fence there and there were some pickets out of the fence, and then on the other side of the fence was somebody else's yard and another house. What I remember doing was running where the pickets were out of the fence, diving through that hole, and when I dived through, half the antenna broke off of the radio. And I just went on through it and got into that house over there.

My first response was to lay down, you know, next to a window with my head below the thing and just try to listen to what was going on. There were several other guys in the house, five or six other guys that had been on the mortars and had done the same kind of thing. It was all hell breaking loose! It was just shooting, bullets flying through the windows, explosions of all sorts. And yelling! Lots of yelling and screaming in German. In the meantime, I remember laying there for about fifteen minutes or so and finally there's still sporadic sounds coming from outside and shooting and explosions, but I'm expecting the Germans to burst through the door any minute or for a hand grenade to come through the window any minute and I don't know what the hell to do. There were no officers there, you know, we were all essentially the same rank and we were all scared shitless. I had the radio and I got on the radio, and I can hear on the radio, these guys are calling for mortar fire. I said, "I can't bring it in. We're being attacked ourselves." Only I remember I was so scared I could barely talk. I mean my voice wouldn't respond to my instructions. But I was able to do it. Well, it turned out that what these guys were doing was calling for mortar fire on top of themselves because they were being overrun, too. And I told them, "I can't do it. We're being overrun. We can't do it. Can you contact the base?" They couldn't get the base, and I couldn't get the base. And I didn't know what the hell to do.

Then I wasn't able to get them any more because I didn't have an antenna and the radio wasn't working well. Then it was very quiet for a long, long time. Then every now and then you'd hear somebody fire something. In the meantime it's gotten very dark and nobody could make a light. And I'm thinking to myself, "You know, this is where I'm going to die." I was sure of it. But I didn't know what else to do. A bunch of us got together, I remember it was up on the second floor. And we figured out how many hand grenades we had, which was two hand grenades, and I had a pistol. Three of the guys had carbines. And that was it—that's all we had. One or two of the guys had hand grenades in their shirt and I was thinking, you know, the hand grenades are maybe what's going to save us, because if they make an attack we can throw the hand grenades out the window, and that will decimate some of them. But I just didn't know what the shit was going to happen. We were whispering to each other because we didn't want to alert the Germans that we were in the house. We thought that they probably didn't know we were in that house, and that's why they weren't literally coming in and attacking. And I didn't know what had happened to most of the guys who were in that house across on the other side of the yard.

Well, this was going on and I get a call on the radio from the base, or I made contact with somebody in the back lines and I told them where we were and what was happening, that we had been attacked. And they said they they would send up an armored car or some armored troops. They were going to send up armored troops, all right? So I alerted the guys that there was armor coming in so we could hold out.

Then it occurred to me or somebody else that the guys in the other house don't know that the armor is coming in and they're likely to fire on them. I felt fairly confident at that time that the Germans weren't there any more, because there hadn't been any firing for an hour or so. As I say, there had been. There'd been all kinds of hell break loose out there. But for over an hour there hadn't been a damn sound from outside, and I couldn't believe they were still there. And I knew that they had been drunk or drugged, so I had to assume that they had left. But I wasn't sure and what I decided that I would do would be that I would go across that way as quietly as I possibly could and somehow alert the other guys without getting shot myself while I did it.

Well, just about the time that I was getting ready to make the run across there, an armored personnel carrier comes into town and drives right past us to the other house. It makes contact with the other house. But I was prepared; I remember being fully prepared to make that run at that point. This is now around dawn. I was waiting for dawn because I didn't want to do it in the dark. I was afraid I would get shot by my own people if they couldn't see me.

The Germans had cleared out. We had shot quite a few of them. What had happened was that, as I say, these SS troopers had come in. I think we lost about five people there, including that guy that I told you about earlier. He was killed. He was one of the people on the machine gun, and the reason that we survived was because of him. He was killed. He pulled the machine gun over to the edge of the house so that it had some protection and shot maybe fifteen of the enemy with the machine gun before they were able to shoot him. Then the other guy pulled the machine gun all the way into the house. Another guy went and grabbed the machine gun and pulled it into the house so they had a machine gun in that house and that's what kept the Germans from being able to break into that house. And they apparently didn't know we were in the house we were in.

The other thing that happened was that after all of this, the lieutenant—you remember that lieutenant I told you about?

AH: Uh-huh.

HH: That son of a bitch was in our house, and he was in hiding under some straw in like a pantry, kitchen. It had some kind of indoor-outdoor pantry kitchen. He was there, not five feet away from us, hearing us talking and making our plans and planning to make that run across there, and that son of a bitch was under that straw the whole goddamn night and never came out until morning. If the war hadn't ended within a day or two of there I would have turned him in. I was so mad about that! But, you know, two or three days later the war ended, officially ended, and I just didn't do it.

AH: Were the other men angry with him too?

HH: Uh-huh. But not so mad as I was, because they didn't know. Most of the other guys had not so much combat as I'd had.

AH: What didn't they know?

HH: They didn't know he was under there. I and one other guy saw him come out from under the straw, you know, but I don't think anybody else knew about it. But that really got me. Because he should have been in charge of the house and been making the decision about what should have been done. Not me. I wasn't an officer.

Then a couple of days later we got word that the war was over. That didn't mean that you could necessarily let your guard down, because there were Germans that called themselves werewolves that would kill Americans even after the war ended, and you had to be careful and cautious. But it was over, as far as . . . that was the last of the actual combat that I ever saw.

AH: Did you meet the Russians?

HH: Yes. Yes, we went to the river. I have some photographs that I showed you of refugees escaping from them. I don't know if I took any pictures of Russians themselves, but I did see some Russians on our side of the Elbe River. I never crossed to the other side. We didn't stay there very long. We went back to some place to rest near Nuremberg, as I recall. We stayed there for quite a while, maybe a month.

AH: A month?

HH: Yes. So that's it.

7 From Southern France to the Elbe

Analysis of Memories

General Dwight D. Eisenhower wanted to engulf the Germans in a vast pincers movement with a landing on the shores of Normandy and a landing in southern France, to be followed by a rapid drive to the heart of Germany. A shortage of landing craft made simultaneous landings impossible, however, so that the invasion of southern France was delayed for almost six weeks. Finally, 77,000 French, British, and American troops were landed on August 15, 1944, in Provence. They met little resistance until they reached the Vosges Mountains. In September they linked up with the main Allied forces from Normandy.

Company C was attached to various divisions of the Ninth and Seventh armies and by December 17 had crossed into Germany. But on December 16 the Germans began a counteroffensive toward the Meuse River and Antwerp which became known as the Battle of the Bulge because of the bulge it created in the American lines.

The Third Chemical Battalion was assigned to Patton's Third Army and rushed to the relief of Bastogne. On December 24 and 25, they traveled 229 miles in convoy. The battle was over on January 28, with heavy losses suffered by both the Germans and the Allies. In February and March the Germans were driven from the highly industrialized Ruhr Valley, and on March 25 large-scale crossings of the Rhine River were made by Allied forces. On April 1, the Third Chemical Battalion crossed the Rhine. By this time Company C had been largely reorganized into Company A. It drove toward Hannover and destroyed a large force of Germans before Hannover after four days of heavy fighting. Hannover fell on April 11. From there the troops moved to the Elbe River, where they continued to encounter heavy German resistance. On April 24 the Allies met the Russians at the Elbe River. (For Allied fighting units involved with the Third Chemical Battalion in the above action, see appendix 3.)

At first, the Germans sought to surrender only to the western

Allies. But General Eisenhower insisted upon total, unconditional surrender, which was finally achieved in the early morning hours of May 7. Officially, Victory in Europe Day was proclaimed on May 8, 1945.[1]

In this section of the narrative it is not so simple to judge the reliability of Howard's recollection because in the second recall document it was decided to force the story out of its chronological sequence in order to ascertain what effect doing so might have on the memory process. In both recall documents Howard described the invasion. In both documents he emphasized that they met no resistance in making the landing, although the second recall document contains more information about the British ship that took them across the Mediterranean. In both documents he also described coming upon wrecked gliders that had landed on poles stuck in the ground: "Guys obviously got killed or wounded. How glad I was that I didn't make the invasion with them."

At this point Howard was asked to go out of chronological sequence and discuss the events associated with meeting the Russians at the Elbe River.

> AH: All right. Let's start with reaching the Elbe River.
> HH: [Long pause] Well, I have to go back up a little bit because one of the most [long pause]—see, I saw the Elbe River. . . . [long pause] We have some photographs of that. . . . Now I have to back up and I don't know how far back to go. There are two incidents just prior to the end of fighting.

Howard's memory for the events of the war seemed to depend at least partly on a time line, and disturbing that organization resulted in considerable confusion for him. For much of the second recall document he described a series of incidents but was frequently confused as to whether they had taken place in France or in Germany. This was not usually the case in the first recall document. In the second recall document after describing an incident he would attempt to reestablish the chronology: "Now do you want me to go on from there to the end of the war?"

The result of forcing the narrative out of sequence was a loss of material. That is, there is material in the first recall document which does not appear in the second. For instance, the story of defending his group from an attack by a rabbit is not recounted in the second document until he is given an appropriate cue:

> HH: Alice assures me that there are gaps in what I recall. I suggest that we ought to see what conditions might bring some of it

France to Germany

*(For combat units to which company was
attached on these dates, see page 188)*

N

HOLLAND

BELGIUM

GERMANY

Apr 23
Restorf

Apr 13
Klotze

Berlin

Apr 11
Hannover Gardelegen

Apr 2
Munster

Elbe

Neinbourge
Apr 1

Mar 3
Krefeld

Feb 9
Linnich

Dec 26
Bastogne

Berle
LUX Jan 10

Dec 24
Longwy Saarburg
Jan 17

Dec 17
Rechtenbach

Paris

Dec 2
Selestat

Nov 2
Biffontaine
Oct 7
Vesoul Vosges Mts.

FRANCE

Dampierre

Quingey

SWITZERLAND

Sep 8
St. Sorlin

Grenoble
Aug 29
Briançon

ITALY

Veynes Gap

Carpentras

Aug 23
Lamanon
Aix Aug 15
St.Tropez

miles
0   100
0   200
kilometers

back. She says that a single word may be an adequate cue to reconstruct one story that is in the first document but not in the second. I'm challenging her to say that word.

AH: Rabbit.
HH: Oh, for goodness sakes! Yes.

Then he proceeds to tell virtually exactly the same story that appears in the first recall document.

Howard was able to recreate all of the missing stories from the first recall document when he was given appropriate cues. "AH: You have described being strafed on this tape. Did something happen right before you were strafed? HH: Yes." He then recounted his capture of the two German soldiers, which appears in the first recall document, in virtually the same words that he used when he told it the first time.

Disrupting the organization of the encoding in memory thus seems to confuse the narrative, causing gaps, omissions, and confusion, but there seems to be organization on another level so that each incident as it is narrated remains intact and is recalled the same way whether it is freely recalled or cued.

In order to study the validity of Howard's memories of the fighting in France and Germany we used a variety of strategies similar to those employed with respect to the memories of the Italian campaign. The most important resource was again the daily log of Company C, Third Chemical Battalion.

Howard did not remember the exact date of the invasion of southern France, but his memory of going in a British ship and of splashing ashore without casualties is confirmed in the daily log. "The personnel on the *Derbyshire* were unloaded at Yellow Beach. . . . No missions fired during day. Casualties: None" (Daily Log, Company C, 16 August 1944).

One of our difficulties was to establish with certainty which company Howard had been with and which platoon. He remembered having been in Company C but was not sure of the platoon. At length we were able to assign him definitely to Company C, Second Platoon, because several highly unusual events had occurred in the First Platoon of which Howard had no memory and several had occurred in the Second Platoon which he had described in some detail. Later in our analysis of the document, however, we suddenly found that nothing in the description of the events in Company C was familiar at all. There was neither recall or recognition for these events. Had we come upon a period of amnesia for events? In the log for March 11, 1945, there is a notation that Company D was combined with Company C and subsequently the Second Platoon of Company C assigned to Company A. When we turned to the records of Company A, not only did the recognition items increase, but once again descriptions from Howard's recall document were reflected in the daily log.[2]

Numerous incidents are thus corroborated by the daily log. On August 23, the log describes a fire which had been smoldering in the woods above the gun position which "was suddenly fanned by the wind and descended rapidly on the platoon gun position. Platoon was forced to move in such a hurry that some small items of equipment were lost. In approximately one hour, the platoon was set up ready to fire on some targets and in two hours all things were in order again" (Daily Log, Company C, 23 August 1944). In Howard's account of this fire in the first recall document, however, he suggests that the officer in charge should have anticipated the fire and should have made contingency plans which would have allowed for more orderly withdrawal. He also described a wild ride over bumpy mountain roads, sitting on top of ammunition from which the firing pins had been removed and hence could have been detonated. The daily log often describes such situations, and the written record puts those in charge in the best possible light.

In one case the log shows that Howard had mixed up the order of events. He thought that a soldier had been accidentally killed during a rifle inspection after the fire (first recall document) before being run over by the Germans at Briançon when, in fact, that incident occurred several days after the events at Briançon. Howard was correct in asserting that it occurred in a place where the battalion had camped for several days. The daily log reports the incident as follows: "The men were informed that a rifle inspection would be held at 1000B. Pvt. Frank Hunter accidently discharged his carbine and shot Pvt. Pat Freeman thru the head. Capt. Fenton, Bn Surgeon, was called and he stopped the flow of blood. Pvt. Freeman was immediately loaded on a W/C and taken North to a Clearing Station where it was necessary to transfer him to an Ambulance headed for Grenoble. Pvt. Freeman died on way to Hospital" (Daily Log, Company C, 6 September, 1944). The log has much detail and includes the name and rank of all of those involved in the incident, but Howard's account includes the human element in the tragedy when he says that these two men were friends and that he had known both of them.

There is one actual discrepancy between the log and the recall documents. Usually the differences between the two documents are due to descriptions of events which Howard either did not experience or does not remember, or conversely there are events which Howard recalled but which are not reflected in the account in the log. But the following is an account where Howard's memory is actually at variance with the report in the log. During the events at Briançon, Lieutenant Jones was ordered to form a patrol in order to find a new location to set up the guns. When they came back, the entire battalion was gone. Lieutenant Jones and his men wandered around for several days and eventually on September 3 were reunited with their company. (See Daily Log, Company C, pp. 5-7, 10.) Howard described this patrol in graphic terms. He recalled watching them leave and begin to climb the mountain. When he described the incident, he stated that he never saw them again. He thought he might have heard that they were captured by the Germans (first recall document). In the second recall document the incident is described in the same way. "I also remember when this thing happened, they sent a patrol up into the mountains to go up and see what the hell was going on. I almost was on that patrol. . . . But the guys who went on that patrol were never seen again, and I heard that they had been captured and spent the rest of the war in German prison camps" (second recall document).

How can we account for this memory failure? It must be seen as a failure because the log includes a detailed account from Lieutenant Jones as to where he was for these four days, what he did, and how he and the enlisted men with him eventually returned to their outfit. Furthermore, one of the enlisted men who was lost with Lieutenant Jones was Corporal Worley, who was a friend of Howard's, was often in his squad, and was someone whom Howard had known in Italy. He is the photographer who took the picture of Howard in the amphibious vehicle and he continued to take the occasional snapshot of Howard throughout the war. How could Howard have failed to register the return of this friend?

One clue to a possible answer may be found in the research of Elizabeth Loftus. She conducted several studies in which she showed slides of automobile accidents to subjects. Then she tested their ability to remember and report what they had seen. In some of the conditions of the experiment she provided false information in the question. For instance, she would ask where the green car was in relation to the damaged vehicle when in fact the car had been blue. She discovered that the false information had a powerful influence on the reports and all the more so if the false information was supplied by an authority figure.[3] I asked Howard to try to picture where he might have been when he remembers, albeit vaguely, being told that the patrol had been captured. He says he has a dim picture of being given this information while sitting in a jeep with an officer.

Another possible explanation is one that we have examined before, namely that some other preoccupation prevented the rehearsal and subsequent long-term store required to install an event in memory. Thus the fact that, within a few days of the missing patrol's return to the company, two friends were involved in a tragic accident in which one of them was killed occupied his thoughts. In the first recall document, he said, "I was very horrified to hear about that [the accident]." In discussing this possibility, Howard added that he had been absorbed with thoughts of how utterly ironic and absurd it was that in the midst of all the danger they were in it was possible to lose your life through such a random and almost prosaic event.

It is also possible that when Howard saw the patrol leave, his certainty that they would be captured or killed made their disappearance a self-fulfilling prophesy so profoundly affecting Howard's mental state that he did not process their return in his memory of events. This hypothesis is in fact a kind of addendum to explanations provided by Loftus, when she found that subsequent information may profoundly alter or affect memory. What we see here is the possibility that one's internal directions or observations may also affect memory in a similar fashion.

One of the events in memory that is not reflected in the log is particularly curious because in the account Howard remembers being told that he had been reported missing to battalion headquarters. Right after the evacuation from Briançon Howard remembers going through the tunnel at Col du Lautaret and then being taken back through the tunnel with about twenty other enlisted men to serve as a forward outpost to watch for the Germans. He remembers being very cold and miserable because most of the equipment and blankets had been abandoned. Much of the information in the daily log is consistent with Howard's memories. Indeed, the accounts are remarkably similar but not identical. On August 31, the log mentions the tunnel, notes a jeep accident which made it impossible to get blankets to the men, and describes in considerable detail several reconnaissance missions but none which reports one private going out with a paratrooper to locate the Germans, as Howard described doing. According to Howard, when he returned, he was told that he had been reported missing. For this reason it seems particularly odd that of the various reconnaissance missions described, not one matches Howard's memory. (See the first recall document.)

We experienced considerable frustration in not being able to verify this memory claim because so much of the memory of the fighting in this part of France is verified by the log and because what is reported in the log so closely parallels Howard's recollections. Moreover, this event is recalled almost word for word the same in both recall documents and is reported in vivid detail and with considerable pride. But the reconnaissance mission with a French-speaking paratrooper is simply not reported in the log. On September 2 the company was relieved by the Free French forces and proceeded toward Grenoble. One possible explanation for the missing mission is that Howard had gone out with a French officer in an American uniform and the report on the mission was therefore made to the paratrooper's unit under French command. The Free French army wore American uniforms and had American equipment; they had been parachuted into France in advance of the invasion.[4] But of course this is speculation.

As with the fighting in Italy, Howard does not report the rest of the fighting in France in much detail. What follows are only those incidents which stand out in one way or another. In other words, we are again observing a primacy effect so that the first days of fighting after the invasion are remembered with considerably more detail than the subsequent period. As Company "C" moved with the infantry up through the Vosges Mountains, the level of German resistance was intense, as can be ascertained from the number of rounds of ammunition fired each day (October 5: forty-three rounds; October 6: twenty-two rounds; October 8: twelve rounds; October 9: thirty rounds; October 10: fifty-eight rounds). The only event during this period that Howard has stored is a memory of being in a house which received a direct hit but in which no one was hurt. This event was confirmed in the daily log as having occurred on October 21. (Daily Log, Company C, 21 October 1944.)

It is of interest that the incident with the direct hit is like several others that are not remembered in a time sequence. Instead they are recalled as individual vignettes which seem to be stored topically rather than chronologically. In the first recall document, the direct hit on the house is recalled as having occurred in Germany and is part of the description of a series of near misses. In the second recall document this incident is triggered by the description of several events which occurred in houses. He recalls a soldier coming into a house where they were holed up with two chickens which he was twirling by the neck, saying,

> "We're going to have chicken tonight." And I could see he was wringing their necks and their bodies were going to start flying all over the god damned room with blood going everywhere. You never saw a bunch of guys fly out of a room so fast as we did there.
>
> And that reminds me of another incident, but I believe it happened in France somewhere. . . . a whole bunch of us were sitting in a room, and all of a sudden a shell hit the wall, and the room was just completely filled with powder and dust, and I thought "My God, I'm alive." And it turned out that nobody was hurt at all, although it was a direct hit on the house. [Second recall document]

Once the memories become more episodic in nature, the cases in which time is confused become more frequent even in the first recall

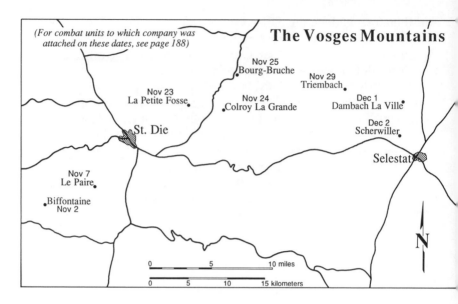

(For combat units to which company was attached on these dates, see page 188)

The Vosges Mountains

Nov 25
Bourg-Bruche

Nov 29
Triembach

Nov 23
La Petite Fosse

Nov 24
Colroy La Grande

Dec 1
Dambach La Ville

St. Die

Dec 2
Scherwiller

Selestat

Nov 7
Le Paire

Biffontaine
Nov 2

0   5   10 miles

0   5   10   15 kilometers

N

document. "We were in the Vosges Mountains, and I remember hearing about Roosevelt's death in a field on the edge of a woods" (second recall document). Howard was certainly in the Vosges Mountains in November, but of course Roosevelt died on April 12, when they were in Germany. The confusion may have arisen from the fact that, while he was in the Vosges Mountains, Howard undoubtedly heard that FDR had been reelected.

Howard described being with the Nisei in the Vosges Mountains and that they were cutting trees. The daily log reports for November 2 that "a position was found but it was necessary to cut some trees. The 442nd RCT furnished ten men to help" (Daily Log, Company C, 2 November 1944). An examination of the records of the 442nd regiment revealed that 442 Regiment Combat Team (RCT), composed of Japanese-Americans, fought through well forested regions of the Vosges Mountains.[6] These comparisons make it clear that, with the exception of certain time confusions, the essential elements in Howard's memories of the battles in France and Germany are the same as in the daily log.

During the Battle of the Bulge when the Third Chemical Battalion rushed with Patton's Third Army to the relief of the troops at Bastogne, and in the fighting thereafter, the mortar crews began to suffer from barrel bursts. "At 1445A an HE shell exploded in barrel of mortar killing Cpl Schoenhoff and Pvt. Farnsworth and wounding Pfc Joyce"

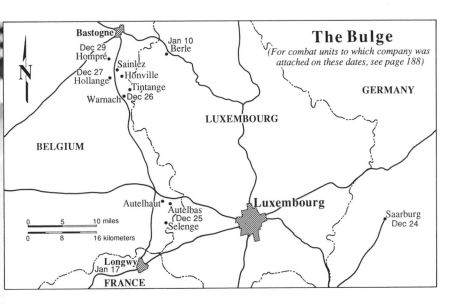

(Daily Log, Company C, 7 January 1945). Howard said, "Around that time [after the Bulge] I lost Jerry Farnsworth. I wasn't with him when it happened" (first recall document). In the summary of the log for the month of January there is a terse account of the barrel bursts.

Difficulties caused by defective 4.2 Mortar ammunition reached a new high during the month of January. Two barrel bursts occurred with HE shell. . . . In a high percentage of shell fired, cartridge container tubes were ruptured. Many of these ruptured tubes remained in the barrel causing misfires which greatly reduced the effectiveness of fire missions. Throughout the month, lot numbers of impounded ammunition were received thru the Army Chemical Officer and on one occasion, 60% of the total HE shells in the Battalion was impounded and returned to the dump. Since dump stocks were similarly affected, expenditure of HE shell was drastically curtailed at a critical time. [Daily Log, Company C, January Summary Report]

Compare the matter-of-fact tone of this account with Howard's description in the first recall document. Howard concluded his discussion of the barrel bursts with the following statement: "Then when I heard, later after the war, about the Garsson Munition scandal, I'm not certain, but I'm willing to bet that Garsson Munitions must have been the people that were making these 4.2 shells, because, as I say, we were really decimated by these things" (first recall document). The daily log supports that statement in that it reports twenty recipients of the Purple Heart for the month of January, which is the highest number of wounded in the company in any month since May 1944.

On July 24, 1946, the *New York Times* reported, "Defective mortar shells of the type which Dr. Henry M. Garsson helped to design and produce in the largest quantity killed American soldiers who tried to fire them in combat and in training, the Senate War Investigating Committee disclosed today."

The investigating committee received letters from veterans who had been in chemical warfare units citing substantially the same facts that Howard reported. One of the letters said: "I do not know whether the Garssons had any contracts for the 4.2 mortar shells. But if they did, you might be interested in knowing that the ammunition we received in Europe was so defective that the Theatre chemical officer had to issue directives requiring that it be fired by lanyard. . . . These orders were not issued, however, until a number of squads had been blown up by their own ammunition" (*New York Times* 9 August 1946).

In another comment reported in the *New York Times* for July 25, 1946, "William G. Mays of Meadville, Pa., former Army officer . . . said today that one of his men was killed and five were wounded by the explosion of a defective shell in a mortar barrel in Belgium. Commenting on testimony before the Senate War Investigating Committee, he remarked: 'It's about time the Army did something about those bad mortar shells.' Mr. Mays said he saw the shell explode in January, 1945, during the Battle of the Bulge."

The testimony before the investigating committee revealed that the Garsson brothers were unsavory characters at best. They had gone into the manufacture of war materiel with limited resources and had built a fortune. Moreover, Murray Garsson had previously been associated with underworld characters such as Dutch Schultz in the brewery business in New York. He had been arrested on charges ranging from disorderly conduct to grand larceny but had never served time in jail. Federal investigators had uncovered overcharges from the Garsson combine of more than $600,000. But the Garssons enjoyed political protection from Kentucky Congressman Andrew May, chairman of the House Military Affairs Committee. At the very time that American soldiers were being killed by defective ammunition, General Alden Waitt, who was in charge of procurement of ammunition for the Chemical Warfare Service, and General William Porter, former CWS chief, were being wined and dined in the Hotel Pierre in New York, and Murray Garsson picked up the tab. General Waitt drew the following conclusions in his testimony before the committee. "I know that serious investigations were conducted at the time to find the cause. Guesses and rumors ran the range from defective fuses to the unpredictable effect of cold weather on the explosives" (*New York Times,* July 24, 1946). General Waitt went on to say that attempts had been made to separate the defective shells to determine whether they came from the same manufacturer but that they had not been able to pinpoint a particular manufacturer as the source.

Whatever the disreputable character of the Garssons, it was not possible politically to make a case for blaming the barrel bursts on avaricious negligence. For one thing, so many people in high places were involved that Congress did not pursue the matter. Meanwhile it was true that, as the bitter cold weather that had characterized conditions at the front during January abated, the barrel bursts also ceased to be a problem. The following July, Congressman May and the Garsson brothers were convicted of extortion and were sentenced to jail for a period of from three months to eight years. (*New York Times* 4 July 1947.)

The log summary for the month of January noted that the Third Chemical Battalion had been in continuous combat since September 11 and that the barrel bursts combined with the long period of combat had created a serious morale problem. It was therefore decided to set up a rest area in Longwy and to rotate each company of the battalion to Longwy for a seven-day break. At this point in the narration there is a curious discrepancy between the two recall documents. In the second recall document, Howard recalled that they were quartered in a kind of gymnasium in Longwy and that he slept on the balcony. While they were staying there, the men had a dance to which local people were invited. During the dance Howard felt tired and went up to the balcony to sleep. A beautiful girl followed him up to the balcony and wanted to know why he was avoiding her. "Well, the next thing I knew we were making it in the sack up there. She took me out and I met her parents and I gave her a ring [the ring which clearly identifies him as the soldier in the amphibious duck in Italy]. I thought I was in love with her, but she wasn't very much in love with me. . . . She just thought I had rejected her and wasn't about to accept it" (second recall document). He then remembered that he had also gone with a bunch of guys to a whorehouse in Longwy because "I'd never been to one. I got inside, and there were just a bunch of guys around reading magazines, and these girls would come and periodically pick one of the guys and call them into the other room. And I took one look at the girls and they were all fat, ugly, and old, and I said, 'No, this isn't for me!' and I picked up and left. That was where I had the picture taken. There was a picture of me with a machine gun" (second recall document).

In the first recall document Howard had avoided describing these incidents along with another previous encounter where he lost his virginity. He may have deemed this inappropriate material to share with the typist and whoever else might read the document. It was not that they were forgotten incidents. It is characteristic of oral history that a certain amount of censorship is employed even as the document is being generated. But it is also typical of oral interviews that, as the process continues and the subject becomes more engaged in an attempt to provide as accurate a portrayal of events as possible, some of this self-censorship is discarded. The absence of these stories in the first interview, however, cannot be explained by a reluctance to discuss these matters with his interviewer/wife because these were stories that had been shared with her on previous intimate occasions.

After February 1945, it became more difficult to compare Howard's memories with the events cited in the daily log. For one thing the log itself tends to be less discursive, and furthermore on March 11 the battalion was reorganized and the Second Platoon of Company C was assigned to Company A. In that company's log there is no mention of the atrocities at Gardelegen, Germany, which Howard described in both recall documents. But in 1978 Howard and I visited Yad Vashem, the memorial to victims of the Holocaust in Israel. Howard stopped short in front of a photograph depicting the atrocity at Gardelegen. It was labeled "Gardelegen, a concentration camp in which 150 prisoners were killed." In Howard's memory, this was incorrect. What the picture depicted was a barn where the Nazis had herded about 1,000 political prisoners. The Germans had been marching them to Hannover, but when they learned that Hannover had fallen rather than let the prisoners go, they set fire to the barn and systematically shot any who managed to claw their way out of the structure.

When we returned to the United States, we searched for some documentary evidence to confirm Howard's memory and found it in *Life* for May 19, 1945. There are the pictures of the horror taken by Margaret Bourke-White. The smoke can be seen rising from the charred bodies. The captions state, "At Gardelegen . . ., the Nazis set fire to a warehouse full of political prisoners. . . . Friday April 13, German guards incinerated 1000 prisoners to prevent their being liberated by advancing Allied forces." Howard sent his findings to Binyamin Armon, director of commemoration and information at Yad Vashem, who responded that the captions to the pictures would be corrected.

In the second recall document Howard recalled the sight as follows: "There were bodies that were just burned terribly. Some of them had on striped clothes, as I recall. I may be making that up about the striped clothes. That's what I've seen in movies and stuff (second recall document). In the *Life* article next to the pictures of Gardelegen are pictures of prisoners of war in striped clothing. At first I surmised, as did Howard himself in recounting the incident, that this was an example of the effects upon memory of subsequent information. Howard did remember having seen this issue of *Life* after the war, so it was easy for us to conjecture that these pictures might have influenced his memory. We subsequently found, however, that Corporal Ralph Worley had taken pictures at the scene, and some of the bodies do, in fact, have on striped prisoner-of-war clothing. Thus the more likely explanation is that Howard at first recalled that they wore striped clothes and then, when he attempted to visualize the scene and did not see bodies with striped clothes in his "mind's eye," assumed that he had been confused by the knowledge that prisoners wear striped clothing.

The essentially accurate nature of this memory may be gauged by comparing Howard's description in the first recall document with the testimony of another eyewitness; Harold P. Leinbaugh, *The Men of Company K.*

> Leinbaugh [writing of himself in the third person] heard of atrocities at Gardelegen and drove to the town, which had been captured hours earlier. Retreating SS troops had herded more than six hundred prisoners, mostly Russians and Poles, into a large tile barn and set fire to hay in the barn with Very pistols. That night Leinbaugh ate with a French commando, a naval officer who had parachuted into occupied France before D-Day as a saboteur. . . . He was the only survivor . . . [and] had crawled to the door to breathe and piled bodies over himself to escape the flames. The dead men were little more than skeletons, but some had clawed holes with bare hands through the tile of the barn and thrust their heads through the holes. Each skull bore a single bullet hole. Inside the barn GIs pressed wet handkerchiefs to their faces—the stench of burning flesh was overwhelming. The 84th and other divisions sent truckloads of men to see the bodies, and German civilians within walking distance were herded gagging and vomiting through the barn.[7]

Note that the only discrepancies between these two accounts concern whether the atrocity was committed by civilians or by retreating SS troops and the number killed, although Howard reported the same number as the *Life* article.

After I had checked Howard's recollections against the daily log and other sources, I attempted to determine whether I could somehow enhance his memory. First Howard was presented with a series of names (the majority of which were those of men from his company). In most cases, the names seemed unfamiliar, and even when a name did seem familiar, it did not elicit new information. There was one notable exception, the name John Moore. Howard recognized that this was the name of the company captain. Furthermore, upon being told that he had been wounded, he was able to describe the circumstances: "It happened on a jeep trip. The jeep got hit" (interview, July 13, 1985, p. 9). The log describes this event as follows: "Capt. John A. Moore and his driver, Pfc George Brown left the 1st platoon. . . . an enemy patrol opened up with small arms fire on the jeep. . . . Pfc Brown was shot through the head and died immediately. Capt. Moore suffered a flesh wound on back of left hand" (12 January 1945).

We then reviewed the daily log, which Howard was seeing for the first time. Here again there were a number of items in the log which he recognized and which had not been previously described in the recall documents, but no new memories were stimulated by exposure either to the daily log or to other documentary sources.[8] He did report, however, that reading the log caused considerable restimulation of the emotion associated with the events described.

We also tried to enhance Howard's memories by showing him a series of pictures which either resembled places where he had been or in fact depicted places where he had been. These pictures were taken from the *Pictorial Record* published by the U.S. Army.[9] In most cases the pictures elicited a recognition response from Howard but no further information. Occasionally, however, a picture yielded something new. The picture apparently needed to be very specifically tied to a memory to bring it to the surface. In response to a picture of a soldier wearing waterproof boots (called shoepacs), Howard stated that he was reminded of when "I was riding in a jeep and it was just bitter bitter cold . . . all we had was blankets and I was feeling very resentful because I knew back in the rear, they had sleeping bags, down coats and shoepacs. I seldom saw that stuff on the front" (interview, September 20, 1985). On that same occasion Howard commented that a picture of a pontoon bridge across the Rhine River did not look familiar because it did not have any trucks on it. It is of interest that the next picture which also showed a pontoon bridge across the Rhine (but this time with a truck on it) prompted Howard to state: "Yes, that's how it looked."[10]

We used one other type of document in an effort to stimulate memory, namely a series of photographs taken by Howard himself. These photographs showed pictures of the dead Germans who had made the desperate, drug-induced attack at Restorf and also pictures of refugees fleeing across the Elbe River to escape the Russians. But even these photographs elicited no new memories. Thus with the few exceptions noted above, our efforts to enhance and stimulate Howard's memory by providing recognition items of various kinds were almost totally unsuccessful.

8 War's End and Return to Civilian Life

First Recall Document

Shortly after the events on the Elbe River, Germany capitulated, and Howard's term as a combat soldier came to an end.

AH: Were you a part of the occupying forces?

HH: Yes. But I didn't have much in the way of . . . I mean, it was this little town outside of Nuremberg with a Kotex factory. [Laughter] We were billeted next to it, and I remember I became a supply sergeant for the company there, and I used to go and swipe all kinds of good food, stuff for my guys, sleeping bags; all the things we never had I would go get for us at the supply depot. And I had an orderly who was an Italian Ph.D. in philosophy. He used to sweep up and he would talk to me sometimes. A young man—not too young—but . . .

AH: An American?

HH: No, he was an Italian. He was an orderly. He was a refugee, and for food and a little bit of money, he would keep the place clean. It was kind of like being . . . you had a lot of power as an occupying soldier. You carried guns—nobody else did—things like that.

And I got to Paris for a few days. Eventually I got down to . . . I think we sailed from Marseille, and we took eighteen days to get back and I went to, I think, Fort Dix, New Jersey, when the boat landed in New York. Then from there I went to Indiantown Gap, and from Indiantown Gap I went probably to Harrisburg and took a train down to Washington and from Washington to Miami. That's how I got home. I got home . . . , I think I got home just before Christmas, sometime around there. The war having ended in what was it? May?

AH: Yes.

HH: But it wasn't until Christmas that I got home. But as I remember that was pretty fast because I had a lot of points compared to most guys, and when they asked me if I wanted to be a member of the Reserves I remember telling them to go shove it! And I did not join the Reserves, and as a result I did not fight in the Korean War. And those that did join the Reserves did fight in the Korean War.

AH: Well, you must have been a fairly long period of time in the occupation though, because the war ended in May, and if you didn't leave until November . . .

HH: Oh, we must have left before November.

AH: You must have been the whole summer in Germany.

HH: Yes. Pretty much. Germany and France. It was slow; we moved from one place. . . . I spent a month or two in this little town outside of Nuremberg and then maybe was another month or so getting down to the boat. But I don't remember; it's all blended together now, what happened there. It must have taken a while to get to that place in Nuremberg, too. We must have gone to several other places before we got there.

AH: How did you occupy your time as an occupying soldier?

HH: Well, I read. I did the supply sergeant bit, ripping off the depots of what I could for my outfit. I fraternized. It really wasn't too unpleasant.

AH: What kind of plans did you start to make for what you were going to do after the war, either while you were still in Germany or when you got to Miami?

HH: Well, when I got to Miami I didn't know what I was going to do. Eventually I made application to the University of Chicago and to Antioch and took a bunch of entrance tests. Those were the only two schools I applied to. And I got accepted at both and eventually went to Chicago the following September. I have never regretted going to Chicago. In a way I always felt that I was educated at the University of Chicago and trained everywhere else. But I have, in a sense, often wondered what my life would have been like had I gone to Antioch instead of Chicago.

AH: Well, what were your feelings while you were down in Miami? I mean, in terms of sort of getting over the experience of having been in combat and so forth? What was your state of mind?

HH: I didn't like Miami. I couldn't believe that these people back in the States had lived such undeprived lives while we were dying over there and that they were so ignorant of what was going on over there. The thing that got me most, I guess, was realizing that some event that I had been through, where I might have lost a friend or might have even been in tremendous danger, would be a line that there were skirmishes on the southern or on the northern border of Germany or whatever. That would be all that would be cited about that in the newspaper.

I couldn't believe that, you know, such terrible things could happen to some people and other people would not have any knowledge of it or even concern about it. But that's the way the world is, I guess. It's hard even now to accept it, but I know that's what's happening. I know that there are brave people in Uganda that are dying tonight, fighting against Idi Amin. And this is happening probably in Iran, too. It's just hard to . . . you can't be [concerned about] all things at all times, I guess.

But I did not like Miami Beach. It took me a long time to stop thinking like a soldier. For years after the war when I would come to a new place I would always be on the alert as to where the Germans were likely to be, where the shelling was going to come from, where would I go if a shell came in, and where would I go if there was machine-gun fire. You kind of instinctively thought about all those things all the time. They were the things that your life depended on, and so you were pretty well trained to keep them in mind. It took me many years to get them out of my system.

Several years after the war I remember an incident when . . . now this was probably in 1954, '55, when we were in Haskins lab up in New York on the second or third floor and there were a bunch of us and I remember we were standing around in lab coats discussing a piece of research when an airplane buzzed the U.N. (we were very close to the U.N.). It sounded like a strafing run or a dive-bombing run, and there I was, I realized I was lying on the floor, you know. I had hit the deck. I felt very sheepish about it because they didn't understand what had happened to me. But that sound was a conditioned stimulus for you to hit the deck. And I had had no chance to extinguish it. By that time I had gotten over jumping and getting ready to crouch when I heard a backfire or a sudden loud noise. That had been extinguished, but I hadn't had anybody fly an airplane near me fast where that sound would have lost its ability to control this conditioned response, so the conditioned response came right back. I didn't think about it. There I was, I was on the floor.

AH: Well, I'm glad you didn't get killed.

HH: Well, thank you very much! I'm glad you're glad.

9 War's End and Return to Civilian Life

Analysis of Memories

The most salient aspect of the memories of the occupation of Germany is how thin they are. In the first recall document they occupy five pages and in the second recall document eight pages. The previous six months from October 1944 to May 1945 filled forty-five pages in the first narrative. This fact is suggestive of the telescopic nature of memory. Not all experience from the past is preserved at the same density. It is probably fair to say that no other year in Howard's life is preserved with the same detail as the year from April 1944 to May 1945. Historians have, of course exercised similar judgment in that the effort to preserve and analyze the events from 1941 to 1945 has occupied more of their attention than any similar period of time in the twentieth century.

The second recall document contains a number of incidents which do not appear in the first. Howard describes, for instance, his feelings upon being told that the war was over: "We were on a road and we had stopped. I remember somebody coming and telling me that the war was over. I could hardly believe it and I can remember sitting around and breaking out a drink of booze of some sort, feeling very jubilant and thinking, 'My God, I am going to live! I can't believe that I'm going to live. I cannot believe it!'" (second recall document). He also described a brief affair with a Polish refugee girl in a Kotex factory. "They just had like from floor to ceiling unpackaged Kotexes. We wandered through the Kotex, it was like being in clouds" (second recall document). The company settled in a small town near Nuremberg. There he met a young German woman and spent time "fraternizing" with her at her house.

Throughout these recall documents there are frequent expressions of wonder and amazement that he had survived: "Anyway we went to a replacement depot down near Marseilles . . . not too unpleasant down there because they had movies and good PXs and you slept on cots, and it was comfortable, and you knew you weren't going to get killed. The war was over and you had survived it" (second recall document).

During the war, Howard's family had moved from Harrisburg to Miami Beach, Florida. The army with its own logic returned Howard to Harrisburg, and he was on his own to get from there to Florida. In both recall documents he described a period of confusion and disorientation. "It took me a long time to stop thinking like a soldier" (first recall document). "It was a very confused, difficult decompression. I really had a lot of problems with my feelings about myself and what I was doing and what my life was about and who I was and where I was going. What I knew for sure was that I didn't appreciate the values of the people I met in Miami Beach" (second recall document).

On the whole the second recall document, although remarkably similar to the first recall document with respect to the description of the events in memory, more frequently expresses the emotional response to incidents. I have no explanation but present this as merely one observation made in the course of this study.

With respect to the validity of these postcombat memories, the only documentary resource that was available to us was a number of photographs which Howard took himself. There are pictures of a softball game and a tug-of-war in a field near Nuremberg and various pictures of Howard and his buddies fraternizing with German girl friends at a picnic. And there are pictures taken at a pool in Miami shortly after he arrived there. The pictures of the sports activities do not prompt Howard to recall the event at all. The pictures of the picnic are recognized but do not elicit any further memories of the event or of the people in the pictures beyond what was already in memory. Just as in previous efforts to use recognition items to enhance memory, these pictures prove to be incapable of eliciting additional information.

Conclusions

This study of memory occupied our attention for approximately ten years. What did it accomplish? Among other things it led us to develop a useful research methodology. Frequently, in studies of autobiographical memory, the researcher lacks a means to determine the extent to which an informant's memories are accurate representations of the events they purport to describe. This study through the use of historical documentation and analysis provided a means to address this issue. We were, of course, not able to confirm all the events in the recall documents, but we were able to obtain sufficient corroboration to indicate that, for Howard, the majority of the events in his memory claim occurred and moreover occurred pretty much as he says they did.

Although the memories presented here are primarily derived from just one individual, they indicate that within the range of human memory it is possible reliably and accurately to recover past events and to amplify and exemplify the existing written record. Howard's memories are not, however, accurate with respect to exact dates or with respect to the exact position where the army was. Moreover, the information they contain is limited in certain respects. For example, Howard's memories of the invasion of southern France incorporate many details, but they are incomplete in that he failed to mention whether the water was warm or cold. In this respect Cornelius Ryan is probably right. Our findings suggest that if one seeks such data from reminiscence, the results will be disappointing. These data must be obtained from other sources. But reminiscences provide detail, analysis, meaning, an identifiable point of view, and emotional impact, all of which are frequently missing from written documents.

Both Bartlett and Loftus have suggested that there are two kinds of rememberers: visual and verbal. They have not suggested that the two strategies are mutually exclusive, but they point out that most people tend to rely more upon one strategy or the other. Howard is a visual rememberer. The process by which he extracts material from memory is clearly delineated in these documents. Unlike the verbal rememberer (I am one), who tends to have a set of words in memory, rather like a tape recorder with no pictures, he calls up a scene and then describes it. Where there are blanks in the picture, he will insert reconstructions based on "what must or might have been" in order to render a coherent narrative. These reconstructions account for some of the error and confusions in his narrative. As Bartlett and Loftus both observed, "seeing is believing." Those who are visual rememberers have great confidence in their memories. Howard tends to feel that, if he doesn't remember it, it didn't happen, and if he does remember it, that's the way it is, in his head at any rate, in spite of evidence to the contrary. That is, he is entirely able to accept the logic of facts that contravene his memory, but the memory itself remains undisturbed.

While long-term memory may be enhanced, modified, reconstructed, and redintegrated, the forty-year-old memories that Howard retains are extraordinarily resistant to change. They appear to have been protected from decay by rehearsal and reinforced by salience so that they have become fixed in the mind. The memories that were elicited by free recall from a period forty years in the past were stable to the point of being set in concrete. It was virtually impossible to enhance or stimulate new memories by any method that we could devise. In a very few instances, exposure to documents, pictures, and conversations with others who had shared the same or similar experiences would, often a day or two later, result in some new memory. But the amount of new material generated over and above what is in the original recall documents is sparse indeed. In order to access this material, it was necessary to find a very specific cue, and that seemed to be largely a hit-and-miss affair. As Marcel Proust said in his great literary study of memory, "The past is hidden . . . beyond the reach of intellect, often in some material object. . . . And as for that object, it depends on chance whether we come upon it or not." [1]

We think that our findings with respect to Howard's memories imply that there is a subset of autobiographical long-term memory which is so permanent and largely immutable that it is best described as archival. From this perspective archival memory consists of recollections that are rehearsed, readily available for recall, and selected for preservation over the lifetime of the individual. They are memories selected much as one makes a scrapbook of photographs, pasting in some, discarding others; they define the self and constitute the persona one retains, the sense of identity over time. They enable us to see ourselves in the image of a sturdy youth, even though the mirror now reveals only the remnants of what once was.

It appears that the impressions stored in archival memory are assessed at the time they occur or shortly thereafter as salient and hence important to remember. Often they are derived from events that were highly emotional. Their special feature is that they must be rehearsed or otherwise consolidated in order to form part of archival memory. At times, subsequent events can lead otherwise unremarkable experiences to be recorded as part of the archival memory of an earlier event. This seems especially likely to occur if the event is perceived as a turning point in life. If the memories of these experiences are rehearsed along with the memory of the event they will become a part of one's permanent memory. We think that this is probably what happens with flashbulb memories. It's not that the so-called flashbulb memory was recorded in an instant (illuminated by a flashbulb, as it were) but that the experiences surrounding it were rehearsed along with the event itself.

On some occasions subsequent events can so occupy one's attention that they prevent the rehearsal of an experience that might otherwise be expected to be in archival memory. Howard has no memory of his experience in the amphibious vehicle when he helped tow a target to sea. He is certain, however, that he would have remembered this experience at the time he was preparing to invade southern France. He thinks that had he not been so preoccupied with thoughts of the invasion he would have rehearsed this experience and it would have become a part of his permanent memory claim.

It appears that the events that become a part of archival memory either are unique happenings or are recorded because they represent the first occurrence of an event which subsequently became more routine. Even occurrences which threaten the very life of an individual may be lost in the stream of events if such an experience becomes sufficiently repetitive and routine. Howard remembers firing the guns only about three times, and these memories are associated with the primacy of the experience or with some unique event, such as a shell's going through his raincoat. In actual fact, of course, he fired the guns hundreds, if not thousands, of times and often under extremely dangerous conditions, yet most of these experiences are lost.

I think that if, for one reason or another, an event is deemed sufficiently salient to one's life, it will be rehearsed either internally or in conversation. It is a commonplace of our language that, when these stories are rehearsed out loud, they often conclude with the words "I shall never forget it as long as I live." Just so—or at least for forty years or more. If the opportunity to engage in this rehearsal is blocked by subsequent events or perhaps by prior events, even relatively important events will not only be unavailable for recall but will also be irretrievable by any ordinary methodology of questioning and research.

Our findings indicate that, for Howard, events which are placed in archival memory are chronologically arranged and are also cross-referenced, sometimes under several headings.

James Jones says: "To accept anonymous death requires a kind of bravery no one has been able to name—for a long time after you are a different person just from having contemplated it." And he suggests that you become a soldier only when you know you are dead and you have accepted this idea. Under these circumstances remembered events have a special heightened flavor.[2] This may account for the fact that Howard remembers an awful lot about the year from May 1944 to May 1945.

I think that studies using procedures similar to those employed here could provide information as to whether density of recall is related to the emotional character of the events. In such studies, alumni could be interviewed. The college yearbooks and newspapers and other records might be employed much as we employed the daily log. In addition, by conducting two or more interviews over several years' time (perhaps at successive reunions) it would be possible to assess the reliability of recall. Moreover, a study similar to this one with individuals who tend to process their memories verbally could provide information on the question of whether the concepts we have postulated might be generalizable to those who tend not to store memories visually.

Vision and hearing are awe-inspiring phenomena of the brain and the sense organs. As Howard tells his students, the eye and the ear are about as sensitive as they theoretically can be. On a dark night at sea, an observer can detect the flare of a single match at a distance of about eight miles. For this recognition to occur, the retina must be capable of reacting to the impact of only a few photons, the smallest units of light that physicists have identified. Similarly, it has been calculated that, for a human to hear a weak tone, the sound need only vibrate the eardrum by a distance that is no longer than the diameter of a hydrogen molecule. We think that memory is also awe inspiring. True, memory may be a selective instrument and the memory of only one individual can provide but one angle of vision on the elusive picture of events in the past. Still, the memory we have studied was able to preserve over a lifetime a set of events with much of the color, tone, and emotionality of the events as first experienced. Moreover, it did so with a degree of accuracy that, at times, exceeded that of the official documents.

This is not to say that archival memory is an unlimited store. On the contrary, we have found, in this example, that it is a collection with well-defined limits. We found material from demonstrated experiences which was not available for either recall or recognition; we found material which, while it is unavailable for recall, can be recognized; and we found a very limited number of events where recognition factors led to stimulated recall.

Another aspect of this body of memories is that it displays a pronounced telescoping effect. Some periods of a week or even a day are remembered more vividly and with greater detail than much longer periods of time. The more vivid memories tend to seem to have filled a greater amount of time than they did. Conversely, the less vivid memories are perceived as having taken up less time. For example, Howard was very surprised to discover that he had been in the occupation army for a period of almost six months, twice the amount of time from the launch of the big push at Cassino to the landing in southern France. This telescoping seems to create a certain confusion in the chronological dating of events.

The conclusions that Howard himself reached, as the subject, are of special interest:

When Alice and I started this project, I had a number of mixed feelings. As a scientist, I was very interested in learning something about the nature of long-term autobiographical memory. As the subject, however, though I was curious about the possible results, I was also apprehensive.

I knew I was going to dig into my memory claim on two widely separated occasions. I wondered if I would be consistent in my recall. Would the stories change on their retelling, and if so, how? Would there be a false progression toward making me something of a hero? It also seemed possible that I might exhibit a loss of memories in the interval between recalls. After all, in my graduate work I had learned that we are born with a full complement of brain cells and that every day thereafter thousands of them die, never to be replaced. Would this be the fate of my memories?

I was also concerned as to how I might react when I would eventually read the daily log. I had a dread that the log might reveal some horrible event in which I had participated or which I had witnessed but which I had repressed. I was also concerned that I might discover that I had fabricated or plagiarized some of what I believed to be my memories. I didn't think this was likely, but I had to acknowledge its possibility. To my relief none of these nasty things happened.

Elizabeth Loftus[3] has shown us that eyewitness accounts are subject to considerable distortion by factors that occur after the events they describe, and Alice alluded to several examples of such distortions in my memory claims. One example was my failure to process and retain information that the lost patrol in the fighting near Briançon had returned. Another example was my failure to recall that the firing at Castelforte began at 11:00 P.M., not 11:00 A.M. as I had suggested.

What seems surprising to me is not that these distortions occurred but that there were so few of them. Perhaps the recollections that survive in archival memory are so well rehearsed that they are less susceptible to distortion than the more recent memories that Elizabeth Loftus studied. Further research, however, will be needed to determine whether this is the case.

Marigold Linton's self-study of her memory of real world events is relevant here.[4] As Alice has noted, Linton concluded that events are likely to endure in memory if: (1) they are perceived as highly emotional at the time they occur; (2) the subsequent course of events makes the event appear to be instrumental or causes it to be perceived as a turning point; and (3) they are unique (not blurred by repetition).

Our study serves to confirm that these elements are also important to the formation of archival memories. This seems especially interesting in view of the differences between Linton's procedures and ours. In Linton's study, the events to be remembered were recorded by a subject, Linton herself, shortly after they occurred. Moreover they were recorded in the context of a study of memory, a factor that could have effected what was selected and what would survive. In our study, I had kept no diary and, at the time of the events, was not engaged in a study of memory. That the two studies should yield such similar conclusions, despite these major differences, serves to underline the importance of the factors they uncovered.

My inability to remember my trip in an amphibious landing craft during our preparations for the invasion of southern France leads to some interesting observations with regard to the question of whether or not all experiences are retained in some kind of permanent store. I know that this event occurred; there is a photograph of it. Moreover, judging from my expression in the photograph, it seems obvious that this was a pleasant experience for me. Furthermore, it was the kind of experience that would have been of special interest to me and hence should have been part of my archival memory. Indeed, I remember having previously seen several such vehicles on the road to Rome (see appendix 1, p. 163). I also remember that, at the time I saw them, I was curious as to how they operated in the water. I had noticed that they had propellers as well as wheels, and I wondered whether the wheels continued to rotate once they were in the water. I must have learned the answer to this question when I helped to tow the target to sea, but I now have no idea of that answer. Nor do I know whether we pulled the target to sea or pushed it. I don't even know whether the target had an anchor and, if it did, whether it was fastened by a rope or a chain. In short, I remember nothing of the experience, even though I have now examined the photograph hundreds of times. Alice has suggested that my subsequent preoccupation with the forthcoming invasion of southern France and/or my emotional reaction to the subsequent flash fire on the beach probably prevented the rehearsal that seems necessary for an experience to survive as an archival memory.

There are those who will argue that rehearsal has nothing to do with it and that the memory is there but that I just can't access it. Some memory theorists would argue that, given enough psycho-analysis, or perhaps hypnosis, I might very well be able to recover this lost episode.

The issue is difficult to assess for a number of reasons. At this stage of my life, psychoanalysis is impractical and I appear not to be susceptible to hypnosis. Several skilled hypnotists have in the past attempted to hypnotize me in connection with various psychological experiments without apparent success. But beyond this difficulty, inherent in the question itself is the Freudian idea that all experience is incorporated in the brain and that failure to retrieve any element of past experience is due either to inappropriate cues or to repression. Moreover, the question also presupposes that hypnosis is an induced state where the powers of the mind are either greatly enhanced or that repression has been removed. Recent research, however, indicates that hypnosis is a relaxed state of neither sleep nor wakefulness in which some inhibitions and repressions may be reduced but not that it is some awesome magical condition in which one may suddenly become able to examine the entire contents of the mind unfettered by inhibition.[5] Elizabeth and Geoffrey Loftus evaluated the evidence that hypnosis and/or psychoanalysis might be able to uncover memory that has previously been unavailable in consciousness. Their review of the literature and their experiments point to the conclusion that, contrary to popular belief, neither of these procedures has such a power.[6]

We began with a set of questions. Is memory reliable over time? This study demonstrates that it certainly can be. With regard to the validity of memory, this study demonstrates that it is essential to apply the standard techniques of historical analysis if the past is to be interpreted as accurately as possible. Moreover, these techniques can also be usefully employed by psychologists as they attempt to understand the basic process of human memory itself.

As a contribution to the taxonomy of memory, we have suggested a class of memories which we have called archival. We have identified this as a separate class because it has its own set of principles or laws. Unlike long-term autobiographical memory, it is unaffected by disuse, is susceptible to little or no decay over time, and because of rehearsal is readily available for recall. It is, however, relatively unaffected by efforts to enhance its elements through the presentation of recognition items. The possible causes of gaps or lapses in archival memory include events subsequent to the experience which might be expected to be memorable and which prevent the rehearsal and redundant encoding of the event. As we have seen in the examination of Howard's memories, such subsequent events may exclude the antecedent from memory's storage or may keep it so buried in the recesses of the mind that there is no practical way of retrieving it.

The causes for such gaps include the fact that the mind tends to extract the gist of an experience and that in doing so it is more careful to preserve events perceived as salient. Moreover, there is a primacy effect. Once events become repetitious, they will tend to decay in the stream of experience. As William James put it, "Forgetting is essential to the health and vitality of the mind."[7] Foreshortening, or extracting the meaning or gist of experience, is essential to the ability to return to the past without having it occupy the same amount of time as the original experience. Finally, substitution of some experience that blocks the rehearsal of immediately prior events will also, apparently, cause gaps in the memory.

Long-term memories may be accessible through the presentation of recognition factors if an appropriate context can be found and if they are not too far remote in time from the subject's current experience. Archival memories, however, would appear to be particularly resistant, at least in Howard's case, to efforts to enhance them in this way. Furthermore there is some reason to believe that his memory may not be atypical in this regard. We have noted that a return to Edgewood Arsenal had little or no effect on his ability to recall additional material from memory of that experience, but likewise all the members of the reunion group who had gone back to Edgewood reported the same experience, and indeed those who had made the trip back to Europe and the scenes of the battle in which they had participated reported that, in the first place, it was difficult to find recognizable sites but that even those found did not stimulate much in the way of new memories.

In the summer of 1989 we also made a trip to Europe and visited Longwy, France, and many of the small Belgian villages where Howard had fought. We visited the memorial museum at Bastogne. The museum is full of memorabilia from that battle: uniforms, weapons, tanks, etc., as well as large photographs taken during the battle. Some of these small towns and some of the artifacts in the museum produced recognition, but none elicited any new memories.

Endel Tulving's work on encoding specificity and its effects on retrieval from episodic memory suggests that "specific encoding operations performed on what is perceived determine what is stored, and what is stored determines what retrieval cues are effective in providing access to what is stored."[8]

An example from our interviewing process may serve to clarify the issue. During the second interview, I deliberately broke the chronological sequence. As a result the second interview contained several gaps or lapses of memory at the point where I did so. When I asked Howard whether he had told me all he could remember, he said, "Yes." But the first interview had given me some very specific cues, like the word "rabbit," which I was able to employ to retrieve the memory of his having shot at some rabbit rustling about in a box in one of the jeeps while Howard was on guard duty. Without that very specific code information, however, it would not have been possible at that time to access that memory.

These results considered in their entirety would seem to have a number of implications for those who wish to collect oral history. First of all, they suggest that the interviewer would do well to ascertain the dominant procedures used by their informants in order more effectively to plan with them the most fruitful line of inquiry.

One of the issues that oral historians have debated at length is how much preparation and detailed knowledge of the issues under discussion is enough to conduct useful interviews. The conventional wisdom is that interviewers can never feel that they have done enough in this regard.

At the 1976 Oral History Association Colloquium, however, the Canadian journalist Barry Broadfoot asserted that everyone has two well-rehearsed stories, and when you have recorded them on tape, you have pretty much all that any one person has to give.[9] His statement offended many careful practitioners of the art of oral interviewing. But he may have made an important observation. If it is true that most people store memories under a number of very specific categories, where they are linked to very specific associations, it will in fact be a chancy business, as Marcel Proust noted, to attempt to find these categories in order to cue the memory. A number of studies, however, show that people have a better recollection of events associated with their prior experience. If you know you are interviewing a plumber, you have a much better guess as to what some of his memory categories and associations might be if you study as much about plumbing as you can. Moreover, the better informed the oral history interviewer, the more likely it is that the necessary cues required to retrieve from either long-term or archival memory will be found.

In addition, candor compels me to observe that skills in interviewing itself will greatly enhance the density of the material retrieved from memory. For example, at one point in the interview where Howard was discussing his memories of Captain Moore, he started to tell the story of the captain's return from furlough in the United States and of his subsequently being wounded in his jeep by gunfire that killed his driver. Howard did in fact remember this incident and started to recount it when he was diverted by another description of the terrain and never got back to the original memory of what had happened to the captain. A more skillful interviewer would have brought the interviewee back to the interrupted narration.

Another, more serious gap in the narrative was caused by the same kind of interruption. Howard was describing the events at Restorf. He had previously described this incident to me and had reported that by the time it occurred he was able to watch a German soldier dying at his feet with little or no compassion. In an effort to correct my error, I reinterviewed Howard on July 4, 1988. The following is an excerpt from that interview:

AH: Howard, I would like to do a little bit of a follow-up interview on your description of the events that took place at Restorf. In the second interview you started to describe hearing the sound of mortars but subsequently discovering that they may not have been the mortars going off but had in fact been the sound of a Panzerfaust being fired at the other house, the house where the rest of your platoon was. You said that the guy who fired the Panzerfaust must have been drunk or on drugs because he held it up to his shoulder and it blew his arm off and killed him. You also said that in the morning "there were several German dead and wounded laying there, but I'll get to that later." This is all in the second interview. The problem is that you didn't get to that later. You got diverted by the description of the lieutenant who hid in the hay. So I'm wondering if you could now tell me—in the morning when you came out of the house, what did you find, and what did you do?

HH: After the armored vehicle came and relieved us, somebody prepared breakfast. I don't remember preparing it myself, but it's possible that I did. I remember that I had some kind of a mess kit, and I remember eating eggs and standing out there, looking at two freshly killed Germans, including one with his arm blown off. I also remember walking over to a third German who was across the road from the other house. He was severely wounded but was still alive. I remember standing looking down at him. His right hand was in his crotch and was constantly moving in a kind of twisting motion and his crotch was all bloody. He had a head wound and was very weak and was really out of it. Every now and then he would say "Wasser," as if he wanted a drink. I remember looking down at him and thinking that he was surely going to die. I was told later that someone gave him water and he died as a result of it. I knew he would die if he was given water because in addition to his head wound, he also had a stomach wound. Later, after he was dead I remember seeing that he had a corkscrew in his hand and he had been jabbing it into his penis and that's why his crotch was bloody. I remember thinking at that time that his head wound must have caused him to react this way. What is amazing to me is that I remember eating my eggs and not being disgusted by what I was seeing. I was so fed up and so hostile about what had happened that night that it didn't make any damned difference at all.

This horrifying memory was available, not repressed, but was also deleted from the narrative when Howard digressed to describe a lieutenant who had hidden throughout the skirmish. This digression would have been noticed by a more alert interviewer.

The density of the material retrieved from memory is also greater when events are taken in the sequence in which they occurred. One of the mind's major organizational categories seems to be chronological.

Bemis Frank, head of the Oral History Program of the U.S. Marine Corps, has interviewed hundreds of veterans. When we started this project we asked his advice. He said, "Begin when Howard first entered the army. It will improve the interview." Certainly when Howard was forced out of chronological sequence, he found it difficult to provide any narrative at all and created a recall document with significant deletions that he was able to redintegrate only after the first recall document had been used to cue other associations and storage categories. The implication is that interviews should not be unduly put off while the oral historian prepares. Probably preparation to engage your informants' attention, to make them feel that you are an informed listener, worthy of their honest and energetic effort, will be adequate. It's relevant here to observe that Howard's conversations with his buddies at the reunion, men who had been where he had been and had experienced what he had experienced, did not elicit much more from Howard's memory than had the simple and straightforward request: "Tell me about the war. And begin at the beginning."

Appendix 1
The Italian Campaign

Second Recall Document

AH: You landed in Naples?

HH: Yes, ultimately. Before we got to Naples we were near . . . the convoy looked like it stopped somewhere outside in Africa, because boats came up, you know, rowboats and canoes and dugouts and stuff came up on us, offering to sell things like fruit and shirts—you know, sport shirts and things like that. But you couldn't really make any kind of contact with the people down there, they were too far. You know those ships are pretty high. I don't remember anybody really able to buy anything from there.

Then a day or so later we docked in Naples. When we landed in Naples . . . Oh, geez, I seem to recall being on a train again, of some sort, but maybe not. I couldn't have gone too far outside of Naples. Naples had been bombed some, but it wasn't completely beat up. I don't remember very much about it, other than coming in there and there being lots of little Italian kids around, seeing women again for the first time in twenty-eight days. And going to the replacement depot, which was a big camp where we were in tents, slept on army cots in tents. Now, I must have gotten into Naples a couple of times, because . . . not into Naples, in around there, maybe it was . . . the name Caserta seems very much on the tip of my tongue, but I'm not sure it was Caserta that we were at.

I do remember going in there and seeing—it was around that time I sent a card to my mother and I've seen the card, the postcard that shows a little Italian kid in the middle of a town. You could get ice cream there; you could get ice cream almost anywhere. If there was a place that was open, they would have some kind of ice cream. Apparently the Italians invented it; it was very popular in Italy. Fresh food, spaghetti, and things like that I think I rarely saw or had an opportunity to get until I got to Rome. But I do remember going around in this area, and I think it was before I joined my company. They did give us some time off, and I was able to get into town and walk around a little bit, see the fountains. And there were always the kids trying to . . . acting as pimps for their sisters. You know, they'd come up to you and ask you if you wanted a "ficky-fick," they would say, or ask you if you had chocolate or soap or C-rations or K-rations they would take. Cigarettes. I didn't smoke at the time, so I could use whatever cigarettes I would get, you know, I'd give them to people for things that I was more interested in. I think I traded cigarettes for a cut cameo, without a frame around it, or little inlaid mosaics and things like this. Those were the souvenirs, very few souvenirs, that I picked up during the war.

AH: Okay, you were describing the replacement depot and what happened there.

HH: What happened there was that I got assigned to . . . eventually I got assigned to the Third Chemical Warfare Battalion. I don't think I was in the replacement depot for more than a week or two. Like I say, I remember we had a mess hall and latrines, showers, and things like that. It was a big place.

AH: Where was your outfit when you got assigned?

HH: Cassino. Somewhere near Cassino. I don't know exactly where. They were not on the line. They were back far enough so that you could hear the guns, way off in the distance, but it wasn't like we were right on the line itself. And I remember joining my outfit and they were in a tent, you know, a tent that was maybe ten or twelve feet across. In fact, it may have even been on a platform like the tents they have at camps, although I don't recall it being on a platform. There were cots, and I was given a cot and introduced to the guys in the thing and I was given a gun. I think a carbine.

AH: These were combat veterans now that you were being introduced to?

HH: Right. Right. They made me feel welcome, told me a little bit about combat but not much. I tried to fit in with them. I don't remember any of the names.

AH: By the way, I meant to ask you, did you get any news while you were on that ship?

HH: No.

AH: Was the paper *Yank* delivered to you or anything?

HH: No.

AH: No war news was given to you?

HH: There may have been a report occasionally, you know, that was read to us, you know, that had come in over the radio to the officers, but very little. And I don't remember anything printed being passed out.

AH: Right. Who was your commander?

HH: I don't know. I don't know who it was. We had somebody who—I keep thinking his name was Cooper, and I think he was from Louisiana, and he was a fairly young man, a captain. But I remember him from much later, from during the Bulge. In fact, it was during the Bulge that he was sent home for a furlough and came back again. And the name Cooper—I'm not sure it's Cooper, because Frank Cooper was the head of Haskins Lab, and I may have the names mixed up, but somehow the name Cooper seems appropriate for Captain Cooper, Captain Something.

AH: This was before the Battle of Cassino?

HH: No, the Battle of Cassino had been going on for months, if not a year.

AH: When did you first get into combat?

HH: May 11, I think, was the day at eleven o'clock in the morning on the day of May, somehow is what I remember. At Castelforte was the first place that I experienced any combat. They brought us up to Castelforte in trucks, and we unloaded hundreds and hundreds of rounds of ammunition, carried it up the mountainside to a place sort of a quarter of the way up the mountain, set up the guns, and then we were told that we were to start firing at a particular time.

Now, I think that we had set up the day before and it was the next morning that we were to start firing and the officer was there with a stopwatch, and he told us when to exactly drop the shells in. And the interesting thing is that just before we fired I could see the guns behind us firing, that is, hear the guns way, way back like the long toms, the 240 millimeter cannons which could fire for miles. The impression I got was that they had tried to time things so that all the shells would land at the same time even though the ones further away would fire sooner. That was the opening of my first experience of combat, was going into that.

AH: What kind of perceptions did you have of what the battles were about? Did any of the officers come to you to tell you that you were to take this strategic place and the reason that it was important was because this, that, or the other? Or were you just blindly told to dig a hole here and dig a hole there?

HH: Blindly told to dig a hole here and dig a hole there.

AH: So you had no sense of whether what you were engaged in was critical or not?

HH: No, none at all. They never told us what the hell we were really doing.

AH: Did the men develop their own ways of figuring out what the situation was that they were in?

HH: Nope. Not that I know of. Nobody knew what the hell was going on. I mean we knew if we had to take a town or if we had to go into, you know, fire at a particular place, but we didn't have any idea of what the big picture was, other than that we're pushing for the Elbe River or we're pushing for crossing the . . . going into Rome, pushing for Rome, something like that. But no knowledge of the big picture; they never told us what the hell we were doing or even where we were.

AH: Okay. Well, why don't you just start in and describe the Italian campaign from your perspective, then?

HH: Well, we fought with a lot of different people. When we made the push into . . . I'll just describe things as I recall them and remember how they happened, with some kind of temporal organization. I remember the firing of the guns at Castelforte, and then eventually, I think, we loaded into trucks and got driven into Castelforte and seeing this completely destroyed village. There was nothing left! Although there were some . . . I remember seeing an old woman and an old man that had somehow been there throughout this terrible bombing. They must have been down in a cellar somewhere and survived it. I remember seeing them. I also remember, you know, moving from the town, so that we were like maybe a half mile from the town in a ravine. And in that ravine there was a little tiny stream at the bottom of the ravine. It had kind of . . . the walls were kind of muddy. I remember having a foxhole dug into the wall of the ravine sort of. And one night—we were there for a couple of days—and I don't remember having the guns even set up there. I recall that everybody got fleas. I had fleas and they would be biting me, especially around under the belt and ankle legs, you know, wherever any clothing was tight against your body. That's where they would tend to congregate and bite. I remember dusting myself with flea powder many times but not being able to get rid of them for quite a while.

I recall one night there was a bombing attack—it couldn't have been too late at night, it must have been in the early evening. I remember this plane coming over and dropping bombs. I didn't see any bombs fall, but I heard them fall. And this plane flew directly overhead and it was low enough so that I could see the big crosses on it. It didn't have swastikas, it had German crosses on the plane, and it was painted white on the bottom or blue, bluish white. And it was a twin-engine plane of some sort, like a Junkers, and not very high; it was maybe 100-200 feet up in the air. I kept thinking, Jesus, what if it drops a bomb right on top of me. But it didn't. And nobody shot at it for some reason. It seemed to be going very, very slowly, but that may be just because of the way I remember it.[1]

I remember being there for a few days, and as I say, the thing that I remember the most is the fleas and getting flea powder to take care of it. We moved from there. . . . Now, it's all very, very hazy. The Italian campaign is really not very clear in my mind. Because I don't remember very often in Italy firing the guns. I remember mostly digging foxholes in various places, carrying ammunition, standing in line to eat, to wash my mess kit, because they would bring food up to us sometimes. You always washed your mess kit; they'd have two garbage pails over a fire, and one of them would have hot soapy water and the other would have regular water in it. You'd dip it in the hot soapy water first and swish it around, and maybe there'd be a brush tied to a chain or a cord and you'd run the brush over it, and then you'd dip it into the next one. Water would come out of a lister bag, usually, chlorinated, with chlorine tablets in it. You might fill your canteen with it. We ate K-rations and C-rations a lot. But we would make coffee, we'd have a pot somewhere, we'd get a pot and make coffee, and we'd often wash in our helmet, and dig foxholes everywhere we'd stop. But the thing that I'm not remembering in the Italian campaign is firing the guns. The only other place I can remember firing guns in Italy was at Pico, oddly enough. Now I remember one place that we stopped, and I remember trying to dig in. It was on a hillside. I can picture it. The thing that I remember about it in trying to picture it in the Italian campaign was that there was so many rocks that I was really almost unable to dig at all, so that what I wound up doing was building a kind of a cairn around . . . kind of a wall of stones and then lying down within that wall of stones and then having a pup tent, shelter half that I put over the top of it. Not because the shelter half protected me but because it made me feel much more safe to be covered.

I had no idea which direction the Germans might be in there or how close I was to the front. The event that I remember from there was that—maybe it's what makes that particular evening memorable—was that there was an air raid and it must have been close to my birthday in time. Because I have some feeling of my birthday being associated with it. And I remember lying on my back— now the shelter half, maybe I must have pulled it back or didn't have it up at that point—and watching the sky and seeing an air raid going on in the distance and hearing it in the distance and seeing all these tracer bullets going up into the sky. It was like eleven or twelve o'clock at night when this happened. Maybe it was earlier, it could have been earlier. But in any event, all of a sudden, a fellow who was a friend of mine, we were all sort of friends, he was—I somehow picture him as being a kind of raw-boned, not very well educated, but nice guy, big, heavyset guy, and young, about eighteen or nineteen, maybe. He jumps up, and he runs over to me, and he says, "Jesus Christ, can I spend the night with you?" And I said, "Yeah, why?" He said, "Something landed right next to my head and I'm just shook up." So I said, "Okay." And he spent the night with me in my foxhole, which was big enough. I don't remember why he did that except he said something had frightened him very much. And the next morning when he went to check, he showed me that there was a hole in his—he had laid down three or four layers of blankets and a shelter half on the ground and he hadn't dug anything in. And there was a hole right next to where his head would have been, maybe two inches from his head. A triangular-shaped cut in the blanket. He pulled the one blanket aside and it was through the next blanket and the next and the next, and then he pulled out of his pocket and he said, "Here's what I found when I dug down into the rock." And he showed me this 50 caliber machine-gun bullet that was bent in half, that had missed his head by maybe two inches at the most.

AH: How did he respond to that?

HH: You saw how he responded the night before. He said something had landed next to him. He carried that around I guess for the rest of his life. I don't know what happened to him ultimately, but I know that scared me plenty to see that thing and to realize what could have happened to him.

I remember from that period the Goumier and the stories about the Goumier. I don't remember actually fighting with them, that is in the sense of . . . because I can't recall firing the guns very much in Italy, but I remember going into places where they had been. For example, a farmhouse where they had been, maybe just a few hours before. I don't know why we were there at that point, but they were very primitive people. You would see them walking along the road, they were the French colonial troops, and they wore turbans, as I recall, and robes of like orange and yellow and red and blue, vertical stripes on the robes. And you would see them, they carried old rifles, the old Springfield rifles, not automatic rifles like we had, M-1s, if we had rifles, and we had carbines. They had the old bolt-action rifles of the sort that we had had for basic training. You'd see them carrying all kinds of loot that they had taken, and it was not uncommon to see a guy walking along with a live sheep on his shoulders with the legs tied in front, a sheep or a goat or making one walk alongside with a string or a rope. And they used to sacrifice them, I understand. I never saw the actual sacrifice, but I was told about it a couple of times, that they would cut the animal's throat and go in and take cups and canteens and things like that and drink the blood directly. They carried knives, wicked knives, and I was told they used to go out on patrol—even in the snow they would go out barefoot, that was the snows of Cassino now. Of course, it wasn't snowing when I was there, but it was sometimes very, very muddy, especially when I first joined the company was when there was so much mud. I do recall trying to walk through that mud and just having it suck on your boots and being ankle deep, or even knee deep in places, and just having a terrible time moving around if it rained, and it did rain a lot at first, when I was first there. But that's going back.

Continuing now with this story about the Goumier. The thing about that farmhouse was that they had defecated in every corner of the room. You know, they could have just as easily gone outside, but obviously chose not to, and making it impossible for us to stay in the house. There was an associated memory with that, there was, outside there, there was white tape with signs saying "mine field." There was an orchard with apples or oranges, I don't recall which, I think it was oranges, maybe. Could have been both, Anyhow I was told that the Goumier would just walk in there and get them even though the place was mined and it was known that they were mined. They would just take the chance and walk in and get the oranges and come out. It was the kind of people they were, fighters. They used to pay them by the ear. Again, this is apocryphal, in the sense that I was told the story, but I never verified it personally. That they would go on patrol, that they would stack their guns and go into the German lines with their knives and that they would kill them with knives and then come back and get paid by the number of ears that they brought back. And that the army had to stop doing that because they began to find their own dead, American dead, up there with no ears, the left ear I think it was that they would take off, one of the ears, had to be the same one. But I remember them walking along the road and us going by them in trucks or jeeps, with us sitting in the weapons carriers.

The next major memory I have really is of Pico. See, I don't remember any battles in between or very much, certainly setting up the guns and fighting. It's more that I recall moving and moving by truck, but I must have been there for a couple of months, even though I'm not able to remember it. What I remember of Pico, and I won't swear that this is the place, but it's the way it was described to me, you know, I remember it as being Pico. We arrived at night and it was a big mountain in the middle of a plain. I mean, all around there was a plain and there was this one big mound, like an anthill in the middle of a field, a large anthill. And we were at the foot of the mountain and the Germans were supposed to be on the other side, and we were supposed to shoot our mortars up over the top of the mountain and come down on the other side of the mountainside itself to hit some Germans and guns that were set up there. As we pulled in, we pulled into the road and then we had to carry our guns over maybe a couple hundred yards up to the edge of the mountain, the guns and the ammo. And there were these big clods of dirt lying in the road that we had to walk around and occasionally would step on to get over to where we were. And I just had the funniest feeling about those clods of dirt, as if there was, that they weren't really dirt, that they were maybe people or something like that. It wasn't exactly. . . . I didn't think it was people. It was that it was curious to see these clods of fresh dirt here and it was something that impressed me at the time that it happened.

So anyhow, we went in and we set up our guns, and I don't know whether I dug in or not, or what, but I recall it was quiet there. There was no shooting that I remember. I remember setting up, you know, my tent, my bedroll, or whatever it was and going to sleep and waking up in the morning with the most godawful odor. It was as if the odor had woken us up at like six o'clock in the morning and it was now beginning to be light. And the odor was just over-whelming, just absolutely. . . . I had never experienced anything like it before, and I don't ever want to experience anything like it again! It was just putrefica-tion of the worst sort. And all of us felt that way. I don't know where the officers were; we were just like a platoon of guys right there. The next thing I know we were given orders that we could move, and we went back and loaded everything back onto the trucks. And then I saw that what I had thought were clods of dirt were actually parts of bodies. Apparently there had been either bombs or machine guns or something had hit—it must have been shells, bombs—had hit several trucks of German soldiers. These were bodies and parts of bodies of German soldiers that were laying around in the road, and they had been there lying in the sun for maybe weeks as far as I know, because they were swelled. There was one guy, he was swelled up and he looked like you took a uniform and you put a balloon inside of it and you just blew it up, including the face. The face was like a big pumpkin, and as big as a pumpkin, smooth and where the eyes were were holes and there was no nose. It was almost just like a big circle. And the flesh was just sort of popping off of it and the odor was just so putrid. The interesting thing is that you could see that the guy had some jewelry on. This was at the beginning of when we were doing this and an hour later somebody in my outfit had gone and cut off the guy's fingers and hands. I don't know how the hell he could get there to get at that jewelry. I mean I can't imagine anyone would have done that. But somebody did it and it had to have been somebody from my outfit. Anyhow that was the first dead bodies that I had ever seen and I was horrified by what it looked like and by what it smelled like. Ugh, it makes me sick to even think about it!

AH: What happened next?

HH: They moved us back, about a half mile back. You could see the mountain in the distance and it was in a kind of . . . there was a little bit of a rise there, not much, and there was a cemetery, an Italian cemetery. They bivouacked us just in front of the cemetery, sort of at the gates of the cemetery, or just in front of the gates of the cemetery, a little bit down below. There was a truck, I remember, like an ammo-carrying truck. There was a little ditch that went along in there, a drainage ditch, but there was no water in it at this time, and I remember going up into the cemetery and looking around and seeing in the cemetery the following: that many of the bodies were kept in crypts in the wall, and there also were many graves, but it was mostly crypts. There were just a few graves, mostly it was crypts with coffins in them. And a lot of the crypts were very small, they had little tiny boxes about a foot by a foot by a foot or two feet by a foot by a foot that contained a pile of bones, and there would be a skull and some of the bones. I don't even think it was necessarily all of the bones of a person, and there was one that I remember seeing that had a kind of a bridal veil, but the rest were bones. In the two kind of rooms, in the gate there were like two gatehouses, and in them was a stone marble kind of platform they must have displayed a body on when they had a wake. Also somebody had pulled aside a trap door, a stone trap door in the floor and we looked down in there and you could see thousands of bones and skulls that had been thrown into this bone pile. Apparently what they would do is they would clean out the crypts in the walls periodically and throw them down in the bone pile and put new people in. That's how they did it. And I considered sleeping in that place. I think one or two of the guys did. But I didn't sleep there. I do remember lying down on the thing and considering it, but I finally made up my mind I was going to sleep down below. It was too eerie. Not that I was really so frightened, but it was kind of eerie. So I went down below near the trucks and I remember that I dug into the ditch and just slept in that ditch, widened it a little bit and slept in it or right next to it. And there was a lieutenant who had set up a little bit in front of me, and there were six guys who had dug their foxholes, they had actually dug foxholes in a star shape. One guy had dug a hole and then four others had dug around him. Now, the reason I remember that is because I went to sleep and I slept well, and the next thing I remember it was morning already and the lieutenant was shaking me and saying, "Get up, Hoffman, we've got to dig out a bunch of guys that have just got hit by a shell." And I get up and I go over there, and there where these five foxholes are is a big pit where a shell has come in and landed in the middle goddamned foxhole and there everybody is. . . . They're there. . . . It's killed all five of these guys. And I don't remember seeing anybody except this pit. And we started digging, mostly with our hands, and we dug up, as I remember, four guys and not one of them was hurt. Now I can't picture it any more. I seemed to think that last time I was able to say that I, you know, helped them up. But now I'm not able to picture reaching down and grabbing them. Like I can't remember that cat [in the gas chamber at Edgewood]. You know, I can't envision that cat, I wouldn't know whether it was a gray cat or a black and white cat. And now I can't remember reaching down and taking these guys out of the ground, but I'm sure that this is something that happened. As I remember, what I remember saying is that we took out four of them and all four were alive, and none of them were hurt, and they had been buried alive. But loosely by the dirt, but now I can't picture it any more. That's a memory that's . . . I can remember sort of standing there, I can remember. . . . I seem to think I have a shovel in my hand, I seem to think I'm pulling, but I can't picture lifting somebody up, coming across a person. The other thing is that the story, I can remember telling the story from four years ago, and I remember. . . . This is what I remember about it, that the shell landed, it had just missed the truck coming in. If it had hit the truck which was loaded with ammo, we'd all be dead. It just missed the truck and landed in the middle foxhole. And the concussion, apparently, went up above all the other guys and covered them without killing them. Now maybe they had been removed from the hole before I came along, but I remember the lieutenant telling, I do remember him physically waking me and saying that I had to come along and help dig these guys out. And the one who was in the middle—we couldn't find anything. And I remember digging and looking, and there was no trace of him. And we assumed that he had just completely disintegrated by the shell. Well, about an hour or two later he comes walking down the hill. He had gotten into a poker game or something the night before with some guys that had found a German dugout outside the cemetery, and he had gone and spent the night in the dugout with those guys. So that all of them were alive.

AH: By this time had you developed considerable camaraderie with these men?

HH: I suppose a fair amount by now, but I can't remember a single person from that group, what they looked like.

AH: You can't recall any names or any people?

HH: No, not at that point. Now later I'm going to be able to recall some names, maybe a name. But at that point I don't. I don't remember anyone.

AH: Okay, so finally they took Rome?

HH: Yes. But there was something to remember before that. I remember two things, two other things from the Italian campaign. One was at one point we were near a Goumier—I think it was Goumier—it may have been the Gurkhas. We fought with the Gurkhas, too, there. And the Gurkhas were British troops, black. We also fought with the Senegalese, by the way, a kind of scarification on their faces. But the Gurkhas I remember were small British—I don't know whether they were from India or where they were from. They wore the flat helmets, and they would not take a knife out but that it didn't draw blood. And I remember they would cut themselves on it. If they took their knife out to cut food or something they would nick their thumb before putting the knife away because it had to draw human blood for some reason. Also there was one thing that I do seem to recall, that either the Gurkhas or the Goumier, one group had white horses that they were on. Some of the men were riding on beautiful white horses and associated with that memory is seeing for the first time these amphibious craft that could go on land and also in the water. And I remember at one point we were in a field or near a field with a road, and on the road were these amphibious landing craft that could also go on land. They were being manned by, I believe, either the French or the British and one of the foreign troops was involved with this. The other thing I seem to remember is that whenever we would stop near a city, not a city, but we were often in Italy near towns, and I do remember that we must not have been fighting all the time in Italy because one of the things I remember—no, that must have been afterward. The garbage pit, we had a big . . . at the garbage pit there would be a rope, it would be roped off, the garbage pit was usually about six feet wide by six feet deep by six feet across and everybody would empty the garbage cans into that, but the kids used to be there and they would be begging for food and they would always have tin cans with a string attached, two holes punched in the top and a string over it, like a number ten, like they put quarts of tomatoes and things like that, and they'd bring these cans and beg us for whatever. . . .

HH: And then the one other memory I have from there that has impressed me so much was, they had a short-arm inspection one time in Italy and it was while we were still in combat. I don't know why they did it, but they had this tent sent up and this was like ten or fifteen feet across, army tent, medical tent. And there was a doctor standing in front of the tent and we all had to line up and one by one we had to "skin it back and milk it forward," is the way they would say it, and that was short-arm inspection. Inspecting for signs of gonorrhea or syphilis. Needless to say, I always passed, unless you could get it from . . . we didn't even have toilet seats. We always had to go in a latrine-type trench that several of us would dig. But in any event what made this so memorable was like it was a morning, maybe a Sunday morning maybe, and there's this line of fifty-sixty guys going by and there, not twenty or thirty feet away, is a whole row of Italian women standing there, watching and pointing and laughing as we went by. And I thought that was terrible. [Laughter] I don't know if they laughed at me or not, but they sure were having a good time.

Well, anyhow, the next thing that I remember about this was that we went into Rome. I remember riding into Rome, a triumphant victor riding on the jeeps, and having people screaming and hollering and cheering us as we went through the thing and throwing flowers.

AH: Very exciting!

HH: Very, very exciting, going into Rome. Because we liberated Rome. But I don't remember fighting to liberate Rome. I just remember going into it and being one of the first people and having the street lined with cheering crowds.

AH: How long were you in Rome?

HH: Not very long. We went into Rome, and we stayed there a couple of days, somewhere in Rome. I don't remember where the hell we were. I remember picking up and meeting this very pretty Roman girl and kind of going on a couple of walks through the park with her in Rome. But then the next thing that happened . . . I think maybe what happened was that we . . . I know what it was, we didn't stay in Rome. We bivouacked outside of Rome on the Appian Way. And I remember there was a big dairy barn and a row of trees on both sides of the road. I don't remember what the road was like, whether it was macadam or stone, but it was the Appian Way. It was outside of Rome by several miles; there was a large dairy barn there, the odor of the manure was clear, and in fact every time I smell cow manure I think of that place. And I remember that I had set up a tent with a close friend of mine right next to the road. We were down there, there were a whole bunch of us down there, but our tent was like ten feet from the road, inside of the field. It was almost a grass field, it was almost like a lawn, it was so nice. The name of the guy I can't remember; I keep thinking of Fernbach or something like that. But whatever his name was, you know, I have this vision of him, he was my age, he came from someplace near Rochester, as I recall, and he had glasses, he wore glasses, and maybe for that reason he was going to be sent home. And I don't remember what it was. It had to do with his eyes. But they considered sending him home. And he was supposed to leave the next day. We celebrated and to celebrate we had somehow gone into town. That's what we would do, we would go into town, hitch a ride into town usually with someone driving along the highway, army jeeps or so. Go into town—I had gotten a bottle of champagne, and we had some scotch, and that night we drank that whole bottle of champagne together in my tent. And it didn't seem like it was very powerful except that when we got up to answer the call of nature, neither one of us could walk. We had to crawl and kind of kneel down and pee and crawl back. We were so drunk. It was powerful, just incredible, because it didn't seem like it was that way. The next day, as I remember, he left and I never saw him again. And he was out of it.

Next I contracted malaria. Now, it's possible it was hepatitis, but they diagnosed it as malaria. What happened was that I got very sick. I had met this lovely girl in Italy. She was young, she was like seventeen or eighteen, as I recall, younger than I was, I think. But I got malaria and got sent to a hospital. I just got very, very ill, high fever, and they sent me to a hospital in Rome in which there were nurses, and it seemed like the nurses didn't speak any English. They may have been nuns at this hospital. And I was in a real bed for the first time in a year, more than a year. And then I was there for a day or two and then, as I remember, I remember being in a room. It was a private room, as I recall, old-fashioned room, old-fashioned hospital. The next thing I knew I was sent in an—I don't remember if I was in an ambulance or how I got there—but the next place I was was down in Anzio. They sent me down to Anzio. We had taken Anzio by that time, you know, everywhere up to Rome. I was in a hospital tent there on a cot with maybe a hundred other sick people. I just remember getting better there gradually and slowly, and we used to have to take Atebrin every day, and I took it routinely, but they diagnosed it. . . . At first they said, "You have hepatitis," but then they said, "You have malaria." And they treated it with quinine, which convinced me that they thought I had malaria. But it was between those two things, because they said I had a swollen liver or something, my liver was not right. And I think that's part of the hepatitis syndrome.

Anyhow, when I was starting to get better, I became friendly with one of the orderlies and one day he appeared, one evening, and he says, "I got something good for us to drink." And I said, "What is it?" He says, "You'll see." And he poured a glass of orange juice out of a can, canned orange juice, for me and himself. Then he reached into his pocket and he took out a little eyedropper with some stuff in it and he squirted it into the orange juice and said, "Here. Drink this." So I drank, and it turned out what he had was ether. And we drank this ether in the orange juice, and I'll tell you, it blew my mind. I got drunk as could be, very quickly. But it smelled like ether, it tasted ghastly, but we did get very drunk.

Eventually I was free to walk around a little bit, and I walked around Anzio, went up and climbed the mountain next to it, and saw where they were—and Christ almighty! you know, the Germans were looking right down their throats. You couldn't go out to take a pee that they wouldn't see you and shoot off your pecker if they wanted to.

AH: At the beach?

HH: Yes, at the beach. We were on the beach. That's where the hospital was, at the beach at Anzio. It was a ghastly place. I'm very glad I wasn't there. It was really destroyed. Also I remember, one thing about there, I remember seeing a village nearby and making a turn and seeing you know, kind of like an inn on the edge. . . . well, this may have been later when we went back near Naples, but wherever it was they told me that the Germans had occupied that place and there had been some kind of a shooting there. They had shot some civilians there.

AH: Do you remember the name of the place?

HH: No. Caserta? No, it couldn't have been Caserta. Well, the next thing that happened is that when I was better, I rejoined my outfit. I don't think I rejoined them in Rome. I think the next thing I knew I rejoined them and they were camped on a beach. I remember one name from the group there on the beach, on the Mediterranean, and that's Harkavy. He was just a very bright young Jewish guy, and what he did eventually, he became a professional card player and ran a bridge club—he used to play bridge all the time when he was there, too. I never played bridge, but down in Miami Beach he set up a bridge club.

AH: After the war?

HH: After the war, and ran it, and my dad knew him. I never saw him again. Oh, well, maybe I met him once after the war. I may have met him once, yes. I seem to remember that. There was one incident on the beach that I remember, and that was, we were firing our guns, practicing. There are several instances that I remember that I ought to tell you about. Can I do this later though?

AH: No. Let's finish, because we are just so close.

HH: What I remember is that we were out there practicing firing the guns; we were actually firing ammo and I remember learning and being able to discover there that I could actually see the shells going along and seeing how far they would go. You could shoot—that 4.2 mortar would shoot about a mile, as I recall—5,000 feet, I think, was the maximum range that it had. And I'm not sure it had that much range, but anyhow, we had the guns down in the beach in kind of dug-in embankments with, I remember, sandbags around them, some sandbags, and lots and lots of ammo and one of the guns, a spark, maybe a cigarette, lit the nitrocellulose that was on the stacked-up shells, and there was a huge flash, not an explosion, but a big flash, whsssssssssh, like that, of fire, a ball of fire, and five or six guys got very badly burned, singed, and burned, and had to be hospitalized. I don't recall if we saw them again.

Two other things that I remember . . .

AH: How many men were in a mortar crew?

HH: I think, the number that comes to mind is something like eight. Now, I remember that there's the guy who drops the shell in and then there's . . . two guys can fire a mortar. One can fire a mortar if he has to. But you need several to keep you supplied with shells.

AH: And these crews tended to stay together, these eight people worked together all the time?

HH: Yes, they tended to.

AH: So you were starting to say something else.

HH: Two other things that I remember from that period. I do remember, I have this strong image of living in this pup tent in this sandy place and kind of enjoying it, going into town occasionally.

AH: What was the town?

HH: I don't know. It was near Naples, as I remember, but I don't remember the name of the town. We were on the beach. It seemed like to the south of us was a city of some sort. Not Naples but an outskirt of Naples. There was also . . . one of the things I remember is going and stealing fruit. We stole some melons from a field nearby one night, a couple of us. I also remember going into the town periodically. I remember there was another incident that I remember and that was that there was a grotto nearby; it was something that had been cut out of the rock right by the sea, maybe like a castle or rooms that had been literally carved out of the rock. There was straw on the floor in some of the rooms. It was reasonably clean, but, you know, it wasn't lived in exactly but had been at some point. I remember going through that with people, and thinking how beautiful it was by the sea there and what it was like.

AH: You mean this was like an old castle or ruin or something?

HH: But it wasn't built. It was carved out of the rock.

AH: Right. But it was from . . .

HH: Prehistoric.

AH: Prehistoric times, or something?

HH: Yes, yes, very, very old. But square. I remember the carving, it was cut like the rooms were square.

AH: Sort of like Mesa Verde?

HH: They weren't built! They were carved out of a solid piece of rock. It was all one piece of rock with these caves carved out of it. The other thing I recall is they had us doing rifle grenade practice. Now, ordinarily when you fire a rifle grenade, you brace the rifle on the ground because the grenade fits on the end of the rifle and it shoots the grenade off with a powder charge and there's a lot of recoil. For some reason I felt that I could fire it from my shoulder without breaking my shoulder, and I did. I remember firing that rifle grenade from my shoulder and being successful with it. I think I was the only one who did it or one of the few that did that. The third thing that I remember from being there was that we were supposed to . . . By now I think I had already started being a forward observer, so I must have had some combat experiences as a forward observer, but I can't remember any of it in Italy.

Appendix 2
Daily Log

Company C. Third Chemical Mortar Battalion

1 May to 31 May 1944: In Italy

1-6 May. The Company remained in Battalion bivouac area 1/2 mile W. of Cappelle(C). On 6 May, S/Sgt. Garland Gore departed for the United States on rotation. Casualties: None.

7 May. The Company remained in battalion bivouac area. At 0001B hours, the Company became attached to the 4th RTT of the 3 DIA per SO #76, CEF, dated 4 May 1944. Casualties: None

8 May. The company remained in battalion area. Capt. Moore, Co. CO, contacted Col. Gilbaud, CO of the 4th RTT and received orders to make a reconnaissance. Casualties: None

9 May. The Company remained in battalion area. Capt. Moore with Lt. Cota, S/Sgt. Cox, of the 1st Plat. and Lt. Muschany and Sgt. Baugh of the 2nd Plat. made a reconnaissance in Castelforte sector and selected OP's and GP's. One OP was selected in Suio and one at 1-1/2 mile S. of Suio. Both the Plat. GP's located in draw at 880991(A). At 2000B hours, two trucks were sent up with advance party to prepare position. Lt. Muschany was in charge of the advance party. Casualties: None.

10 May. The Company spent the day in preparation for the move to the forward area. The Company departed from battalion bivouac area at 2100B hours. There was much traffic on the road. The last truck was unloaded at the gun position 0230B hours, May 11th. The night was quiet and no enemy shelling. Casualties: None

11 & 12 May. The men were busy digging in gun positions and moving ammo. during the morning. Both platoons ready to register at 1300B. Lt. Muschany and Lt. Saint were at OP in Suio. Lt. Cota was at OP located at 877975(Al) and had radio control. Registration took place at 1730B. The ammo. was prepared for three missions starting at 2300B, 11 May. The 2nd Plat. started initial concentration at that time. The attack was slower in progressing than expected and required more Mortar support than scheduled. At one time the ammo. was nearly exhausted but more ammo. was reported to be at the old "A" Co. dump by Capts. Hoffman & Fallwell who visited the Regimental PC about 1200B, 12 May. More ammo. rolled in by 1400B from "A" Co. dump and also from Bn rear near Cappelle which was hauled up by "C" Co. trucks. The trucks crossed the Garigliano in broad daylight. One truck was kept near CP to facilitate any moves of ammo. or personnel. Communications were established with "D" Co. by cooperation of "D" & "C" Co. communication sections. The line was about 5 miles long and very difficult to maintain. After registering in, the GP received about 12 rds of Jerry Mortar fire. Powder rings on prepared ammo. were ignited. Pvts. Aciz, Devivi & Masterson succeeded in removing the burning shells to a safe distance from the other ammo. Pvt. Aciz was badly burned on his hand but refused to be evacuated. The Regimental PC moved at 1800B. Lt. Jones was the Company's liaison officer and moved with them. Radio communications to the PC were established. One of Co. "C" men on duty with Hq Co. Smoke Detail near Tiger Bridge was a casualty. The missions of both platoons from 2300B, 11 May thru 12 May were as follows:

Platoon	Target	Time	Rounds Fired
2nd	852999(B)	2300-0700	1037 HE
1st	861001(C)	1015-1025	252 HE
1st	861001(C)	1145-1200	200 HE
1st	855995(D)	0831-0836	220 HE
1st	861001(C)	1025-1030	279 HE
1st	855997(E)	0640-0650	87 HE
1st	Hill 185	1600	4 WP
		Total	2075 HE & 4 WP

The firing for these two days was in support of the 4 RTT of the 3 DIA. Casualties: Two

13 May. Both the 1st & 2nd platoons fired missions during the early morning. The missions were ordered from the Regimental PC by radio, Cpl. McCorkle operating. A heavy concentration was ordered from 1155 to 1205B. This mission was called off at 1145B as French troops now occupied the area. 800 rds of ammo. had been prepared. Orders were received to make a reconnaissance N.W. of Castelforte for new Mortar positions. A suitable position was found in S.S. Cosma e Damiano-846994(F) and Lt. Cota had 1st Plat. in position before dark with 500 rds ammo. Bad road congestion was caused by tanks on road ready to break thru Damiano. The 2nd Plat. remained in present position to be ready to shuttle by 1st Plat. A few snipers continued to fire into Damiano but were cleaned out before morning. A few shells threw rocks and debris into gun position of 1st Plat. during the night. The missions of the day were as follows:

Platoon	Target	Time	Rounds Fired
1st	860001(G)	0800-0805	104 HE
2nd	859998(H)	0700-0710	50 HE
2nd	857999(I)	0700-0710	50 HE
			204 HE

The missions were in support of 4 RTT of the 3 DIA. Casualties: One.

14 May. No missions fired. Capt. Moore went to the Regimental CP in the morning. Lt. Cota returned from his OP on Hill 298 with bad shrapnel wound in right bicep. He received treatment at Regimental Aid Station. He was then

taken forward to the 3rd Cml Bn Aid Station by jeep. Both Lt. Cota and Cpl. Harkavy believed the shelling to be a heavy barrage from 120 mm Mortars. After preparing excellent gun positions Jerry was on the run and completely out of range. Prisoners kept pouring into the Regimental PC faster than they could be evacuated. The count by noon was 320 and still rising, including many officers. Prisoner officers from "C" & "D" Co. target areas reported that they had never before been subjected to such barrages. They estimated more deaths than casualties. Lt. Quarantillo, CO of Co. "D" moved in vicinity of 2nd Plat. during the afternoon. Lt. Saint is liaison officer with 4 RTT as his platoon is very close by. The 4 RTT is now in reserve and reorganizing. Both the platoons of the Co. are resting. Casualties: None.

15 May. No missions fired by either platoon. Capt. Moore, Co. CO visited 4 RTT in the morning. No new developments. The 4 RTT is in reserve. The 1st Plat. is in S.S. Cosma e Damiano(J). The 2nd Plat. is still near Pantano(J1). The Co. is maintaining liaison with Regiment by SCR 300 radio, a distance of about 2 3/4 miles. The radio communication works very well. The reception is always clear. The scrambled alphabet code is used with good results. The afternoon was quiet. At about 2215B, the Luftwaffe tryed to work over Castelforte and S.S. Cosma e Damiano. From the CP at Pantano they seemed to be landing directly on the 1st Plat. Capt. Moore together with Sgt. Edmondson and T/5 Gustavson traveled part way up there by jeep and walked remainder of the way. An ammo. dump 150 yds S. of 1st Plat. had been hit and was ablaze. The Regt. reported that parachutists had been dropped in the town. The remainder of the night was quiet. Casualties: None.

16 May. No missions fired. Liaison officer from 3 DIA delivered message for both "C" & "D" Cos. to move up toward Ausonia, both Cos. being atchd to 3 RTA. Capt. Moore & Lt. Quarantillo, CO of Co. "D" prepared to contact the 3 RTA CP. Capt. Fallwell, 3rd Cml Bn S-3, arrived and the two Co. Comdrs. and he traveled to Castlenuovo where Col. Linares gave them more specific orders. One platoon was all he needed at the time to fire on area N. of Monte Bastia, in support of 2nd Bn, 7 RTA. Reconnaissance was made and GP selected near Selvacava. It was decided to move 2nd Plat. of "D" into GP while "C" Co. and rest of "D" Co. move up to vicinity of Coreno, in readiness. While CO Co. "D" established liaison with 2nd Bn, Capt. Moore went back to bring up the Cos. "C" Co. moved into bivouac at 817033(A) at 1800B. Capt Fallwell furnished liaison at the Regt. for both Cos. The battle for the Northern slopes of Mt. Fammera was watched from the Co. bivouac. Casualties: None

17 May. Capt. Moore & Capt. Fallwell, Bn S-3 visited the 2nd Plat. of Co. "D". They had fired for the 0530B attack but at the present were out of range. The Regimental CP received orders to move the Cos. to area 1-1/2 miles N. of Ausonia(B), completed move at 1130B. Capt. Moore spent the afternoon at the Regimental CP watching the battle and awaiting developments. The French troops occupied Esperia at 1300B. At 1800B, Capt. Moore received orders from Col. Linares to make a reconnaissance for gun positions. Targets hadn't yet been fired upon but general direction of fire was to be N.W. Position was selected at 739093(A). The trails into the position were several feet high with rocks and debris, so two squads of men were sent in advance to clear the roads. The Co. completed the move by 2300B and was ready to fire by 2400B. A preparation of 1/2 hour duration was to be fired on 4 targets. 540 rds HE were fired. After the push at 0400B 18 May, no other targets were in range. A few enemy Mortar shells dropped in the position and quite a number in S. Pietro, but caused no casualties. Casualties: One.

18 May. No missions fired. Capt. Moore contacted Col. Linares and Col. Guilband, the 4 RTT CO at Via Bergamaschi 1 mile SE of Monticelli. There was a conflict in the division orders as to which Regt the Co. is atchd to. The Co. became atchd to 3 RTA and rec'd orders to prepare for a move. At 1600B, trucks moved up and loaded both platoons and pulled into assembly area close by at 752090(B). Quite a few Jerry shells dropped below the area during the night. The Co. has maintained contact with Lt. Jones, Ln 0 at the Regt by means of radio. Casualties: None.

19 May. No mission fired. The Co. was awakened at 0520B by a heavy enemy shell burst close by that sounded like a delayed action bomb. Several men called for help about 20 feet away. Sgt Edmondson was lying with a lump of dirt the size of a bedroll on his chest and with a cut on his face. Capt Moore found no severe cuts on him so ran to the other calls and found Pvts Ryan and McGrady, the two first aid men, and Pvts Depresco and Childress buried in their slit trenches with only their heads exposed. Sgt Toscano's squad was summoned for help and the two First Aid men were soon on their feet and uninjured. Pvts Depresco and Childress, however, were deeply buried and Pvt Aciz worked some 15 or 20 minutes digging them out. Pvt Childress was lifted onto a stretcher but Pvt Depresco, who was underneath and somewhat protected, scrambled out and onto his feet. Sgt Edmondson, Pvts Childress and Depresco were sent back to Bn Forward Aid Station. Since the Jerries were on the run, the Regt. had no definite mission for the Co. and, therefore, was moved North of Ausonia to 788075(C). Capt Moore reported back to Col. Linares and rec'd orders to make a reconnaissance in area of Monticelli for gun positions. No suitable GP's were found there but found a good position near S. Oliva. However, the bridge across the river was just under construction and the rain was continually washing out the approaches. They thought it would be pass-able by 2000B. The 2nd Plat. under Lt Muschany, was brought into position at 698131(B) by 2400B, 4 guns being all that were required. The Plat atch'd to 2nd Bn, 3 RTA. Casualties: Two.

20 May. No missions fired. The French troops pushed beyond the mortar range soon after daylight without requiring any support. The 3 RTA CP was located in S. Olivia. The Co. has orders to stand by for possible move, but roads to the N.W. looked doubtful for the trucks. Co. Linares offered mules but declined, knowing that the French troops need them. Capt. Moore was with 2nd Plat. located near S. Oliva. Everything was very quiet during the day. The 3RTA expected to be placed in reserve soon. Capt. Moore was ordered to make reconnaissance for new gun positions. No good positions were found. The only possibility was a draw at 683153. The Co. was ordered to move up but found that one platoon could do the job. Casualties. None.

21 May. The 1st Plat. moved into position at 683153(C). The move was completed after midnight. The initial mission to be fired at 0700B was called off and guns were placed on a defensive sector. At 1900B, the 1st Plat. was reld from 2nd Bn and atch'd to 3rd Bn, 3 RTA. The radio communications were not clear and the line was not yet in when Jerry formed a tank and infantry force to storm Mt. Leucio. Capt. Moore made it back to the 1st Plat. GP in record time and Lt. Saint soon had his guns blazing. 155 rds HE were fired at 685175(D), between 2030 and 2045B. This mission put Jerry and his tanks out of commission or else back across the Liri River. Total rds fired: 155 HE. Casualties: None.

22 May. No mission fired. The 1st Plat. now practically out of range. A big push toward S. Giovanni was planned which would require the support of the whole Company. No suitable mortar positions were found, but a spot behind Hill 227(E) was selected for the 2nd Plat. and another position located at 667177(F) was selected for the 1st Plat. The 1st Plat. was able to start moving in during the afternoon but observation prevented the 2nd Plat. from moving until dark. However, before they could complete their move, the first objectives were taken by the French with ease and the 1st Plat. would be able to give all the support needed. Telephone communications were established with the Regimental PC which was only a few hundred yards away on HIll 227. The 1st Plat. was ready to fire by dark, but no missions were given until the following morning when the attack was made. Casualties: One.

23 May. The 1st Plat. fired for the early attack as follows:

Time	Target	Rds Fired
0445-0455B	654189(G)-663191(H)	150 HE
0500-0515B	647198(I)-655196(J)	235 HE
0955-1010B	647198(I)-655196(J)	*363 HE*
	Total	*748 HE*

The above missions were fired at enemy infantry and mortars in support of 3 RTA, 3 DIA. The progress of the attack was slow as stiff resistance was met. At 0950B, the French broke thru. At noon a counterattack was feared on the right flank and the mortars were set up on that sector and ammo. was prepared. At dusk, the 1st Plat. was given another sector to defend, but were never called on to fire. During the morning, PFc Ashley & Pvt M.J. Miller received serious shrapnel wounds. The Jerry fire was intense throughout the day. Casualties: Two.

24 May. No missions fired and Co. remained in position. The Co. was awakened at 0330B by Jerry planes. The sky was lit up by their flares, planes were directly overhead for 1/2 hour or more but all their eggs were laid a safe distance away. Casualties: None.

25 May. The 1st Plat. fired an early mission for the French attack from 0910 to 1010B. The target was 647203(A) (Overlay #20) and a total of 140 rds HE & 40 rds WP were fired. The GP located at 667170(K) (Overlay #19). The target was a road cut, where enemy troops and vehicles had been observed entering. The observation was very good from Hill 227; with phone control to the GP. The mission itself had been given to Lt. Jones, Ln 0 at 3 RTA and was practically out of range. Capt. Moore contacted Col. Linares about 1300B and was given new targets. Another GP would be necessary so sent back to S. Oliva for the 2nd Plat. The Plat.streamlined and moved up on jeeps and trailers for a 1730B attack. Reconnaissance was completed by Capt. Moore, Lt. Muschany and Sgt. Baugh. A good GP was selected at 648182(L) (Overlay #19) and the 2nd Plat. moved in and guns were set up. However, the objectives were taken without the need of mortar support and once again were out of range. Another GP was selected at 626188(B) (Overlay #20) and by 2300B the entire 2nd Plat. was set up ready to fire on the sector North of Mt. Cervaro. The opposition again crumbled without a shot being fired. Total expended during day: 140 HE & 40 WP. Casualties: None.

26 May. No missions fired. Capt. Moore was ordered to make a reconnaissance for GP to cover targets well to the North of S. Giovanni. Col. Linares was contacted just before starting on reconnaissance and it was learned that the 3 RTA had been reld. A Company bivouac area was located at 654166(C), both platoons moved in together with the Company Rear. The entire Company was in bivouac by 1900B. Casualties: None.

27 May. The Co. was reld from atch'd to 3DIA at 270000B and reverted to Bn control per Order #91, CEF, dated 27 May 1944. Capts. Hoffman & Fallwell visited the Co. during the morning and informed Capt. Moore that Co. would have to move. Later in the day it was learned that all Cos. had been reld and that Bn was placed in Corps reserve. Capt. Hoffman secured permission for the Co. to remain in present area. Casualties: None.

28 May. The Company remained under Bn control. Usual bivuoac duties. Hot cakes were served for breakfast. Casualties: None

29-31 May. The Company under Battalion control. Remained in position(C) and performed usual camp duties. Casualties: None.

3rd Division Infantry Algerian
General Order No. 162

Officer, Non-commissioned officers and Soldiers of 3 DIA, of 7 RCA, of 17/27, 21/26, 15/31 Pack Cos of the 2 Armoured Group, of the 3 Chemical Battalion, of the Meyer and Godfrey Artillery Groupments, following your magnificent successes at Monna Casale and Belvedere, the High Command reserved a place worthy of you in the battle of Italy.

This was to collaborate in the breaching of the Gustave line and to push straight on as far as possible, without permitting the enemy to reorganize.

You accomplished this task in a magnificent way.

After having broken through at Castelforte, you defeated the enemy wherever he tried to stop you; you smashed through the fortified Adolf Hitler line and you went far beyond the objective which was assigned you, thus aiding the attack of those on our flanks.

In vain the enemy hurled in front of you reserves drawn from distant sectors and his best troops, from his elite grenadiers to his most modern tanks.

Castelforte, Coreno, Ausonia, Esperia, Monticelli, San Oliva, Pico, San

Giovanni, are among the victorious names which mark the glorious road that you opened—the road to Rome.

The example of your heroes who fell in this operation will soon open the road to France.

CP 29 May 1944
General de Division de Goislard de Monsabert
Commanding 3 Algerian Infantry Division
signed: de Goislard de Monsabert
Official: Lt. Colonel Pardes
Chief of Staff
G-1
/S/ Pardes

Distribution:
C.O. 3 Chemical Battalion.

Certified a True Translation
(Signed) W. P. Galvin
Capt. Infantry

Excerpts 15 August to 30 August 1944: In Southern France

15 August. The Company became atch'd to the 30th Inf Regt of the 3rd Infantry Division while in Italy and trained with the Regt for the Amphibious Operation in Southern France. Company "C" Liaison party unloaded on Red Beach with 30th Inf Regimental Hqs at H plus 80 as scheduled. The Infantry had light casualties. Company "C" made landing without any casualties. Lt. Slater stayed with Regt and Lt. Plaster remained on beach to bring in any men or vehicles if they unloaded. Lt. Muschany and 11 E.M. got off on Red Beach at 2000B. No missions fired during day by the Company. Casualties: None.

16 August. Lt. Plaster learned that Red and Yellow Beaches had made contact and he got a ride to Yellow Beach to meet the 10 drivers and Jeeps which unloaded about 2000B, the previous day. Sgt. Hogg and 5 E.M. with him for the Smoke Detail mission unloaded at approximately H -15 on D Day on Yellow Beach. The personnel on Derbyshire were unloaded on Yellow Beach at 1200B. Two E.M. unloaded on Red Beach with 2, 2-1/2 Ton Trucks at approximately 2000B. No missions fired during day. Casualties: None. One E.M. RTD 5 Aug 1944.

17 August. Lt. Slater was given one Jeep and Trailer. Lt. Plaster took 2nd Plat. and endeavored to contact 30th Inf Regt. He left from Bn assembly area 4 miles S. of St. Tropez. He first went to Collobriers, but Regt had moved to Gonfaron. He then proceeded to Gonfaron but Regimental Hqs had moved to Flassans. Lt. Plaster pulled off road approximately 2 miles S. of Flassans and contacted the Regt at about 1800B. The Regt atch'd the 2nd Plat. to 2nd Bn of the 30th Inf Regt, which had their CP set up near Brignoles at 057295. The Bn CO had the Plat. go in position at 044296(B) (See Overlay #2), to prepare to fire on Brignoles and surrounding valley and hills 567 and 436. Brignoles had an unknown number of Jerries in it. A German 88 knocked out an American Tank about 300 yards ahead of the CP on the road. The Plat. was not called on to fire and everything was comparatively quiet during the night. Casualties: None.

18 August. The American Infantry and Tanks kicked off from their line of departure at 0700B. Line of Departure was on the 04 Grid. The 2nd Plat. fired 10 rds HE to register in on Town of Brignoles at 0630B, and saw some Jerries run about. At 0710B, Plat. fired approximately 50 rds WP and put down a beautiful smoke screen in rear edge of Town to screen advance of Tanks and Infantry. A large enemy ammo. dump in Town was hit by one of the Platoon's Mortar shells which caused it to start burning and after about 10 minutes went off with a terrific explosion, sending timber, clouds of smoke and dust hundreds of feet into the air. A Major in the 2nd Bn, 30th Inf Regt was well pleased. Lt. Hull went back to Bn to get ammo. and rations. The 2nd Plat. moved their GP to better defilade. Lt. Plaster went back to the rear to see Lt. Muschany. It was decided that the 1st Plat. would move up with the 2nd Plat. on 19th August. This position was at 047296(C). Total Ammo. fired during day: 10 rds HE & 50 rds WP. Casualties: None.

19 August. Town of Brignoles was cleard of Germans by 1000B. The 30th Inf Regt CP moved into Town about noon. The 2nd Plat. was reld of support of 2nd Bn. The Company moved in afternoon to just East of Tourves. The first Elements of 30th Inf Regimental Hqs moved to St. Maximum during the evening. This included Liaison Section. Lt. Plaster contacted Lt. Slater in St. Maximum and then moved Company near St. Maximum at 864326 (A) (See Overlay #2), on S. side of road. Three trucks sent to old Company dump to move Ammo. The morale of the Company continues to be excellent. No missions fired during the day. Casualties: None.

20 August. Lt. Plaster contacted Regt at St. Maximum about 0730B. Received orders for 1st Plat. to support the 2nd Bn which was moving up Highway #7 towards Aix. The 3rd Bn to have 2nd Plat. atach'd and to move up thru Pourrieres, Vauvenavgues and St. Marc towards Aix. Both Platoons moved out approximately 0830B and contacted their respective Regimental Commanders. The 2nd Plat. went into position at 544425 (D) at 1300B. They received sporadic small arms fire at their position for a short time. The Plat. observer gave orders to fire on advancing enemy troops. They fired 15 rds on the target and was credited with killing or wounding fourteen out of fifteen Krauts. The Regimental CP ordered unobserved fire on an enemy 88 mm AA gun located in the outskirts of Aix. 60 rds rapid fire were delivered on said target and Plat. was credited with a hit on the gun. The 2nd Plat. then stood by for further orders the remainder of the day. The 1st Plat. went into position at 553400 (E) at 1600B, but did no firing. The 2nd Plat. fired 75 rds HE. Casualties: None.

21 August. The 1st Plat. began interdictory fire on RR Trestle in the area of 530395 (F) (See Overlay #3), aiding the mission of the supported units. Mission was completed at 0900B, 87 rds HE & 1 rd WP expended. At 1600B, the 1st Plat. changed Battalions and was put in support of the 1st Bn, 30th Inf Regt. The Plat. moved to an assembly area N. of Aix at 501442, move completed by 1800B. The 2nd Plat. was alerted at 0600B to support attack on City of Aix. The 2nd Plat.

observation party entered Aix with Bn observation party at 0845B. No resistance met except a few rds of small arms fire. The Plat. did not fire during the attack, but was given march order at 1330B, moved into Aix, and ordered to move into position 1 mile N. of Aix to support road block. Moved into this position at 1800B. At 2000B, Plat. was ordered to move with 3rd Bn, 30th Inf Regt into position 1.3 miles NW of Ecuilles, and moved out of convoy at 2130B. Total Ammo. expended by 1st Plat. 87 rds He & 1 rd. WP. Casualties: None.

22 August. The 1st Plat. left assembly area N. of Aix at 0400B and arrived at another assembly area (450423) just before daylight. They were informed by Lt. Plaster at 0900B that Plat. was reld from support of 1st Bn and put in support of 2nd Bn. They moved into position at 358421 (G) and set up guns on Road Junctions to N. & W. in support of Road Blocks. No rds were fired. At 0600B, Plat. received march order, approximately 0800B moved into an assembly area at 378436 and also at the same time received orders that it was once more with the 1st Bn. 250 rds HE, 150 rds WP on vehicles and 138 rds HE & 106 rds WP in area at 358421. The 2nd Plat. arrived in position 1.3 mile NW of Ecuilles at 0430B, stood by for further orders and at 1630B moved into new position NW of Ecuilles. Platoon received another march order at 2000B and moved into position on the outskirts of Salon, where they set up firing by Company on this date. Casualties: None

23 August. At 0030B, Capt. Hunt from 30th Inf Regt arrived at 1st Plat. assembly area and guided it to the 1st Bn, 30th Inf Regt. The 1st Plat. was in position at 243596 (I) by 0800B. At OP was established at 237597 (J). At 1230B, orders were rec'd to set guns on targets near Lamanon. Lt. Saint went with Company "A" and sent fire orders back by telephone (radio communications failed). At 1430B, 1st Plat. received orders for a barrage preparatory for the attack. 30rds HE & 4 rds WP were expended. The mission was completed in 15 minutes, but all guns were out of action because of soft soil on slope of Hill. The American Infantry reported that they occupied the Town without casualties which could not have been done without the preparatory barrages of Mortar and Artillery fire. At 1600B, a fire which had been smouldering in the woods above the gun position was suddenly fanned by the wind and descended rapidly on the Plat. GP. Plat. was forced to move in such a hurry that some small items of equipment were lost. In approximately one hour, the Plat. was set up ready to fire on same targets and in two hours all things were in order again. The 2nd Plat. moved to position S. of Salon at 1030B, and awaited orders remainder of the day and did no firing. Total Ammo. expended during day: 30 rds HE & 4 rds WP. Casualties: None.

24 August. The 1st Plat. maintained position until 1200B, when the guns were placed on Azimuths 5700, 5800 and 5900 to aid in support of Road Block to the North. The OP was maintained at 237597 until 1800B. No firing during the day. The 2nd Plat. remained in position S. of Salon throughout the day, but did no firing. Platoon was alerted for movement at 1930B, but did not move. No missions fired by either Platoon. Casualties: None.

25 August. Lt. Plaster was informed by a Lt. Col, the 30th Inf Regt Exec O, that the Company had been released and was to pass to control of the 3rd Cml Bn for a road movement to Apt. Both platoons were notified and returned to Bn, arriving there at 1200B. The remainder of the day devoted to care and cleaning of equipment. No firing during the day. Casualties: None.

26 August. The Company was under Bn control. Headquarters, "C" & "D" Companies pulled out of bivouac area W. of Aix at 0900B. The route followed was: Aix, Veneilles, Mayrargues, Peyrolles, Mirabeau, Pertuis, Cadenet and Apt. A bivouac area was set up for the night about 2 miles W. of Apt. No firing.

27 August. Hqs, "C" & "D" Companies moved out at 0830B from bivouac area. The route followed was: Pernes, Les Fountains, Carpentras and pulled in a bivouac area about 3 miles E. of Beaumes at 1030B. Both Protestant and Catholic services were held in the area at 1115B. The Company stood by all afternoon for orders. The Company was alerted about 1800B and informed that Companies "A" & "B" were atch'd administratively to the 7th & 15th Inf Regiments respectively and that the remainder of the Bn was atch'd to VI Corps and would be used as part of a Task Force. The Bn (-Cos. "A" & "B") was to move out for VI Corps as soon as gasoline arrived. Gasoline finally arrived and Company got on the road at approximately 2315B. No missions fired by the Company. Casualties: None.

28 August. The Bn moved N. thru Malaucene, Vaison, Nyons, Rosans and pulled in an area about 1 mile E. of Serres at 0530B. The men had their breakfast there and Bn pulled out at 0730B & traveled route - Serres, Veynes, Gap, Chorges, Embrun, L'Argentiere & pulled in bivouac about 2 miles S.W. of Briancon (L) at 1400B. Lt. Plaster was informed by Major Ramsay that Company "C" was in the Bibo Task Force Reserve. The Company stood by for further orders the remainder of the day. No missions fired by the Company. Casualties: None.

29 August. The Company was alerted at approximately 0900B. Previous to that time the Company heard considerable small arms fire and Mortar fire in the vicinity of Briancon. About 8 rds of Mortar fire landed in the general area. Lt. Plaster went with Maj. Ramsay to Task force Hqs in Briancon at 0930B and learned that Lt. Col. Bibo wanted one platoon to go in position in Briancon to fire on fortress located at 94072966 (M), which was occupied by Germans. Lt. Saint, 1st Plat. Leader brought the Plat. in position at 1045B and ranged in on the Fort. The Plat. fired 10 rds HE at 1100B and then fired 50 rds HE at 1130. They drew a lot of fire from other Mortars or Howitzers. The enitre Town was being shelled heavily by noon and the road between Town and 2nd Plat. area was getting almost impassable because of enemy fire. Maj. Ramsay called for Lt. Plaster and informed him that the Lt. Col. wanted two Mortars of the 2nd Plat. set up to fire on the draw at 940294 (N). He also wanted the remainder of the Plat. to form a Patrol and reconnoiter the Town of Villar St. Pancrace and set up a strong point beyond it to obtain observation of the draw at 940294. Lt. Hatfield from the 2nd Plat. took two Mortars and set up in the area of 9372940 (O). Lt. Jones took the remaining three squads and formed a battle patrol and brought with them a 536 Radio to maintain contact withthe remainder of the Plat. The Patrol crossed the Durance River at 937294 (P) and proceeded toward Villar St. Pancrace. At approximately 1300B, a messanger contacted Lt. Plaster at the 2nd

Plat. GP & stated that Maj. Ramsay wanted to see him at once. Lt. Plaster contacted the Major in Briancon and was informed that the Germans had infiltrated into part of the Town and to the Right Flank and possibly the rear. The Major ordered that all excess personnel and equipment get out of Briancon and take Highway No. 91 out of Town about 2 miles and establish a Company bivouac. The Major received this order from the Task Force Hqs. Lt. Plaster returned to the old Company area at 937294 and got all excess equipment and personnel loaded and headed out of Briancon on Highway No. 91 about 2 miles out of Town. Lt. Stewart, Bn Commo. O was contacted and he informed Lt. Plaster that the situation was growing much worse and that Maj. Ramsay ordered that all personnel evacuate immediately even if it was necessary to leave equipment. Lt. Stewart reported that Lt. Saint had been notified. The personnel riding the Jeeps were unloaded and started walking and all five Jeeps turned around and went after another load. Upon returning to the 2nd Plat. area, Lt. Plaster told Lt. Hatfield to send runners after the Patrol. The runners were sent. The five Jeeps were reloaded with personnel and made the run thru Town to about two miles out on Highway 91, where they were unloaded and returned to the area again. Several of the men from the Patrol had returned and were questioned as to whether or not all the Patrol had returned, but no one was sure. Everyone present was loaded on the Jeeps and they once again ran thru Town and out Highway No. 91. Each time the Jeeps made the trip they narrowly escaped direct hits. All the men riding were transported to a Bn Assembly area about 4 miles out of Town and left there. The men that were walking were shuttled up. A thorough check was made by the 1/ Stg. and it was found that the following O & EM were missing: 1st Lt. Donald Jones, Cpl Olin F. Sanders, T/5 Worley, Pfc Prenevost, Pfc Ieradi, Pfc Arthur, Pvt Leonard and Pvt Sabori. The 1st Plat. was ordered to set up a GP near le Casset, to effect a Road Block. The 2nd Plat. acted as Infantry in front of them. Later in the day the Company was all reld except Lt. Hatfield and 20 EM who went forward with the reconnaissance group and Lt. Saint & 20 EM went into position halfway between le Lauxe & Col de Lautaret (Q). They also acted as Infantry and had two Machine Guns with them. The balance of the Company slept in a Hotel in Col du Lautaret. Total Ammo. expended by 1st Plat: 60 rds HE & 10 rds WP. The 2nd Plat. expended none. Approximately 500 rds of Ammo, 4 Mortars, two 300 radios, four 536 radios, 6 telephones and considerable wire and personal equipment were losses for the day. Casualties: None.

Summary of Lt. Jones' Experiences at Briancon. "At approximately 1200B on August 29th, I was ordered by Lt. Plaster to take a Patrol, including myself and three Squads, cross the River and enter the Town of Villard St. Pamcrace, neutralize any enemy resistance, establish strong points and locate a suitable OP.

At approximately 1230B, I moved out. My Patrol consisted of Sgt. Raymond, Cpl. George and Cpl. Sanders and the men in their Squads, with Pfc Prenevost as my Radio Operator to maintain contact by a 536 hand set radio.

At approximately 1300B, just outside of the Town of Villar St. Pancrace, I sighted what I would estimate as one Squad of Germans. I was unable to contact the Company by Radio to report same. At this time I sent back a runner ordering up my Squad Leaders to explain my plans for advance. It was soon thereafter that I was contacted by Cpl Worley with a message from Lt. Plaster ordering me to return to the Company immediately. I returned to the Company position at approximately 1330 B and found the Company had moved out. At that time, I had seven EM with me listed as follows:

Cpl Sanders, Olin L. (Squad Leader)
Cpl Worley, Ralph L.   "   "
Pfc Prenevost, Neil R. (Radio Operator)
Pfc Arthur, Paul
Pfc Ieradi, Edmond
Pvt Leonard, George E.
Pvt Sabori, Ernesto G.

Soon after I arrived at the area, I made a complete inspectiion of the area and found that bedding rolls, rations, ammo. and communications equipment had been left behind.

I then went to the Town of St. Blaise and inquired from the FFI as to the situation, and was informed that the Germans had entered and were fighting in the Town of Briancon.

At approximately 1430B, I stopped a 6 x 6 heading for Briancon on Highway No. 94. The vehicle driven by Pvt. Forman and as assistant driver, were both C Company men of the 3rd Cml Bn. Pvt. Dorman had been told by an Officer of the 2nd Cml Bn that the 3rd Cml Bn had moved and that he could contact them by going to the Town of Briancon and going North on the Grenoble road.

Having been informed by the FFI that the Germans had taken Briancon, I turned the truck around and into the Company area and loaded the truck with communications equipment, including two 300 radios, three 536 radios and six telephones and wire, rations, bedding rolls, musette bags, etc.

I then moved my men and equipment out and South on Highway No. 94. On Highway No. 94, I met a second 6 x 6, an 83rd Cml Bn vehicle heading for Briancon to pick up a Company. The driver of this vehicle had a field order by Lt. Col. Markham ordering all American Troops out of the area, that did not get out the Grenoble Road, and to report to Lt. Rosenberg, 117th Recon. at St. Crepin on Highway No. 94.

I had the driver of the 83rd Cml truck turn his vehicle around facing South West on Highway 94 and then walk on into the Town of Briancon to locate his Company. Due to heavy machine gun fire the driver was unable to enter the Town of Briancon, so he returned as directed to St. Crepin.

After receiving the Field Order by Lt. Col. Markham, I continued on Highway 94 toward St. Crepin. On the way I picked up two Ack Ack men. Stayed in St. Crepin the night of the 29th.

The morning of the 30th, Col. Markham put me in charge of eleven 83rd Cml Bn men, two Ack Ack men and the nine of my own men to be used as security and attached to the Company "D" of the 2nd Cml Bn.

29 August (Cont'd) At 0900B on the 30th, my men had been equipped with two grenades and 1 box of Carbine ammo. each and had moved into position in support of Company "D", the 2nd Cml Bn, whose mission was to set up and maintain a Road Block. The road block was located on Highway 94 about 4000 yds southwest of previously located 2rd Cml Bn bivouac area. This position was maintained throughout the day of the 30th and till 1730B on the 31st, at which time the Task Force commanded by Lt. Col. Markham was relieved by the French Army.

Lt. Col. Markham then relieved me from duty with the 2nd Cml Bn and ordered my return to the 3rd Cml Bn. Lt. Col. Markham in addition ordered that I take all the 83rd Cml men and the two Ack Ack men and return them to their respective units.

The night of the 31st was spent in St. Crepin. At about 1900B on 1st of September I arrived in Grenoble and returned the 83rd Cml men to their unit. On the 2nd, the Ack Ack men were left at a ration dump at Reeves where their organization drew rations. About 1800B I contacted the 3rd Infantry Division and was told to bivouac nearby as the 3rd Cml Bn was moving into this area. The night of the 2nd was spent in the School House of the Town of St. Sorlin. At approximately 1100B on the 3rd of September I was contacted by Major Ramsay, CO of 3rd Chemical Battalion."

30 August. Lt. Muschany and T/5 Caton obtained a Jeep load of blankets and started toward the position near Le Casset occupied by Lt. Hatfield and his men who were with the reconnaissance group. They ran into a large shell crater which had knocked away half the road and rolled over a cliff about 100 feet high. This accident occurred at approximately 0000B. Lt. Muschany was uninjured but T/5 Caton was badly cut about the forehead and cheek. Lt. Muschany and T/5 Caton caught a ride up to the position occupied by Lt. Hatfield, delivered the blankets and returned with the Engineer Jeep to Col du Lautaret were T/5 Caton was given first aid. The Jeep was a complete wreck. Lt. Hatfield asked for relief early in the morning. The remainder of the Company was alerted to reinforce Lt. Saint's position. It was decided that it would be better to send 20 fresh men to relieve Lt. Hatfield and let he and his men, in addition to the remainder of the Company, reinforce Lt. Saint. This change took place about 0900B and Lt. Slater took Lt. Hatfield's place. This left about 45 at the position between Le Lauxe and Col du Lautaret under Lts. Saint and Hatfield and 20 men under Lt. Slater near Le Casset. The day was spent in acquiring and improving Machine Gun positions. The Task Force Hqs called for a listening post below the tunnel at about 2000B and Maj. Ramsay sent up Sgt. Horsey and five men from Headquarters Detachment. Lt. Plaster posted them. There was no action and no casualties during the day or night, but several alarms which turned out to be French Maquis or Civilians on the road. Bn Hq & Co. Rear moved to Villar d' Arene (S). Casualties: One LIA.

Excerpts 19 October 1944 to 23 April 1945: In Germany

19 Oct (cont'd). Total expenditure for the period: 230 rds HE & 22 rds WP. Casualties: None.

20 Oct. The 1st Plat. remained in position in support of 141st Inf. The following missions were fired:

Time	Target	Rds Expended	Target Description
1000A	268557(H)	36 HE & 19 WP	Ey troop concentration in woods
1000A to 1010A	267536(I)	24 HE & 41 WP	Ey troop concentration on hill
1545A	263551(J)	*47 HE & 2 WP*	Hill 501
	Total	107 HE & 62 WP	

The 2nd Plat. GP moved at 1800A to new GP in Town of Champ le Duc, 244554(K), set up 4 guns on 2 targets, but did not fire during the day. The Co. CP in Town of Laval (K), with good communications to both Platoons and Regimental Hqs of the 143rd Inf. Considerable enemy shelling throughout the day. Total expenditure during the period: 107 rds He & 62 rds WP. Casualties: None.

21 Oct. The 1st Plat. remained in GP of previous day, but fired no missions. At 1030A, 2 German Planes strafed in vicinity of the Plat. position. The 2nd Plat. remained in position and in support of 2nd Bn, 143 Inf. Their missions were:

Time	Target	Rds Fired	Target Description
1115A	267550(L)	3 HE	Ey positions in nose of Hill
1600A	" "	*30 HE*	" " " " " "
	Total	62 HE	

After the above missions, Infantrymen from 2nd Bn, 143 Inf could hear the Germans yelling for their Medics. The enemy shelled the Town of Champ le Duc all day. One shell hit the house in which one of the Squads were staying. Total expenditure during the period: 62 rds HE.

22 October. The Co. CP remained in Town of Laval. The Co. continued support of 143 Inf. At 1600A, the 1st Plat. moved 2 Squads to new GP located in vicinity of Champ le Duc, 248555(M). The other 2 Squads remained in the old GP at 228545. An enemy SP Gun shelled the Town between 1400A and 1500A. The 2nd Plat. remained in position of previous day. No missions during the period. Casualties: None.

23 Oct. At 1400A, the Company was reld from support of 143rd Inf and placed in support of 141st Inf. At 1600A, both Sections of the 1st Plat. set up in position at 248555(MN). The 1st Plat. GP was shelled at 1700A, a considerable amount of Shell fragments fell in the area but no damage was done. The 2nd Plat. remained in position and received light enemy shelling throughout the day. No missions fired. Casualties: None.

1 November. The Company continued support of 36th Inf. Div. At 0615A, 1st Plat. moved from Champ le Duc into new GP at 331586(A), setting up 2 guns. Trees had to be cut in order to get field of fire. The 1st Plat. in support of 100th Bn, 442nd RCT. Lt. Jones was Ln O with 100th Bn. Lt. Hull was Ln O at 442nd RCT. Numbers 1 & 4 guns moved from Champ le Duc into Town of Belmont(B) in order to be closer when called upon to move into the line. The Plat. ranged in on reported enemy troops at 361565(C), expending 2 rds HE. About 20 rds enemy shells fell around the position after the Plat. ranged in. Pvt. Casimano got hit in his left hip at the time of the shelling. Major Hoffman, Capt. Fallwell &

Lt. Plaster were 100 yards away at the time shelling took place. The only protection they had was their jeeps. The ey barrage lifted in approximately 2 min. T/4 Porrell, Company 1st Aid Man, administered 1st Aid to Pvt. Casimano, and after treatment, Pvt. Casimano was evacuated. At 1830A, a fire fight took place 500 yds from the Plat. GP. The enemy Artillery barrage continued throughout the night, but no casualties were caused as the men were dug in deep. The 2nd Plat. remained in Town of Biffontaine with 4 guns set up and well scattered behind houses, GP at 310576(D). At 1030A, Plat. fired 39 rds HE & 3 rds WP at 321574(E). The mission was in support of 143rd Inf. At 1430A, Plat. fired on 333568(F), expending 10 rds HE again for support of 143rd Inf. The enemy had observation on Biffontaine, so it was necessary to deliver rations to the 2nd Plat. at night. Total expenditure during the period: 51 rds HE & 3 rds WP. Casualties: One. One WLA 30 October 1944.

2 November. The Company continued support of 36th Inf Div. The 1st Plat. remained in position but did no firing. The 2nd Plat. also remained in position. Lt. Plaster & Lt. Saint went on reconnaissance at 1300 A to look for new GP. A position was found, but it was necessary to cut down about 20 trees. The 442nd RCT furnished 10 men to help. After one hour of wood cutting, the enemy commenced shelling, probably 81 mm Mortars. The shelling continued so the wood chopping detail was called off. At 1500A, a French girl come into Town of Biffontaine on a bicycle and informed Lt. Slater that enemy had Mortars set up behind a house which could be seen from the CP. The Artillery was informed, they opened fire on Kraut Mortars at 1545A, using 8 inch guns, and blew the enemy held house to bits. The Artillery accomplished this mission because the target was not in the Company sector. Cpl Miller, Company Communications man was wounded by an enemy shell which hit. The wound was in his back, 2 inches from the spine. At the same time the shell landed, an enemy S-Mine exploded nearby. Cpl. Miller was evacuated. No missions during the period. Casualties: One

3 November. The Company continued support of 36th Inf Div. the 2nd Plat. remained in position and fired missions in support of 100th Bn, 442nd RCT. They were as follows:

Time	Target	Rds Expended	Target Description	Results
1600A	331568(G)	42 HE & 25 WP	Ey personnel	Satisfactory
1700A	332571(H)	*20 HE & 10 WP*	Hillside & Trail	"
	Total	62 HE & 35 WP		

7 January (Con'd).

Time	Target	Expenditure	Target Description
0930A-1500A	P581540(I)		Ey pers on trail &
	P583537(J)	158 HE & 87 WP	Trail junction 1 mi
	P584535(K)		NE of Lutrebois
1530A-1715A	P579539(E)		
	P579537(M)	*59 WP*	
	P581533(N)		
		158 HE &146 WP	Total

At 1445A an HE shell exploded in barrel of mortar killing Cpl Schoenhoff and

Pvt Farnsworth and wounding Pfc Joyce. The 2nd Plat. remained in position continuing support of 3rd Bn. At 0800A the Plat. opened fire on Road, ey personnel and MG on trail vic of Lutrebois, P574538(O), P575526(P) and 569519(Q), expending 125 rds HE & 60 rds WP. Their mission completed at 1700A. Total expenditure during period: 283 rds HE & 206 rds WP. Casualties: Three.

8 January. The Co. was reld from 134th Inf Regt, 35th Inf Div at 0900A and placed in support of 357th Inf Regt, 90th Inf Div. The 1st Plat. for support of 1st Bn and 2nd Plat. for support of 2nd Bn. The 1st Plat. in position of previous day, opened fire on trail junction in woods 1/2 mile E. of Lutrebois, P581533(N). Expended 97 rds He and 43 rds WP between the hours of 0900A and 1200A. Both Platoons moved out of their respective positions at 1400A and closed in assembly area at Rambrouch, Luxembourg, P650386, arriving at 1600A after a 15 mile move. Total expenditure during the period: 97 rds HE & 43 rds WP. Casualties: None.

9 January. The Co. cont'd support of 357th Inf. The Co. Rear moved out at 1500A and arrived at Lannen, P634340 at 1630A. At 0315A both Platoons left Rambrouch and went into position in Bavigne, Lux, P645490(U) and P645489(V) respectively. Closed in after a 12 mile move. At 1635A the 1st Plat. registered on target 1/3 mi N. of Berle, P652526(W), expending 5 rds WP for support of 1st Bn. The 2nd Plat. did not fire any missions. Total expenditures during the period: 5 rds WP. Casualties: None.

10 January. No change in attachment. All elements of Co. except 2nd Plat. remained in their respective locations. At 1600A the 1st Plat. opened fire on enemy personnel in wooded area 1 mi. W. of Berle, P636518(X), expending 3 rds HE & 8 rds WP for support of 1st Bn. The 2nd Plat. in support of 2nd Bn fired a mission from 0900A to 1200A on ey personnel 1/2 mi. NE of Berle, P658524(Y), expending 70 rds HE & 50 Rds WP. At 1830A the 2nd Plat. left Bavigne and closed in new GP 1 mile NE of Bavigne, P655508(Z), arriving at 1900A. At 1045A, 2nd Lt. Milavitz was lightly wounded in right elbow by shell fragments from enemy fire. At 1310A, T/5 Hunter was lightly wounded by enemy shell fragments which lacerated his chest. Both of the wounds occurred at Berle, Lux. They were given first aid treatment at 1st Aid Station. Total expenditure during period: 73 rds HE & 58 rds WP. Casualties: Two.

8. Notes & Comments:

a. Difficulties caused by defective 4.2″ Mortar ammunition reached a new high during the month of January. Two barrel bursts occurred with HE shell. Three "tracers" from WP shell were observed. In a high percentage of shells fired, cartridge container tubes were ruptured. Many of these ruptured tubes remained in the barrel causing misfires which greatly reduced the effectiveness of fire missions.

Throughout the month, lot numbers of impounded ammunition were received thru the Army Chemical Officer and on one occasion, 60% of the total HE shells in the Battalion was impounded and returned to the dump. Since dump stocks were similarly affected, expenditure of HE shell was drastically curtailed at a critical time.

b. Continuous combat since 11 September 1944 had so affected the combat efficiency of this Battalion that Corps decided to relieve one company at a time for rest, rehabilitation, and repair of equipment. A rest area was set up in Longwy, France on 15 January and at the close of the period, three companies had completed a 7 day break. At Longwy, hot showers were always available and, under the direction of the Battalion Officer, movies and entertainment were available every night.

The lift in morale and efficiency exhibited by the companies after the rest period was very noticeable.

7 March. The Company continued supporting the 334th Inf Regt, 84th Inf Div. All elements of Company remained in their respective locations. No missions fired. Casualties: None.

8 March. The Company was reld from attach'd to 334th Inf Regt, 84th Inf Div 072400A March and reverted to Battalion control. At 1000A both Platoons left Homberg and moved to Co. Rear in Stahldorf, Germany (A179018). Closed in at 1200A. Remainder of period devoted to care and cleaning of equipment. No missions fired. Casualties: None.

9–10 March. The Company remained under Battalion control. No missions fired during the period. Casualties: None.

11 March. Battalion reorganized under new T/O & E3-25, dated 29 September 1944. Company C Personnel transferred to various Companies as follows: Company Headquarters to Headquarters Detachment, 1st Platoon to Company B, and the 2nd Platoon to Company A. At close of period, Company C, 3rd Chemical Battalion Mtz ceased to exist. Casualties: None.

[When Company C was dispersed, Howard was assigned to Company A, 3rd platoon. The following excerpts are from the daily log of Company A.]

1 April. Company continued attachment 17th Airborne Division and support of 194th Glider Infantry Regiment. CP Group moved to Town of Schapdetten (A778709). Traveled distance of 12 miles and arrived in new area at 2130A. The 1st Plat. continued support of 1st Bn, 194th Glider Inf Regt. Left their position in Dulmen and moved 14-1/2 miles to new position 1/4 mile E. of Schapdetten (A787608). Arrived at 1730A. The 2nd Plat. continued support of 2nd Bn, 194th Glider Inf Regt. At 1615A left Nottuln and moved to a position 2-1/2 miles NE of Nottuln (A753731), arrived at 1635A. Guns were set up but no missions fired. At 1500A the 3rd Plat. left their position vicinity Dulmen and moved 8-1/2 miles to Appelhulsen (A783673). The 3rd Plat. was detached from 3rd Bn, 194th Glider Inf Regt at 1730A and was placed in support of 513th Parachute Regt. Company fired no missions during the period. Casualties: None.

2 April. The CP Group moved to Nienberge (A879781). 1st Plat. attchmt–No change. Moved 9 miles to Nienberge (A876783) at 1300B. Plat. set up guns and at 1500B fired 41 rds HE and 15 rds WP at enemy personnel and an antiaircraft battery at A902767. Plat. credited with knocking out a battery of four 88's and one 20 mm flakwagon. At 2000B Plat. left their GP and moved 2 miles to HS Wilkinshege (A897768). No change in atchmt of 2nd Plat. Plat. left Nottuln at

0500B and traveled 17 miles in convoy to Nienberge (A880781). Moved again at 2000B and traveled 4-1/2 miles to Munster (A916758) at 2300B. The 3rd Plat. in support of 513th Parachute Regt. Left Appelhulsen at 0800B and moved 6 miles to Albachten (A845697) at 0900B. At 1100B Plat. was placed in support of the English Coldstream Guards per VOCO 513th Parachute Regt. At 1200 B Plat. left Albachten and moved 3 miles to Mecklebeck (A896703) at 1245B. Guns were emplaced but no missions fired. Several prisoners were taken by Company during period and turned over to proper authorities. Pvt Paul Lindsey met a German Soldier who refused to surrender. Lindsey fired and wounded the Kraut in shoulder. The German then gave himself up, was treated by T/5 Forrest Hamby, and turned over to PW Enclosure. Company ammo expenditure during the period: 41 rds HE & 15 rds WP. Casualties: None.

3 April. The CP Group remained in area of previous day. The 1st & 2nd Platoons remained in positions of previous day. At 2100B both the 1st & 2nd Platoons reverted to 3rd Cml Mortar Bn control. At 0800B the 3rd Plat. was reld from support of English Coldstream Guards and placed again in support of 513th parachute Regt. Plat. left Mecklenbeck at 100B and moved to assembly area in the outskirts of Munster (A888737) at 1145B. At 1630B moved to a GP at A887754, a German barracks at Kloppenburg. At 2000B fired 21 rds HE & 12 rds WP on enemy personnel and positions in wooded area at A873765. Plat. reld from atchmt at 2400B and reverted to Bn control. Again several prisoners were taken by Co. and turned over to Regimental PWE. Total expenditure during the period: 21 rds HE & 12 rds WP. Casualties: None

4 April. Company in Bn resersve. The CP Group left Nienberge at 0800B and moved 3-1/2 miles to Company assembly area in Munster (A916758). Arrived at 0900B. The 1st Plat. left Wilkinshege at 0900B and moved into Co. assembly area at 0930B. The 3rd Plat. left Kloppenberg at 1000B and arrived in Co. assembly area at 1030B. At end of period all elements of Company in assembly area. No missions during the period. Casualties: None.

23 April. Company placed in support of 3rd Bn, 335th Inf Regt at 0830B. The CP Group left Gartow at 1610B and moved 2-1/2 miles to Holtorf(538992). The 1st Plat. left Gartow at 1000B and moved 3 miles to Holtorf at 1030B. At 0840B, 2nd Plat. fired 23 rds WP on a group of houses at T-428027 where an enemy GP & enemy personnel were located. The 2nd Plat. left Gorleben at 1120B, and moved 11 miles to Holtorf(T527998) at 1300B. As a result of above mission, several of the buildings were set on fire. At 0005B the 3rd Plat. fired 4 rds HE on enemy personnel at T-497037. Results were not observed. *At 0230 the Plat. GP was overrun by an enemy combat patrol of approximately 60 men and a fire fight started which lasted until 0400B. Cpl Carl Wilson, 35257505, was killed instantly by a bullet which penetrated the left side of his throat.* Pfc William H. Moriarity, 36060625, was wounded in upper left leg and after first aid treatment was evacuated to Regimental aid station. Pvt Wiley J. Grier, 44035616, was hit in palm of left hand, hit in the back by numerous bits of shell fragments and glass and also suffered lacerations in the forehead. He received first aid and was evacuated thru Regimental Aid Station. Pfc Lloyd Wentling, 38542609, was slightly wounded in left finger and sent to Company Rear after receiving first aid treatment. S/Sgt

Herbert H. Baugh, 34012670, was slightly wounded in right leg and evacuated to Company Rear. Pfc Bernard L. Tobin, 37199613, was slightly wounded in right ear but remained at GP after first aid treatment. Most of the above wounds were caused by enemy bazooka shell which exploded near a window. The Plat. remained at Restorf(T491005) during the period. Four German soldiers were found dead near the Plat. GP. Total expenditure by Company during the period: 4 rds HE & 23 rds WP. Casualties: Three.

2. *Summary of Operations:*

On 25 March 1945, the Allied Armies in the West began large scale crossings of the Rhine, initial crossings were made North of the Ruhr in the vicinity of Wesel. Enemy opposition was surprisingly weak and the expected delay for a buildup of forces was not necessary.

On 1 April, 2rd Chemical Mortar Battalion (Company A) crossed the Rhine in convoy with the 84th Infantry Division while Company A was moving into position to support the attack on Munster by the 17th Airborne Division. The City was cleared on 2 April after a sharp fight while columns of Armor and Infantry which had bypassed Munster to the South and East were well on their way to Gutersloh. Bielefeld and Herford fell after a short battle and our troops were in force along the West bank of the Weser on 5 April. On the East bank of the Weser, the enemy was strongly entrenched on the heavily wooded Ridge commanding the Autobahn and was supported by a considerable number of 22 mm and 128 mm guns.

Nevertheless, the 84th Infantry Division with Companies B and C, 3rd Chemical Mortar Battalion attached, crossed the Weser, cleaned the first three miles of the Ridge and then bypassed to the left of the opposing forces and continued the attack towards Hannover. The 102nd Infantry Division with Company A, 3rd Chemical Mortar Battalion attached, engaged the bypassed force which numbered about 3000 men and destroyed it after four days of very heavy, close in fighting.

Hannover fell on 11 April after a short fight on the Western outskirts and our forces continued the advance against scattered opposition to reach the Elbe River near Stendal on 14 April. Plans for a crossing were made but a standfast order was received and our forces on the River settled down to await the Russians.

During the advance from Hannover to the Elbe, many thousands of PW's were taken but other thousands hid in the thick forests covering a large part of the terrain. Under the energetic leadership of General Unrein, Division "Clausewitz" infiltrated 50 miles behind our front, with the mission of cutting our communications lines and forcing its way South to the Harz Mountains.

Division "Clausewitz", well supplied with tanks, assault guns and armored vehicles, intercepted our convoys at widely separated points forcing us to change our MSR frequently and to provide armored protection for our supply trains. When the XIII Corps CP was closely threatened on the night of 19 – 20 April, Company C, 2rd Chemical Mortar Battalion fired almost 700 rounds of WP in order to burn the woods to the South and thus deny the enemy approach to the Town. A considerable force was diverted to contain the enemy and Division "Clausewitz" was finally destroyed on 23 April by the 5th Armored Division and the 29th Infantry Division after a life of 13 days. Regiments from the 84th and 102nd Infantry Divisions were also engaged in containing the enemy behind XIII Corps CP. In contrast to the usual Nazi methods, prisoners captured by this enemy force were well treated and were voluntarily released as quickly as possible.

The XIII Corps boundary was shifted to the left and the 84th Infantry Division attacked on 21 April to clear its new zone up to the Elbe River. The ferry sites at Schnackenburg and Lenzen were hotly defended and on the night of 22 – 23 April the enemy launched a counterattack which carried 3 kilometers into our lines before it was repulsed. The 3rd Platoon, Company A, 3rd Chemical Mortar Battalion engaged the enemy in a small arms fight at the Platoon Mortar position in Restorf. Daylight disclosed several enemy dead in the gun position.

As the Russian advance neared the Elbe, demoralization of the enemy became rampant and whole units crossed the River to our lines. As the month ended, our forces were disposed along the West bank of the Elbe with activities limited to occasional patrolling. Artillery and Mortar fire East of the Elbe was restricted due to the proximity of the Russians and the presence of several enemy hospitals near the River and even on barges in the River.

Appendix 3
Combat Units Supported by Hoffman's Company

Date(s)	Location/Route	Unit Supported
	The Road to Rome (p. 78)	
5/1-5/23/44	Cappelle-San Giovanni	7th Army, 3rd Div. Infantry Algerian
	France to Germany (p. 126)	
8/15-8/23/44	St. Tropez-Lamanon	7th Army 3rd Div. 30th Inf. Regt.
8/27-8/28/44	Carpentras-Gap	[Btn. Control—road convoy]
8/29/44	Briancon	7th Army, Task Force BIBO
9/6-9/8/44	Grenoble-St. Sorlin	[Btn. Control—road convoy]
9/10/44	Quingey	7th Army, 3rd Div. 7th Inf. Regt.
9/13/44	Dampierre	7th Army, 3rd Div. 30th Inf. Regt.
10/7/44	Vesoul	7th Army, 36th Div. 141st Inf. Regt.
11/2/44	Biffontaine	7th Army, 36th Div. 442nd Inf. Regt.
12/2-12/17/44	Selestat-Rechtenbach	7th Army, 103rd Div. 409th Inf. Regt.
12/24/44	Saarburg	[Btn. Control—road convoy]
12/26/44	Bastogne	3rd Army 4th Armored Div. 51st Regt.
1/11/45	Berle	3rd Army, 90th Div. 357th Inf. Regt.
1/17/45	Longwy	[Btn. Control—7 days Rest and Rec.]
2/9-3/3/45	Linnich-Krefeld	9th Army, 84th Div. 333rd Inf. Regt.
4/1/45	Neinbourge	9th Army, 17th Airborne Div. 194th Inf. Regt.
4/2/45	Münster	17th Airborne Div. & Coldstream Guards
4/11-4/13/45	Hannover-Klotze	9th Army, 102nd Div. 406th Inf. Regt.
4/18/45	Gardelegen	[Btn. Control—road convoy]
4/23/45	Restorf	9th Army, 102nd Div. 406th Inf. Regt.
	The Vosges Mountains (p. 132)	
11/2/44	Biffontaine	7th Army, 36th Div., 442nd Inf. Regt.
11/7/44	Le Paire	7th Army, 36th Div. 142nd Inf. Regt.
11/23-12/2/44	La Petite Fosse-Selestat	7th Army, 103rd Div. 409th Inf. Regt.
	Battle of the Bulge (p. 133)	
12/24-12/25/44	Saarbourg-Autelhaut	[Btn. Control—road convoy]
12/26-12/27/44	Warnach-Sainlez	3rd Army, 4th Armored Div. 51st Ar. Bn.
12/29/44	Hompré	3rd Army, 35th Div. 134th Inf. Regt.
1/10/45	Berle	3rd Army, 90th Div. 357th Inf. Regt.
1/17/45	Longwy	[Btn. Control—7 days Rest and Rec.]

Sources: Daily Log of Company C, Third Chemical Battalion and (for April 1945 entries only) Daily Log of Company A, in the same group of battalion records. (On 3/11/45 the Third Chemical Mortar Battalion was reorganized and Company C ceased to exist; Howard was assigned to Company A.)

Notes

Foreword by Charles T. Morrissey

1. Michael Frisch, "Oral History, Documentary, and the Mystification of Power: A Case Study Critique of Public Methodology," *International Journal of Oral History* 6, no. 2 (June 1985): 119.

2. Trevor Lummis, *Listening to History: The Authenticity of Oral Evidence* (London: Hutchinson Education, 1987), p. 123.

3. David Lowenthal, *The Past Is a Foreign Country* (Cambridge: Cambridge University Press, 1985), p. xxvi.

4. Michael S. Gazzaniga, *Perspectives in Memory Research* (Cambridge, Mass.: MIT Press, 1988), p. ix.

5. Arthur Mann, *LaGuardia: A Fighter against His Times, 1882-1933* (New York: J.B. Lippincott, 1959), p. 335.

6. Paul Knaplund, *Moorings Old and New: Entries in an Immigrant's Log* (Madison: State Historical Society of Wisconsin, 1963), p. x.

7. John W. Blassingame, *Slave Testimony: Two Centuries of Letters, Speeches, Interviews, and Autobiographies* (Baton Rouge: Louisiana State Univ. Press, 1977), p. xxxvi.

Introduction

1. Thucydides, *The History of the Peloponnesian War,* translated by Richard Livingstone (London: Oxford Univ. Press, 1946), pp. 44-45.

2. Charles Morrissey, introduction to David K. Dunaway and Willa K. Baum, eds., *Oral History: An Interdisciplinary Anthology* (Nashville: American Association for State and Local History in cooperation with the Oral History Association, 1984).

3. *The Second National Colloquium on Oral History at Arden House, Harriman, New York, November 18-21, 1967* (New York: Oral History Association, 1968), p. 88.

4. Ibid., pp 13-16

5. Alice Hoffman, "Reliability and Validity in Oral History," in Dunaway and Baum, *Oral History: An Interdisciplinary Anthology,* pp. 67-74. Ryan uses the word "reliable" when "valid" would be closer to his meaning.

6. Robert R. Brooks, *As Steel Goes . . . : Unionism in a Basic Industry* (New Haven: Yale Univ. Press, 1940), p. 9.

7. John Mullen, interview with Alice Hoffman, February 1966, Pennsylvania State Univ.-United Steel Workers of America Archives, University Park, Penna., pp. 8-10.

8. U.S. Senate, Committee on Education and Labor, *Hearings on Violations of Free Speech and Rights of Labor,* 75th Cong., 1st sess., pt. 14 (Washington, D.C.: U.S. Government Printing Office, 1937).

9. Charles Cofer in his important compilation *The Structure of Human Memory* (San Francisco: W.H. Freeman, 1976), omitted history from his list of the fields concerned with memory "It is beyond the scope of this book to deal with memory as it concerns

psychiatry, psychoanalysis and literature. Philosophy does not enter directly either" (p. 1). History and psychology have come together in only one area, the domain of psychohistory. In this area the concepts of psychoanalysis have been applied to the character study of historical figures, such as the psychoanalytic study of President Woodrow Wilson (Sigmund Freud and William C. Bullett, *Thomas Woodrow Wilson: Twenty-eighth President of the United States* [Boston: Houghton Mifflin, 1967], and Edwin A. Weinstein, *Woodrow Wilson: A Medical and Psychological Biography* [Princeton, N.J.: Princeton Univ. Press, 1981]). These studies have, however, been based upon the medical model of Freudian analysis and have not drawn upon current experimental psychology.

10. John Neuenschwander, "Remembrance of Things Past: Oral Historians and Long-Term Memory," *Oral History Review* (1978), p. 53.

11. Hermann Ebbinghaus, the first researcher on memory, did a self-study. More recently Marigold Linton did a systematic study of her own memory. See Hermann Ebbinghaus, *Memory: A Contribution to Experimental Psychology* (1885; repr., New York: Columbia Univ., Teachers College, 1913), and Marigold Linton, "Real-World Memory after Six Years: An in vivo Study of Very Long Term," in M.M. Gruneberg, P.E. Morris, and R.N. Sybes, eds., *Practical Aspects of Memory* (London: Academic Press, 1978).

Biographical Note on Howard S. Hoffman

1. William Styron, *Lie Down in Darkness* (New York: Bobbs-Merrill, 1951).

2. H.S. Hoffman, M. Fleshler, and P. Jensen, "Aversive Training: Long-Term Effects," *Science* 138 (1962): 1,269-70.

1. A Psychological Overview of Memory

1. Charles Cofer, in his introduction to *The Structure of Human Memory*, states, "Most of the work reported in this book is . . . more in his [Bartlett's] tradition than in the tradition of Ebbinghaus" (p. 4).

2. Hermann Ebbinghaus, *Memory: A Contribution to Experimental Psychology*, p. v.

3. Quoted in Cofer, *The Structure of Human Memory*, p. 3.

4. F.C. Bartlett, *Remembering* (London: Cambridge Univ. Press, 1932), p. 60.

5. Elizabeth Loftus, *Eyewitness Testimony* (Cambridge, Mass: Harvard Univ. Press, 1979), p. 148-50.

6. Bartlett, *Remembering*, p. 6

7. Psychologists have disagreed as to whether this represents two parts of a unitary system or two separate interrelated systems. See Alan Baddeley, *Your Memory: A User's Guide* (New York: Macmillan, 1982), p. 63.

8. Michael Howe, *Introduction to Human Memory: A Psychological Report* (New York: Harper and Row, 1970), pp. 78-80.

9. Ibid., p. 83. Also see Larry R. Squire, *Memory and Brain* (New York: Oxford Univ. Press, 1987).

10. D.B. Bromley, *The Psychology of Human Aging* (Baltimore: Penguin, 1966), p. 216

11. Wilder Penfield, "Consciousness, Memory, and Man's Conditioned Reflexes," in Karl Pribram, ed., *On the Biology of Learning* (New York: Harcourt, Brace and World, 1969).

12. Baddeley, *Your Memory: A User's Guide*, p. 63.

13. Ibid., p. 105.

14. Duncan Godden and Alan Baddeley, "When Does Context Influence Recognition Memory?" *British Journal of Psychology* 71 (1980): 99-104.

15. Baddeley, *Your Memory: A User's Guide*, p. 69, and I.M.L. Hunter, *Memory: Facts and Fallacies* (Baltimore: Penguin, 1957), p. 270.

16. H.P. Bahrick, P.O. Bahrick, and R.P. Wittlinger, "Fifty Years of Memory for Names and Faces: A Cross-sectional Approach," *Journal of Experimental Psychology: General* 104 (1975): 54-75.

17. Ibid., p. 75.

18. Robert G. Crowder, "Commentary of Endel Tulving," *Behavioral and Brain Sciences* 9 (September 1986): 566.

19. W.B. Witten and J.M. Leonard, "Directed Search through Autobiographical Memory," *Memory and Cognition* 9, no. 6 (1981): 579.

20. Endel Tulving, *Elements of Episodic Memory* (Oxford: Clarendon Press, 1983), p. 9.

21. Ulric Neisser, ed., *Memory Observed: Remembering in Natural Contexts* (San Francisco: W.H. Freeman, 1982), p. 6.

22. Ibid., pp. 23-40.

23. Floyd E. Bloom, Arlyne Lazerson, and Laura Hofstadter, *Brain, Mind, and Behavior* (San Francisco: W.H. Freeman, 1985), p. 190.

24. Michael McCloskey, Cynthia G. Wible, and Neal J. Cohen, "Is There a Special Flashbulb-Memory Mechanism?" *Journal of Experimental Psychology: General* 117, no. 2 (1988): 171-81.

25. Neisser, *Memory Observed*, p. 26.

26. Elizabeth F. Loftus, *Eyewitness Testimony*, p. 104.

27. Neisser, *Memory Observed*, p. 139.

28. Endel Tulving, *Elements of Episodic Memory* (Oxford: Clarendon Press, 1983), p. 1.

29. David C. Rubin, ed., *Autobiographical Memory* (Cambridge: Cambridge Univ. Press, 1986).

30. William F. Brewer, "What Is Autobiographical Memory?" in Rubin, *Autobiographical Memory*, pp. 39, 40.

31. Endel Tulving, "The First 100 Years of Memory Research: A Survey of Accomplishments" (paper distributed at the meeting of the Psychonomic Society, November 22-25, 1975, Boston).

32. Marigold Linton, "Ways of Searching and the Contents of Memory," in Rubin, *Autobiographical Memory*, p. 66.

3. Stateside Experiences: Analysis of Memories

1. Public Relations Office, Camp Sibert, *This Is Camp Sibert* (Camp Sibert, 1943).

2. Leo P. Brophy and George J.B. Fisher, *The Chemical Warfare Service Organizing for War* (Washington, D.C.: Department of the Army, Office of the Chief of the Military History Department, 1959).

3. William James, *Psychology* (Cleveland: World Publishing, 1948), p. 300.

4. Brophy and Fisher, p. 303.

5. The picture appears in Brophy and Fisher, *The Chemical Warfare Service*, p. 387.

6. Studs Terkel, *"The Good War": An Oral History of World War II* (New York: Pantheon Books, 1984), pp. 151-59; Keith Winston, *V . . . Mail: Letters of a World War II Combat Medic* (Chapel Hill, N.C.: Algonquin Books, 1985).

5. The Italian Campaign: Analysis of Memories

1. W.G.F. Jackson, *The Battle for Rome* (New York: Charter Books: 1969), pp. 122-23.

2. "History of Company C 3rd Chemical Battalion . . . " Records of the Adjutant General's Office, 1917—. Entry 427 W.W. II Operations Reports, 1940-48. National Archives, Suitland, Md. Hereafter cited, by date, as "Daily Log."

3. Conversation between Ralph Worley and Howard Hoffman, taped by Alice Hoffman 21 September 1985.

4. Thomas Parrish, ed., *The Simon and Schuster Encyclopedia of World War II* (New York: Simon and Schuster, 1978) p. 313.

7. Southern France to the Elbe: Analysis of Memories

1. Parrish, *Encyclopedia of World War II*.

2. Company A's log is to be found in the same group of Operations Reports described in note 2, chapter 5.

3. Loftus, *Eyewitness Testimony*, pp. 118-20.

4. Jacques Robichon, The Second D-Day, translated by Barbara Sherey (New York: Walker, 1969) p. 101

6. "Ops. in France, October, 1944." Records of the 36 Inf. Div. 442 Infantry Regiment are to be found in the same group of World War II Operations Reports.

7. Harold P. Leinbaugh and John D. Campbell, *The Men of Company K: The Autobiography of a World War II Rifle Company* (New York: Bantam Books, 1987), pp. 275-76.

8. Martin Blumenson, *Breakout and Pursuit. The European Theater of Operations. U.S. Army in World War II* (Washington, D.C.: Office of the Chief of Military History, Department of the Army, 1961); Hugh M. Cole, *The Ardennes: Battle of the Bulge. European Theater of Operations. U.S. Army in World War II* (Washington, D.C.: Office of the Chief of Military History, Department of the Army, 1965).

9. *The War against Germany: Europe and Adjacent Areas: Pictorial Record: The U.S. Army in World War II* (Washington, D.C.: Department of the Army, Office of the Chief of Military History, 1951).

10. Ibid., p. 340.

Conclusion

1. Marcel Proust, *Remembrance of Things Past: Swann's Way* (New York: Random House, 1934), p. 34.

2. James Jones, *World War II: A Chronicle of Soldiering* (New York: Ballantine Books, 1975), p. 85.

3. Elizabeth Loftus, "Leading Questions and the Eyewitness Report," *Cognitive Psychology* 7 (1975), pp. 560-72.

4. Marigold Linton, "Transformations of Memory in Everyday Life," in Neisser, *Memory Observed*, pp. 77-91.

5. Peter W. Sheehan and Perry W. Campbell, *Methodologies of Hypnosis: A Critical Appraisal of Contemporary Paradigms of Hypnosis* (New York: John Wiley, 1976).

6. Elizabeth F. Loftus and Geoffrey R. Loftus, "On the Permanence of Stored Information in the Human Brain," *American Psychologist* 35:5 (May 1980), p. 409.

7. James, *Psychology*, p. 300.

8. Endel Tulving, "Enclosing Specificity and Retrieval Processes in Episodic Memory," *Psychological Review* 80:5 (1973), p. 369.

9. I recall Barry Broadfoot's having made this comment at "History Shared through Memory," a colloquium that represented the eleventh annual meeting of the Oral History Association, which took place at Le Château Montebello in Quebec, Canada. Broadfoot had written a book based upon his interviews. It was entitled *Ten Lost Years*. His remarks at the colloquium are summarized in the *Oral History Review* for 1977 on pages 58 and 61.

Appendix 1.   Second Recall Document: The Italian Campaign

1. In the first recall document at the point where the same incident is described, Howard says, "And there were people shooting up at him." This is probably an example of the reconstructive aspects of memory. When Howard was asked to account for the discrepancy, he said, "I don't think anyone shot at him. Now that I think about it, I think I said that people were shooting at him because I thought they should have been shooting at the plane. I reconstructed it that way in my memory."

Acknowledgments

In order to work on this study, Howard was awarded a paid sabbatical leave from Bryn Mawr College while Alice took an unpaid leave of absence from The Pennyslvania State University. We are especially grateful to Bryn Mawr College for this support. Many people assisted us in bringing this long-term project to a conclusion. May Smith, the transcriptionist at the Labor Archives in the Pattee Library at the Pennsylvania State University, contributed her expertise in transforming tape-recorded speech into intelligible typescript. Jean Grimes and Doris McCullough also cheerfully typed and retyped numerous versions of the manuscript.

The staffs of the following archives were unfailingly patient and helpful: the U.S. Army Military History Institute in Carlisle, Pennsylvania; the National Archives and Records Service at Suitland, Maryland, particularly Fred Purnell; and the History Office of U.S. Army Armaments, Munitions, and Chemical Command at the Aberdeen Proving Ground, Maryland.

Our friend and colleague Charles Cofer read an early version of the manuscript and made many helpful comments on the psychological overview of memory. We of course remain responsible for any errors of fact or interpretation. We also thank Charles Morrissey and Forrest Pogue, not only for their insights, expressed here in their forewords, but also for their support and encouragement. This project had its origin in discussion with Forrest Pogue, the biographer of General George Marshall, and his persistent encouragement has been much appreciated. Charles Morrissey's wide experience in the field of oral history and his penetrating and insightful analysis of the contribution that oral history may make to historiography made discussions with him of our hypothesis and conclusions enormously stimulating.

The men of the U.S. Third Chemical Mortar Battalion and their wives and families were also most helpful. Near the end of the project we learned that this unit was having reunions and we met with its members on several occasions. Their input and encouragement are much appreciated. We particularly thank Ralph Worley, who shared many combat experiences with Howard and who had the foresight to preserve some of them photographically. He was most generous in making his pictorial record available to us.

Finally we thank the membership of the Oral History Association. For more than twenty years, the annual colloquia have provided the joy of a shared intellectual endeavor, the satisfaction of charting new territory, and challenging and precious friendship.

Alice M. and Howard S. Hoffman

Index